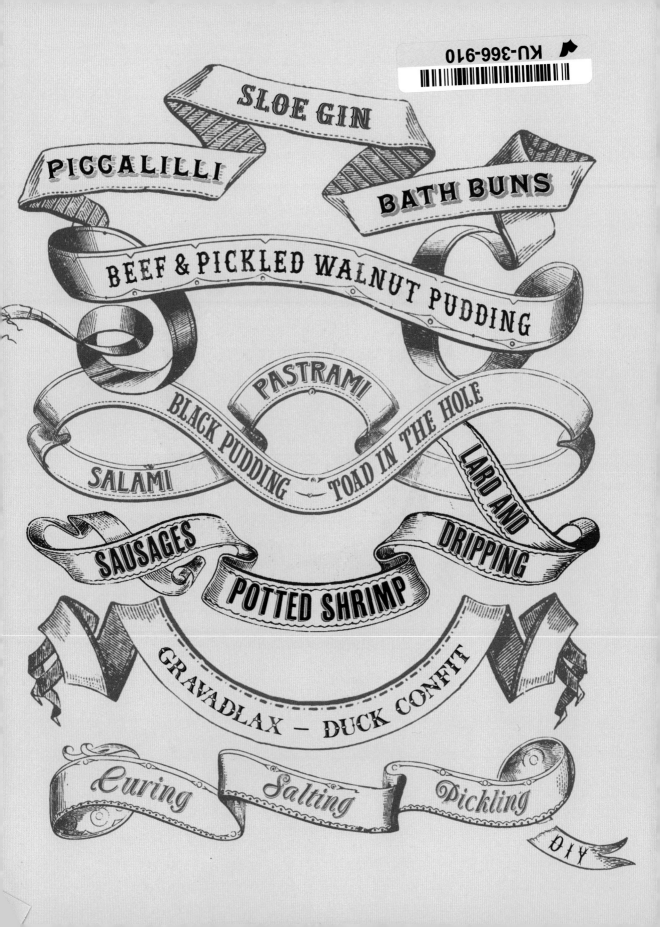

FOR ALISON AND LIBERTY

FOOD DIY

HOW TO MAKE YOUR OWN EVERYTHING:
SAUSAGES TO SMOKED SALMON,
SOURDOUGH TO SLOE GIN,
BACON TO BUNS

TIM HAYWARD

Photography Chris Terry

Illustration Nicholas John Frith

PENGUIN
FIG TREE

FIG TREE an imprint of PENGUIN BOOKS

Published by the Penguin Group

Penguin Books Ltd, 80 Strand, London WC2R 0RL, England

Penguin Group (USA) Inc., 375 Hudson Street, New York, New York 10014, USA

Penguin Group (Canada), 90 Eglinton Avenue East, Suite 700, Toronto, Ontario, Canada M4P 2Y3
(a division of Pearson Penguin Canada Inc.)

Penguin Ireland, 25 St Stephen's Green, Dublin 2, Ireland (a division of Penguin Books Ltd)

Penguin Group (Australia), 707 Collins Street, Melbourne, Victoria 3008, Australia
(a division of Pearson Australia Group Pty Ltd)

Penguin Books India Pvt Ltd, 11 Community Centre,
Panchsheel Park, New Delhi – 110 017, India

Penguin Group (NZ), 67 Apollo Drive, Rosedale, Auckland 0632, New Zealand
(a division of Pearson New Zealand Ltd)

Penguin Books (South Africa) (Pty) Ltd, Block D, Rosebank Office Park,
181 Jan Smuts Avenue, Parktown North, Gauteng 2193, South Africa

Penguin Books Ltd, Registered Offices: 80 Strand, London WC2R 0RL, England

www.penguin.com

First published 2013
001

Text copyright © Tim Hayward, 2013
Photography copyright © Chris Terry, 2013
Illustrations copyright © Nicholas John Frith, 2013
Photograph page 112, copyright © Bob Zook; page 263, copyright © CoolCulinaria.co.uk

The moral right of the author has been asserted

Typeset in DinPro, Veneer and Wood Bonnet Antique No. 7
Colour Reproduction by Alta Image Ltd
Printed in Italy by Printer Trento

A CIP catalogue record for this book is available from the British Library

ISBN: 978-1-905-49097-4

ALWAYS LEARNING   **PEARSON**

THE PATRON SAINT OF FOOD GEEKS

BARON JUSTUS VON LIEBIG

Justus von Liebig was the father of organic chemistry and discovered the importance of nitrogen as a plant fertilizer...but that's not the reason he's one of my great culinary heroes. He discovered a way of extracting the nutrients from cheap offcuts to feed those who couldn't afford real meat and started the Liebig Extract of Meat Company – later trademarked as OXO. His discovery that yeast could be extracted in the same way means he also gave us Marmite. Were this not enough, his company was the first to develop and ship canned corned beef from its factory in the Uruguayan town of Fray Bentos.

WE SALUTE YOU.

CONTENTS

CHAPTER 4: SMOKING 116

Hot-smoking – Pulled pork / Coleslaw / Bonus beans / Smoked mackerel / Arbroath smokies / Cullen skink / Omelette Arnold Bennett

Cold-smoking – Smoked salmon / Smoked haddock / Finnan haddie / Smoked haddock chowder

CHAPTER 5: BAKING & FERMENTATION 154

Daily bread / Sourdough starter / Sourdough bread / Pizza / Quick rye bread / Crumpets / Bath buns / Char siu steamed buns

CHAPTER 6: PASTRY 178

Short and sweet pie pastry / Fruit Bakewell tart / Hot water crust pastry / Gala pie / Game 'cutting' pie / Crab pasty / Beef and pickled walnut pudding

CHAPTER 7: PRESERVING 203

Fruit in alcohol / Fi's vin d'orange / Gin / Sloe gin / Rabbit confit / Partridge escabeche / Duck confit / Pâté de campagne / Potted lobster / Chicken liver parfait with Madeira jelly / Potted shrimps / Faggots / Damson cheese / Preserved figs

CHAPTER 8: OUTDOOR COOKING 226

Beanhole baked beans / Hog or lamb roast / Deep-fried turkey / Éclade des moules / Clambake

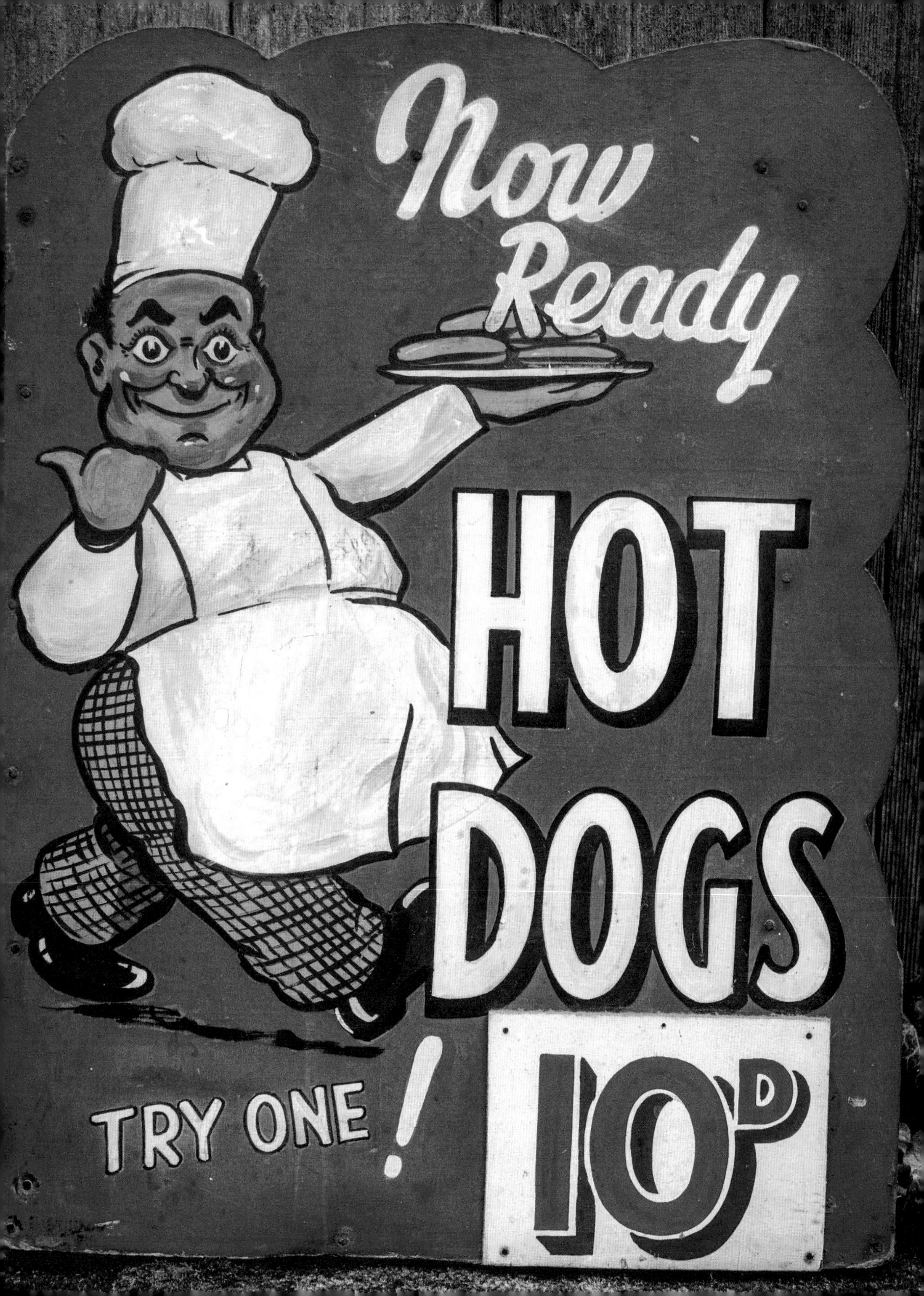
Now Ready
HOT
DOGS
TRY ONE!
10d

DO-IT-YOURSELF

In the corner of my office is an ugly little bookcase. It's about 60cm long, the sides are not quite at right angles to the bottom and it wobbles. I don't throw it out because I made it. In fact it's one of the first things I remember making. Obviously there had been embarrassing hand-coloured Christmas cards for Mum and one of those desk tidies made of toilet rolls for Dad, but the bookcase, made in a school woodwork class, was the first thing I remember planning, cutting, fitting, fettling and finishing, the first thing I took home to my family with a surge of pride.

The bookcase was the beginning of a life of making things. I was an obnoxiously practical little kid, always assembling and disassembling anything from Airfix kits to pet rabbits. In fact, in a childhood that sometimes felt disorientating and scary, I grew to trust a basic mechanical understanding. If you understood how things worked, how they fitted together and why they did what they did, there were fewer unexpected and unpleasant surprises.

I made model planes, fixed bicycles, learned to strip down car engines and outboards. I screwed up plenty of things but I learned a lot more. Later I was lucky enough to go to one of those art colleges where you learned everything from welding to screen printing, from film-making to letterpress. In none of these individual skills did I particularly excel – I wasn't destined for a career in stained glass or botanical illustration – but I and the people around me set great store in understanding. Each creative action improved our appreciation of our materials, of practical design, of the history of a craft and of art in general and our place in a seemingly endless descendancy of craftsmen. I wasn't a tailor but I knew enough about cutting a suit to talk to one. I wasn't a mechanic but no one was ever going to tell me a gasket was blown when only the timing needed adjusting, and I'd always be able to clear a blocked drain.

In spite of my ugly bookcase I didn't go on to be a cabinetmaker, nor a car mechanic, a tailor or a carpenter – these days, in fact, I write about food – but though I love the flavours, the smells and the sensual pleasures of cooking I'm still fascinated by the craft elements. Quite aside from how bloody marvellous it tastes in a sandwich, home-cured bacon is an opportunity to understand more. Butcher the pork and understand the animal better, brine the meat and feel how its texture changes and how its chemical makeup becomes hostile to bacteria. Watch the meat firming up and connect with the generations of smallholders who killed their prized pig and stored its meat through the winter, and, finally, whack off a thick slice and cook it up for the family.

There's quite marvellous bacon to be had from your local artisan butcher, from the deli or even, at a pinch, from the supermarket, so nobody is suggesting that you cure your own, once a month, for the rest of your life. But just once is enough to make the connection. To understand bacon, its history and its cultural significance in a far deeper way than from the glib rubric on the back of the pack.

Across much of the world, 'Food DIY' is a way of life. Hunting and fishing don't have the same aristocratic connotations as they have in the UK and are enjoyed by all sorts of people. In the US and Europe recreational hunters are used to butchering their kill, smoking, drying or otherwise preserving it, often in a suburban garage with equipment bought from a local hardware store. While in the UK air-drying a ham might be considered either an obscure hobby or something left to specialists, in Italy or Tennessee you're just as likely to find one hanging in the garden shed as a bike or a lawnmower.

What's most noticeable is that in other food cultures, these exercises in preserving are not seen as the weird pursuits of a food freak but just part of the seasonal duties of the household, like clearing the gutters or burning dry leaves.

In the UK, where food preservation is taking place it's seen firmly as a rural pursuit, something that goes with a Barbour and an Aga, but in US cities recently there has been something of a movement towards Urban DIY. Perhaps mirroring an increasing interest in a craft movement, food lovers have begun building smokehouses on balconies, bread ovens on rooftops and hanging salamis out of windows to dry. These new urban DIY-ers couldn't be further from the image of the *Little House on the Prairie* homesteader or back-to-the-land hippy, sporting tattoos, piercings and getting very, very serious about meat. There's even a political edge, a sort of punk/anarchist 'seizing the means of production' that recalls the Diggers, or the allotment movement.

Now, as then, there's something empowering about grasping back food production from industry and middlemen and a dignity in providing for your family – feelings a thousand miles from the unhealthy way food has become another branch of consumerism; conspicuous consumption in the most literal sense.

The instructions can be treated as ordinary recipes but it's better to take them as starting points for your experiments. I treat cooking and preparing food as an adventure, so, instead of trying to be comprehensive, I've shamelessly picked out those projects that are the most fun, the most rewarding, and which, I hope, will inspire your own adventures.

Of course, you might get bitten. There are artisan bakers, charcutiers, microbrewers and cheesemongers at farmers' markets all over the country who have rediscovered these techniques and used them to change their lives. But, to begin with, at least, let's just acknowledge that, in a strange, geeky way, some of these skills are a pleasure in themselves and worth trying if only once.

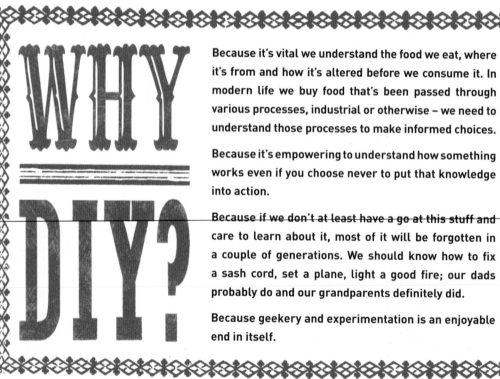

WHY DIY?

Because it's vital we understand the food we eat, where it's from and how it's altered before we consume it. In modern life we buy food that's been passed through various processes, industrial or otherwise – we need to understand those processes to make informed choices.

Because it's empowering to understand how something works even if you choose never to put that knowledge into action.

Because if we don't at least have a go at this stuff and care to learn about it, most of it will be forgotten in a couple of generations. We should know how to fix a sash cord, set a plane, light a good fire; our dads probably do and our grandparents definitely did.

Because geekery and experimentation is an enjoyable end in itself.

A NOTE ON MEASUREMENT

I shifted over completely to gram measurements a few years ago. Imperial measurements have died out even in the building trade – pray God we cooks are less reactionary than brickies – and the volumetric system the Americans use was always bonkers, so, for me, metric is the way to go. I weigh everything in grams – including liquids.

Most liquids we use in the kitchen weigh in at roughly 1ml = 1g – at least, that's good enough for the first trial of an existing recipe and better than trying to get a sensible measurement from something printed on the side of a fifty-year-old plastic jug.

I use domestic electronic scales from a department store for around £40 – they are fine for measurements from around 10g to 5000g and stow in a drawer. I have a special pocket electronic scale, accurate to 0.1 of a gram, which I use for the small stuff. These are popular with baristas and drug dealers and can be had for around £20 wherever bongs and incense are sold (or on the internet).

When I give a 0.5g measurement in a recipe, I'm not necessarily expecting the reader to weigh it any more than I expect them to whip out a micrometer when I say 'chop carrots into 1cm dice'. I do expect people to be able to judge and I give them the best information with which to do so. Given that we've never standardized teaspoons, tablespoons, dessertspoons or coffee spoons in the UK, they are an extremely ineffective way to communicate and far less accurate in the long run than an intelligent grown-up judging 2.5g.[1]

I give internal temperatures because they are the only scientific way of working and, though a few years ago a probe thermometer was a piece of science-fiction kit, they are now absolutely standard in the catering industry and can be had for as little as £12 from a catering supplier. (I favour Thermapens, which are a bit more Rolls Royce at around £50.)[2]

---

1 If you would like to use traditional kitchen measurements you'll find that the smallest quantity specified in the book is 2.5g – roughly half an average teaspoon.

2 You can buy a digital probe thermometer from most kitchen supply companies, either domestic or professional. All are a lot more accurate than traditional thermometers and will revolutionize your cooking. Do be aware, though, that having to wait for every reading can become wearing after a while, so go for the 'instant read' type. The Thermapen is instant and can handle fats and boiling sugar syrups. The only downside is that pulling out the neatly folded probe – which automatically switches it on and off – can be a bit fiddly. I live in permanent hope that they'll develop some sort of sprung 'flick-knife' version which will revolutionize chefs' lives.

By law, food served to the public has to have its internal temperature checked and recorded, which means that the pub barman, the dinner lady at school, the bloke in the hotdog wagon and the kid in the paper hat and acne at McDonalds all use probe thermometers, routinely taking and judging internal food temperatures. If they can do it, we can, and our home cooking and the results of our recipes will improve immeasurably.

Proper, accurate measuring kit is now cheap and widely available. You don't have to buy a Thermapen and an electronic scale, but I think, if we're going to take the business of cooking seriously enough to buy cupcake machines, breadmakers, water filters and juicers, we should probably bite the bullet and get the measuring tools up to speed first. I wouldn't suggest you took up carpentry without a ruler and a square, because without correct lengths and angles it fails. Cooking is all about quantities, times and temperatures – we can no more work without accurate scales and thermometers than we could without a clock or watch.

I've given regular oven temperatures in recipes throughout this book. If you have a fan oven, set it 10°C below the suggested temperature to compensate. Here are, also, some rough[3] Gas Mark conversions.

Regular oven	Fan oven	Gas Mark
120	110	½
140	130	1
150	140	2
170	160	3
180	170	4
190	180	5
200	190	6
220	210	7
230	220	8
240	230	9
250	240	10

---

3 The original Gas Marks were calculated from Fahrenheit temperatures in 25°F steps. Modern ovens have their dials calibrated in Celsius rounded to the nearest 10°C, so you'll see that a chart like this jumps in irregular steps. If you ever need evidence of how hopelessly unscientific cooking is, come back to this page and take another look at the chart.

A NOTE ON HERBS

Traditionally recipes have given two different quantities for herbs, one for the nice fresh stuff, another for the dried-up old dust that's been in the back of the cupboard since 1978. Today supermarkets have revolutionized the supply chain for herbs, so something like thyme will be available alive in a pot, in a cut bunch, freeze-dried, as a paste with oil or from the freezer cabinet. With the woody/oily herbs (thyme, rosemary, sage, juniper) I find that all forms (except the '78 vintage dust) work equally well. These are the quantities I've given here but, as with all flavourings, the amounts are guidelines only – perhaps the single most important DIY technique to develop is constant tasting.

A NOTE ON FOOD DIY AND KIDS

Like most food writers I'm unhappy with the way we teach our kids about food and eating, so I try to involve my daughter (Liberty, ten) in cooking whenever I can. To us, though, one of the unexpected bonuses of a DIY approach to cooking has been that, in viewing food in an experimental way, we're both building a greater understanding of first principles – the basic science – and placing everything in a cultural and historical context.

DIY cooking with kids isn't just about recipes, it's about spending time together, about science, history, culture, art, physical competence with tools and heat, about learning to enjoy sensory pleasures, taking responsibility for how we treat our bodies and those of other living things, all the stuff we learned from our parents and from experience and want to pass on.

For generations people have taught their kids through doing – taking a more DIY approach to food is a brilliant way to carry it on.

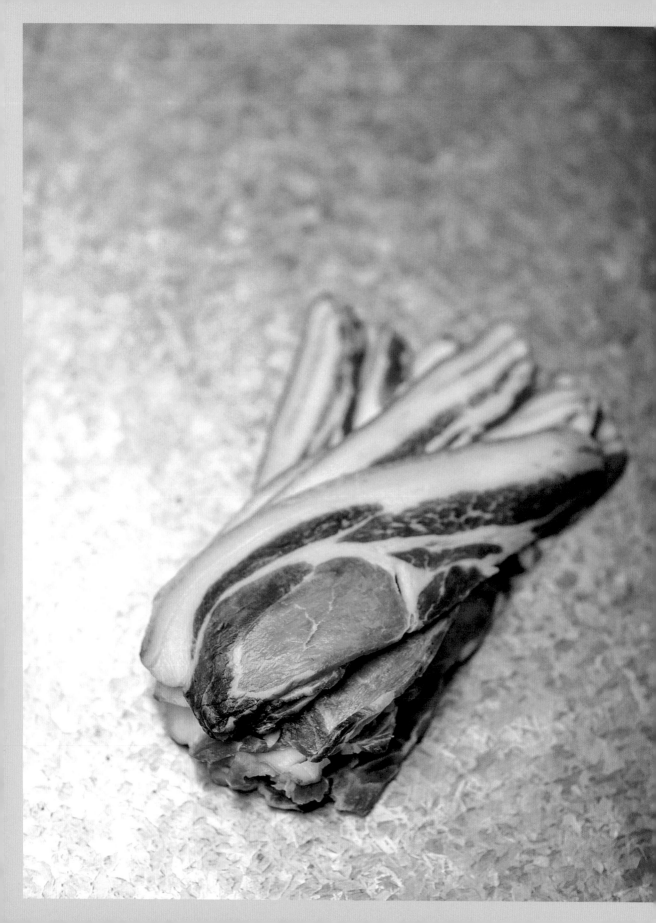

Curing & Salting

CHAPTER ONE

Most of us, at some time, will have experienced what happens to a piece of meat or fish when it's left unattended for too long. Decay is not something that you're likely to forget. Preserving is the art of managing decay, so it's worth looking at what happens in animal flesh during slaughter and afterwards.

The meat or fish we eat is largely composed of muscle – along with some fat, connective tissue and other bits. Animal muscle operates by burning oxygen, supplied from the lungs by the circulatory system, and turning it into movement. As with any chemical reaction there are waste products, in this case lactic acid, which can build up in the muscles until it is carried away, also by the circulatory system, to be excreted.

If you run, or work out at a gym, you may be aware of the 'burn' that occurs in a freshly worked muscle as the lactic acid builds up and begins to attack it – provoking a feeling of irritation or pain. When an animal is slaughtered, the circulatory system immediately stops and lactic acid can no longer be flushed from the muscles. If an animal has been in a state of muscular tension prior to death (and that can mean standing and moving rather than asleep), then the resulting, built-up lactic acid will continue to attack the muscles and connective tissue.

Take, then, a piece of well-shot game or a cleanly slaughtered cow, hang it some-where that's not freezing, and it will, without any further intervention, begin to break down its own fibres. This process, sometimes called 'hanging' or 'ageing', is used in a controlled way to make meat more tender in texture and to develop flavour.

As the lactic acid begins to break down cells in the tissue, enzymes are released that also attack or consume surrounding tissue, a process called 'autolysis'. At the same time bacteria will establish a hold on the meat, usually at the surface, followed by other organisms, from moulds and fungi to insects. As this process continues, with the meat being consumed from within and by outside agents, we begin to experience the signs we interpret as rot, festering, decay or putrefaction.

Bacteria cannot survive at temperatures above about 65°C – which explains one of the reasons we cook things – but they also can't function below a moisture level of around 13%. For this reason, a food product that has been dried can have an effectively indefinite life – food has survived burial in the dry conditions of Egyptian tombs. In climates where food cannot be dried immediately by the sun or wind, salt or sugar can be used to 'suck' moisture out by osmosis. Because bacteria themselves are also subject to osmosis, they may be destroyed by the concentrated sugar or salt.

Cooking food halts the process of self-consumption but, once it has cooled, it is still open to bacterial attack, so methods of sealing the surface – with oil, syrup, fat or an impermeable membrane like sausage skin – physically block access.

Strongly acidic environments are lethal to bacteria, so pickling in vinegar or citrus can preserve some food well. Acidic solutions are also used as a topical treatment for undesirable moulds during, for example, drying and salting.

Smoking, the final method of preservation, creates an atmospheric environment hostile to organisms – nothing wants to fly through acrid smoke to lay its eggs on a ham – which enables the process of gentle air-drying to take place. In other cases it actually deposits a layer on the surface of the food which is toxic to bacteria.

Our various methods of preservation have been evolving almost as long as man has been eating, so many recipes and techniques combine elements of more than one process – a ham can be aged, salted, air-dried, smoked and eventually be wrapped airtight and frozen. Understanding all of them is man's way of conquering decay.

BACON

Let's start, as all the best days should, with bacon. According to *The Grocer*, a magazine that specializes in such arcana, the average Brit eats bacon three times a week – a rise in sales due to the growing popularity of 'premium and organic bacon'. That's marvellous news both for the producers and for those discerning souls who still reckon that a piece of bacon should sizzle when it hits a hot pan, not yield a great puddle of milky fluid and a vague smell of fish.

We do, however, pay dearly for our discernment. Fashionably artisanal bacon from organic pigs can cost anywhere between £12 and £18 a kilo – about twice the price of the pork it's made from. That's an impressive mark-up for one of the oldest and simplest processes of meat preservation.

People have been salting since ancient Egypt. The technique of powdering flesh with salt and 'natron' (that's saltpetre) and burying it in sand to dry out worked just as well for hams as it did for the bodies of kings. All over the world, from the beams of a Tennessee cabin to the lofts of Parma, salt pork hangs drying. It's not some high-tech mystery; any peasant with access to a pig and salt has made bacon in whatever hut, yurt or hovel they called home. Hell, my granny salted pork in a council house.

Bacon used to be home-cured in sides or 'flitches', which, I have to admit, is a tempting thought, if a little unwieldy for the domestic setting. William Cobbett, in *Cottage Economy* (1821), reckoned that owning a flitch or two did wonderful things to the morals of the peasantry: 'The sight of them upon the rack tends more to keep a man from stealing than whole volumes of penal statutes.'

A domestic pig would live in close symbiosis with its owner, foraging for its own food as well as neatly hoovering up any waste the family produced. After a year of fattening the pig was slaughtered and every bit, from bristles to blood, was used in some productive way. Without refrigeration, though, preservation was vital. Pigs were usually slaughtered at the beginning of the winter, when cold weather kept the meat fresh during processing, but mainly so that there would be a stock of salted products to carry the family through the tough months of annual famine.

The most common method of salting was to pack pieces of pork in a barrel of dry salt. Osmosis drew liquid from the meat, which leached out of the bottom of the barrel, creating an environment in which bacteria couldn't survive. This kind of rough salted pork was the winter staple wherever pigs were kept. It was also a vital part of the rations aboard ships and for armies on the move.

It wouldn't suit our modern palates. Much like salt fish, it would have benefited from a long soaking in 'many waters' to wash out enough salt to make it edible. This strong saltiness was probably the reason people experimented with sweeter cures once refined sugar and molasses became available and, eventually, inexpensive. They have a similar preservative effect to salt but can balance it on the palate. Most modern cures combine salt and sugar in varying proportions, depending on taste.

WHAT IS THAT WHITE LIQUID?

Many years ago butchers discovered that a syringe-like device could be used to inject pork with brine. This made the curing process quicker and ensured that all the meat was properly salted right through. Butchers, of course, are not without guile, and it didn't take long for them to work out that, while dry-cured bacon loses weight as it cures,[4] injection curing could actually increase the weight of the meat and thus profit.

When we think we're paying for bacon in a supermarket, we're all too often buying water – well, not exactly 'buying', more 'renting', because the minute that juicy rasher hits your frying pan it dumps its load in that dispiriting pool of milky white liquid in which it proceeds to poach into a disappointing, leathery scrap.

Your own bacon won't yield any water in the pan, an experience you may initially find disorientating. Please be brave though, keep your eyes on the prize and plough through. If bacon was meant to have that much salty water in it, pigs would have evolved gills.

NITRITES

The main noticeable difference between traditional salt pork and modern bacon is the colour. Cured pork is an unappetizing grey and cooks up to a thrilling beige. Modern bacon owes its healthy pink to sodium nitrite.

In commercial curing, nitrites are added to maintain the colour and, more importantly, as a kind of total insurance against botulism in an industrial production environment. Some scientists believe they have established links between heavy consumption of nitrites over long periods and some forms of cancer, but not to such an extent that governments have done anything more than give recommended maximum dosages.

Some home-curers work entirely without nitrites – in fact, many give the avoidance of nitrite additives as the main reason they cure. I'm a nitrite fan. Removing the tiny risk of botulism is a reassuring benefit, and grey bacon is harder to sell to children and dinner guests. But this is an entirely personal choice.

---

4 *Pigs for Breeders and Feeders*, by Sanders Spencer, with chapter on bacon curing by Loudon M. Douglas (London: Vinton [1908]), ends with the following warning: 'It must be borne in mind that the longer either bacon or hams hang in the smokehouse the greater will be the loss of weight.'

PASSING DOWN RECIPES

Like many folk recipes and much farmers' wisdom, curing methods were generally passed on verbally. Butchers, slaughtermen or pig farmers who sold bacon to their customers would often keep a particularly successful or tasty method of curing as a family secret, denying it to commercial competitors.

It's only when salted and preserved meat becomes politically and strategically important – when government local or national, the Navy or the Army begin to stockpile supplies and demand consistent quality – that recipes start to be recorded.

Even today, textbooks on curing rarely agree on amounts of salt, sugar or nitrites, on a wet brine, a dry cure or any combination.

So let's start by trying to understand the different approaches.

The dry cure uses salt in high concentrations to draw the liquid out of the meat, and aggressive salting creates a surface environment in which no bugs can flourish. The meat is set up in such a way that the liquid flows away and the joint remains dry. In circumstances where the meat is likely to 'go off' quickly, the dry cure gets it stable much faster, though it leaves little time for any subtle flavourings to penetrate. A period of dry salting is often the prelude to more complex curing processes.

CURE FLAVOURINGS

Many of the strong-flavoured 'oily' herbs – rosemary, thyme, juniper and sage in particular – are considered, even today, to have antiseptic properties. This is probably why they appear so commonly in traditional cures. In Europe, garlic is a more common addition and, as spices became more readily available, they also began to appear, particularly in dry cures.

Most of the cure recipes in this book are intentionally simple, usually with a single flavouring element. This is the best way to conduct a first experiment, a clear starting point from which to develop your own variations over time.

BASIC DRY CURE

500g salt ★ 300g sugar ★ 2.5g Prague Powder #1 per kg of meat to be cured[5]

Older recipes recommend saltpetre. This contains sodium nitrate, which partially converts to nitrite during curing. It has been used for centuries, but the actual quantities of nitrite that eventually remain in your meat are less easy to control with saltpetre.

On the farm, dry-curing would have taken place in wood or stone troughs or sometimes barrels, and the liquid leached from the meat would be able to run out on to the curing house floor. That will be a bit messy in a modern kitchen, so you could persuade your local wine shop to give you one of those flattish wooden crates, the sort that store wine bottles on their sides – a lid is nice but not essential – and rig up some way of catching the liquid in a bucket or bowl. Mix up your cure in a big enough quantity to create a thick layer on the bottom of the box, then lay in your pork piece and heap more cure over the top.

A dry-curing box like this is closest to the original farmhouse method. Any liquid from the meat drips through the bottom of the box and it's easy to check the state of the cure regularly. Perhaps a more modern approach is to buy two of those large plastic boxes from the pound shop that are so good for storing tools, toys and clothes. Stack them one inside the other, then drill holes in the bottom of the top box. This will now take cure and meat, which will remain clear of the liquid as long as you remember to empty the bottom box regularly.

---

5 Available from the supplier listed on pages 370–71, Prague Powder is a mixture of 6.5% sodium nitrite in common salt. The nitrite itself is toxic in large quantities but the Prague Powder is easier to keep, to measure and to use safely. You can obviously leave this out entirely if you wish. The Prague Powder you buy will come with full instructions. If the manufacturers' recommendations vary from mine, please follow theirs.

BASIC WET CURE

In wet-curing the brining ingredients are dissolved in water and the meat is fully immersed. Butchers used to favour this method, as it required less attention than dry-curing and possibly led to less weight loss in the meat through dehydration. If you want to wet-brine, a single pound-shop plastic storage bin is a good choice of container. Pick something into which your meat can fit easily, without touching the sides, but don't overdo the size – it has to be filled deep enough with liquid to completely submerge the meat, and that can get expensive.

'It is desirable to maintain the brines in the cisterns at a uniform strength for pickling purposes and in order to determine this strength a salinometer is used. A jugful of the brine is taken out, and the salinometer floated in it. The strength of the brine is at once indicated on the scale, and this should never be allowed to exceed 90º or 95º.' [6]

Again you'll need:

500g salt ★ 300g sugar ★ 2.5g Prague Powder #1 per kg of meat to be cured

But this time dissolve it in boiling water and perhaps add a few flavourings. Bay leaf, peppercorns, crushed juniper berries would all be traditional. As the meat is going to be in the brine longer, the flavourings will have much more chance to penetrate. In this case the salty brine on the surface of the meat is inhospitable to bugs but the liquid also excludes air, making it even more difficult for them to survive.

Cool the brine before pouring it over the meat – you don't want to parboil it – and then store it in a cool dark place. It's easy to create a brining set-up small enough to go into your fridge, and modern butchers might well keep big brine barrels in their walk-in fridges, but traditionally a cool larder or cellar would have been fine, particularly in the cooler months. If you're wet-brining for a long time it's worth draining off the brine once a week, bringing it up to a rolling boil to kill anything unpleasant, then allowing it to cool before pouring back over.

---

6 Sanders Spencer, *Pigs for Breeders and Feeders.*

VAC-PACKS

The vacuum-packer is the DIY-er's secret weapon. About the size and shape of a small A4 printer, it sucks all the air out of a special plastic food bag and then welds it closed and airtight. Curing fish and maturing smoked products in the fridge can be a smelly business, but vac-packing means you can share space with fluffy desserts and stinky cheeses without cross-contamination.

Some gadgets can seem pointless, but a vac-packer replaces a small suite of carefully ventilated curing rooms, hanging cellars, a salting trough and half a dozen other things that no longer exist in the average non-stately home. Retailing at between £50 and £100 for a domestic model, it constitutes a pretty serious tool investment, but look at it this way: once you can professionally pack homemade smoked salmon, salami and bacon to give as gifts to grateful family, it'll pay for itself in the first Christmas.

Both meat and fish can be dry-cured in a vac-pack and the anaerobic environment adds an extra level of security against bacteria. Curing sides can be stacked in the fridge and turned daily to ensure even penetration of salt.

THE EASY CURE

The most efficient and least fussy method of modern home-curing comes halfway between wet-curing and dry-curing.

Get hold of a nice fatty piece of belly pork – any size you fancy as long as you can find a ziplock freezer bag that it will fit into. Rub the dry cure hard into the meat. Put the meat into the bag and pour in the rest of the cure. Zip it up and put it into the fridge. Turn it over every day and, after a week, rinse it off and pat it dry.

That's it. Bacon in a paragraph, using ingredients and equipment you probably already have. Not difficult, is it? The advantage of this method is that the whole process is sealed, so the 'packages' of curing meat can be stacked in the fridge and allowed to do their work with minimal intervention. As moisture leaches out of the meat it dissolves the dry-cure ingredients, so for half the curing time it's being wet-brined.

SMOKING BACON

For many of us, proper bacon is smoked. (You can find out how to build a smoke chamber in Chapter 4.) After curing, leave the bacon piece uncovered in the fridge overnight. This allows the meat to dry out a little and develop a sticky coating.

Hang up your bacon in the smoker or lay it on racks and smoke to taste. I like to give both belly and back bacon a good 8 hours in the smoke, which develops a strong flavour, but many people prefer shorter times for a more subtle effect.

Whatever time you smoke it for, the bacon will benefit from 'resting' for a couple of days wrapped and in the fridge. This enables the smoky flavours deposited on the surface to equalize throughout the meat.

The natural home for smoked bacon is the bacon sandwich (see page 41), or, at a pinch, the BLT, but a small quantity goes a long way in a salad. 'Lardons' work particularly well with bitter salad leaves like chicory or, better still, dandelion, as you need something robust to take the fat. The traditional French technique would be to 'deglaze' the pan in which the bacon had fried with a splash of wine vinegar, and use the resultant liquid as the base of a dressing. You can also make up a simple vinaigrette – heavy on the mustard – and use the leftover bacon fat to fry up a few stale bread croutons. Well, we wouldn't want to see it go to waste, would we?

SALAD WITH LARDONS

1 generous serving of bitter leaves such as dandelion, endive, chicory and radicchio ★ 50g smoked bacon ★ 15g red wine vinegar

1. Cut the bacon into small batons, a couple of millimetres square in section. Try to include both fat and meat in each piece. Fry them briskly in a dry pan, which will make the outside crisp without completely melting away all the fat.

2. Remove from the heat, and scatter the lardons over the leaves.

3. Add the red wine vinegar to the pan, stir, then pour over the salad.

BACON CUTS

I have a beautiful old brochure from the British Bacon Council pinned up over my desk. It's dated around 1960 and shows the range of cuts from a whole salted side of pig.

Names of meat cuts are notoriously confusing – there are regional and national variations, and today even many butchers won't remember the old terms, but it's worth working our way round a side just to see how things used to be. A good fat pig is conveniently rectangular in shape. Looking at the whole side, in general the front end and underside – the cheaper cuts – will be cured hard and called 'bacon'; the rear end and top side, more premium cuts, will be 'gammon', with a more refined, lighter cure and a shorter shelf-life – better for roasting and boiling. These latter are literally 'high on the hog'.

Starting at the top front is the end collar and directly behind it the prime collar, rare cuts these days but with a complex muscular structure and good fatty cover. Delicious as a frying rasher or boiled.

Moving backwards along the top of the pig we now have top back, back and ribs and short back. Today, supermarkets tend to use the generic term 'back' to describe premium rashers with less fat and a big central eye of solid lean meat. Our grandmothers would have known that the meat gets more tender and can be lighter cured as we move towards the rear, and would have tongue-lashed any butcher who dared to pass off something from further forward.

Getting back around the hog's hips are two further distinct cuts. First is the oyster, regarded by aficionados as the best slicing bacon, with a thick fat layer for excellent grilling, but also, as we're perilously near gammon territory, an ideal small baking joint. Secondly we have the long back, which begins to look leaner as we move into the haunch or buttock area.

Finally, we have corner gammon, the top corner of our rectangular side, the top end, as it were, of the bottom. The large muscles of the hind leg and haunch are the sort that would be used for an expensive and refined air-dried ham so, unsurprisingly, they make premium boiling or roasting joints, take light salting and can even be served cold after cooking as gammon ham.

PANCETTA AND GUANCIALE

Pancetta could be described as Italian bacon. It's belly pork, dry-cured, sometimes with the addition of herbs and garlic, but perhaps Italy's most exciting contribution to the world of bacon is guanciale, cured and air-dried pig cheek. Guanciale is as simple as bacon to cure but, among bacon aficionados – of whom there are a worryingly large number – it's regarded as a kind of piggy holy grail. Once you've tried pasta amatriciana with your own, home-cured guanciale, there's no going back.

GUANCIALE

2 pig's cheeks ★ 500g coarse sea salt ★ 500g sugar ★ 3 sprigs of fresh thyme ★ 15g black peppercorns

1. Trim the pig's cheeks carefully. You're looking to create a neat shape and to remove any odd-looking bits. Ragged edges are a temptation to bacteria, and glands and bits of blood vessel are just unappetizing.

2. Mix the salt, sugar and thyme leaves in a bowl and add the peppercorns, roughly crushed with the back of a spoon.

3. Rub the dry cure into the cheeks as hard as you can. It feels like an expensive exfoliation regime for a reason – you're making sure the cure can penetrate. Heap the cure over the cheeks and leave them, uncovered, in the fridge for 5–7 days.

4. Find a dry, airy spot where you can be sure the temperature won't rise above 16°C (a garden shed or cellar works well in the winter months), and hang the cheeks on strings to dry for 3 weeks.

5. When you're ready to eat, cut them down, scrape off the salt coat and enjoy. Guanciale can be used in the same way as bacon, but is shown off to its best advantage in a rich carbonara (bacon, eggs and cream) or a simple amatriciana.

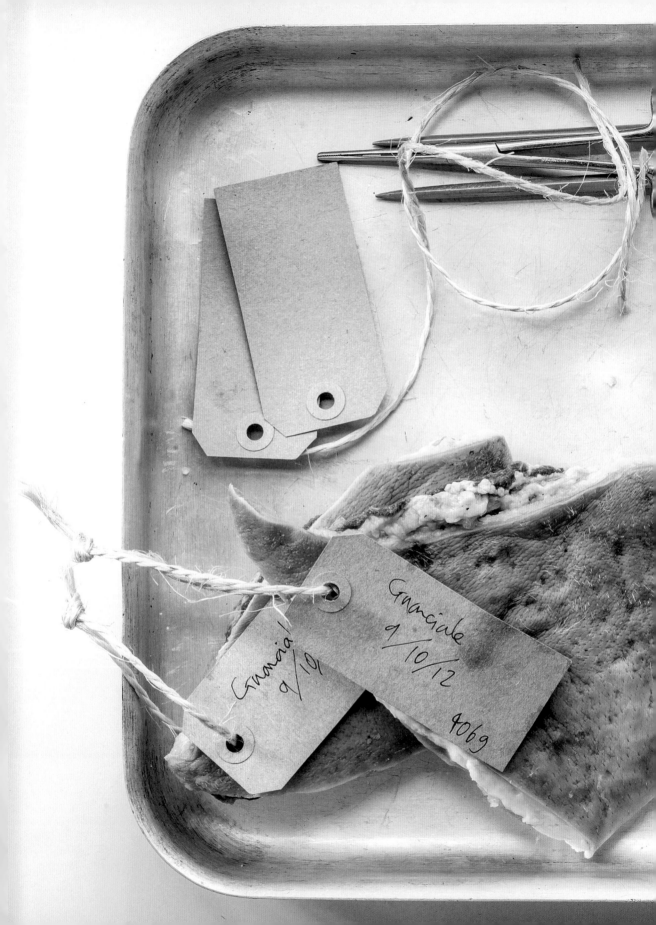

PENNE AMATRICIANA

350g guanciale (see page 33) ★ **15g olive oil** ★ **1 onion** ★ **1 clove of garlic** ★ **1 dried chilli** ★ **75g white wine** ★ **1 x 400g tin of tomatoes** ★ **400g pasta** ★ **100g pecorino** ★ **plenty of grated Parmesan**

1. Cut the guanciale into cubes or batons roughly 0.5cm thick. Fry them gently in the olive oil until they're crisp but haven't lost all their fat. Scoop out the meat and put it to one side.

2. Chop the onion finely and soften it in the fat left in the frying pan. Take your time over this so that the sweetness develops.

3. Throw in the chopped garlic and chilli (deseeded if you prefer less heat) and drop the heat. The garlic, particularly, will burn and become bitter if 'fried'. Just let them stew for a minute in the hot oil.

4. Add the white wine, about a glass of something crisp and not too fragrant, and bring the heat back up so that it bubbles fiercely and reduces. Once the wine is below the level of the chopped onions, pour in the tomatoes and their liquid, breaking up large chunks with a fork. Drop the heat again and allow to barely simmer for 20 minutes while you cook the pasta.

5. Choose a pasta to which the sauce will cling well – I like penne rigate (ridged). If you can get the really premium stuff that's been formed with a bronze die so it has a rougher surface, it will be worth the extra few pence.[7] The sauce goes further and seems even more delicious when it coats properly.

6. Stop the pasta just short of fully done and drain it (save a cupful of the liquid), then put it back into its pan with a shot of olive oil. Pour over the sauce, add the pecorino and stir over a low heat for another minute.

7. Check and adjust the seasoning – if you like things a little more runny, add a splosh of the pasta water to loosen everything up.

8. Serve to 4 people, with plenty of grated Parmesan.

---

[7] Garofalo is a good brand, made with bronze dies and widely available in UK delis.

LARDO

Health fiends like their rashers lean, but a real bacon freak knows that all the flavour is in the fat. If that's true, then lardo di Colonnata must be the acme of baconly delight. This Italian salume is pure backfat, at least 3cm thick, cured with salt and herbs. Colonnata is a district of Carrara, where the beautiful white marble of which much of Rome is built was quarried. Traditionally the lardo is cured in tanks made of Cararra marble. The sight of a slab of pure backfat, nestling in a tub of blinding white marble, might well have greeted Michelangelo when he nipped into the quarry for a lump to carve his *David*. Somehow I find that thought immensely pleasurable.

If you are lucky enough to spot a piece of pork at your butcher's with a serious, unbroken fat layer, seize upon it like a dropped tenner. Although proper lardo di Colonnata is made from specially bred pigs, those occasional finds of pieces more than a couple of centimetres thick can be quickly turned into something just as glorious.

Trim the fat of any shreds of meat and pare away the skin. Lay two or three disposable wooden chopsticks in the bottom of a non-reactive dish, then bury them in a layer of salt seasoned with fresh thyme and maybe a crushed juniper berry or two. Lay the fat on top of the salt layer and cover it thickly with more of the seasoned salt. The fat will not yield quantities of liquid like meat, so the chopsticks are usually sufficient to keep the meat in contact with the dry salt. Cover with clingfilm and leave in the fridge, turning, draining and re-burying every couple of days. After 10–14 days the lardo should be ready to eat as charcuterie – slice it very thinly while still at fridge temperature, then eat it draped on grilled bread on which you've rubbed a cut clove of garlic – but the Italians leave it much longer.

Cured backfat has an excellent shelf-life, much extended by modern refrigeration, but I've never managed to keep a piece in my fridge for more than a fortnight without eating the lot.

Lardo is also excellent for larding other meats.

PIG FATNESS

There are wonderful engravings of pigs made in the eighteenth century, when selective breeding was becoming an art-form across the country. Giant beasts with evocative names (The Empress of Blandings), bred for staggering size and enormous fatness. In more recent years, though, breeders have selected for leanness and consistency in a pig, and as a result it's almost impossible to find pork with a really hefty fat layer. Rare breeds, allowed longer productive lives and selectively mated for a better fat covering, are beginning to supply better fat pork but it is still an inexact science. Rare breed pigs are remarkably like humans – their ability to form fat seems frustratingly unpredictable, with some animals in a litter putting on pounds of lovely fat and others remaining irritatingly sylphlike. If you know your butcher or pork supplier well, you can wait patiently and pounce when a fat beast is slaughtered, but sadly it's going to be many years before we can reliably go into a butcher's and order a pork chop with a good inch of fat like our grandparents did.

LARDING

Although it's fallen out of favour with modern cooks – perhaps because it sounds so spectacularly unhealthy – larding is a useful technique for reintroducing good fat to lean cuts of meat. If you're choosing your beef well and from a good butcher, you'll see plenty of natural fat distributed through the tissue – what's often called 'marbling' – and it's in the fat that much of the flavour and juicy mouthfeel lies. Loin of venison, on the other hand, or even a sirloin, can often lack any fat, so a larding needle is used to thread matchstick-section lengths of lardo or backfat either right through the meat along the grain or in and out of the surface, like fatty little hair transplants.

A properly larded joint is a beautiful thing to serve. It says a lot about your generosity as a host when your guests can see you've taken the trouble to add fat to their dinner rather than parsimoniously paring it away.

PORK BUTCHER

Aficionados of salami, of rustic pâtés, of chorizo and of Westphalian ham often opine that England has no tradition of charcuterie, but your grandmother would always have distinguished between a 'butcher' and a 'pork butcher'. Until the advent of the supermarket, any high street big enough to sustain them would have had two separate shops. The butcher specialized in raw meat, beef, lamb and occasionally pork, but the 'pork butcher' went further, curing, salting, making sausages, cooking pies and in some cases even smoking hams. The two professions, though related, kept a respectful distance.

IT'S GOTTA BE PIG?

Though, today, we Brits regard bacon as a solely porcine product, other kinds of meat have been made into bacon by other cultures and further back in our own food history. In South Africa, beef bacon is popular. In many Scandinavian countries mutton or lamb bacon is a favourite. In medieval England, goose legs were 'poudred' or salted to make a sort of bacon, and in rural areas some cuts of badger found their way into the brining tub. In America, where health obsessions can lead to odd manufactured solutions, turkey bacon has gained popularity, as have a wide range of 'bacon-alikes' based on vegetables or mycoprotein, a kind of benign fungus – yes, that'll be mushroom bacon.

THE BACON SANDWICH

The bacon sandwich probably deserves a chapter of its own as a national treasure, corrupting temptation of vegetarians, sovereign hangover cure and, if we had the death penalty, surely the most requested last meal of any True-born Englishman.

Food writers love to waffle about flavours 'balancing each other', but in a bacon sandwich the equilibrium between pork, salt, carbohydrate, crunchy burnt bits, the sweetness and the acid bite of ketchup is the definition of sublime. It's as near to a religious experience as I allow myself.

You may well have a favoured bacon sandwich recipe of your own, one you've evolved over many years. Everyone can and should have their own favourite way, because we live in a country that values freedom of expression and tolerates difference. That doesn't of course make you any less wrong.

Here's how I like my bacon butty.

Heat a cast-iron pan, quite dry, and then drop in your rashers. They will, of course, release absolutely no liquid at all because they will be either homemade or artisan-crafted bacon that hasn't been reinforced with injected salty water and worse. It actually matters little whether you prefer smoked or unsmoked. Both are pretty wonderful. Back is nice if it has a sufficient fat layer, but streaky is guaranteed and also tends to crisp better.

Flip the bacon constantly and neurotically, keeping the heat high and the meat moving until you begin to see signs of scorching at the edges. At this point and not before, cast in a knob of butter about the size of a child's thumb. This will melt immediately and somehow encourage the fat in the bacon to run. Whip out the bacon at this point and allow it to rest for a few moments on a plate.

Cheap doughy white bread is compulsory here. Not just 'Oops, I went to the supermarket and I bought the non-sourdough boule, darling' – no . . . properly vile, white sliced, sealed in polythene and with-a-shelf-life-of-a-month bread. The kind of thing you could munge into a giant, dense ball and use as bait for elephant seals. I'm fairly sure the sugar content of dreadful bread works in some mysterious way against the salt in the bacon and I'm positive that the preservatives extend your life.

Take 2 slices and drop them into the hot fat for a couple of seconds. Only fry one side of each slice. Lift the bread on to your plate and smear one piece with ketchup or brown sauce – I like both, though obviously not at once.

Do not be tempted by clever-clever homemade 'ketchups' or artisanal gloops made from 'seasonal-and-local' tomatoes. The actual fruit content of the ketchup is entirely immaterial – a mere figleaf of healthiness covering the staggering amount of sugar syrup and MSG that you really need in your butty.

Finally, lay on at least 2 layers of bacon – it would be idiotic to scrimp at this point – and drop on the lid, the concrete cap for your culinary Chernobyl.

Serve with arrogant pride and a breathtaking lack of guilt.

(If there happen to be lettuce and tomato in the fridge I have been known to divert at the last moment to a BLT – there's something about the chilled lettuce that cools a head boiling with hangover – but I understand that many will justly regard this straying into the vegetables as morally questionable.)

BACON FRENZY

In recent years, bacon seems to have taken on an online life of its own, a kind of nerd mass-hysteria. Googling 'bacon' brings up bacon martinis, bacon bikinis, bacon perfume, 'Bacon Lube',[8] a scarf and hat knitted to look like rashers and thousands upon thousands of new ways of consuming the sublime meat. Perhaps my favourite is the Bacon Bomb, recipes for which usually feature a kilo of sausage meat, dressed liberally with barbecue sauce and then wrapped in a woven bacon blanket before being cooked on a barbecue or smoker.

Most of the recipes are as simple as they are unappetizing, but here's one that might just tempt you.

---

8 No, really, www.baconlube.com.

BACON JAM

750g streaky bacon rashers (smoked or unsmoked) ★ 300g white onions ★ 200g espresso ★ 100g muscovado sugar ★ 75g cider vinegar ★ 75g maple syrup ★ 3 cloves of garlic, finely chopped ★ 2 dried chipotle chillies, crushed

1. Preheat the oven to 160°C. Chop the bacon roughly and cook in a large frying pan until well browned. Drain the fat and store it for nefarious uses.

2. Put the cooked bacon and all other ingredients into a heavy-bottomed pot. Cover with foil and then the lid and place in a medium oven. Start checking at 3 hours, but it may take up to 4.

3. On removing the lid, the smell should drive you insane with pork lusts, but retain your composure. The contents should look like a lumpy, treacly brown chutney. If it's insufficiently dark or sticky for your taste, put it on a high flame on top of the stove, uncovered, stir compulsively to prevent burning and whip off the second everything looks dark and glossy.

4. You can blitz the jam to whatever consistency you like. I like to let it cook to rags and retain a certain rude chunkiness, but I realize more refined souls might want it completely smooth.

5. Pour into sterilized jars (see page 68) while still hot, then seal and refrigerate. Bacon jam should last around a fortnight, but let's not kid ourselves here … nobody's ever kept any long enough to check. You might want to let it come to room temperature before serving so that the bacon fat is less ferociously set and you can achieve a sufficiently erotic spreading consistency.

There's no real meal occasion for something as bonkers as bacon jam. It's good on some cheeses, like a chutney, spread on a croissant like Nutella or dolloped on your fried eggs like ketchup. Some people eat it straight from the jar with a spoon. I like to think that, in a fair and just world, dining etiquette will eventually catch up with bacon jam and we'll have specially made silver spoons.

"I'M A DANDY, BUT I'M NO DUDE."

HAM (BAKED)

Ham is a more much complicated issue than that brutal monosyllable might lead us to believe. The thick upper thigh of the pig can be processed in countless ways. Salted and hung to dry for a year or so, it becomes prosciutto, Bayonne or jamón; dry-cured and smoked, it becomes what the Americans call country ham, the Germans schinken; boiled and lightly smoked, it becomes York ham – the bright pink favourite of the British tea table. This, by the way, is by no means a comprehensive list. Variations in cure and cooking are as many as the countries which dig on swine, but the traditional ham many families favour for high tea, funerals or particularly Boxing Day is a gammon joint, boiled, coated with a highly seasoned basting paste and then baked to a crisp crust.

Gammon can be bought either 'green' or smoked. You can also buy it on or off the bone. There are dozens of recipe variations for the crust, which really needs enough sugar to ensure a toffee-like glaze, and whichever aromatics you favour. I've gone with a simple mix of honey and English mustard with the traditional light studding of cloves (fewer than usual – too many and it tastes like licking a Christmas air freshener), but you could experiment with citrus versions, baroque combinations of Chinese five-spice (see recipe on page 172) and maple syrup, or the ever popular Coca-Cola glaze which has retained trailer-trash cachet, in spite of the gentrifying endorsements of Nigella Lawson. I usually add a teaspoon of cornflour to the glaze, which, though it initially looks a little unappetizing, actually cooks out completely, thickens the glaze and helps it adhere during cooking.

BAKED HAM

1kg boneless gammon joint (smoked or otherwise) ⭐ **1 onion** ⭐ **1 leek** ⭐ **1 stick of celery** ⭐ **1 carrot** ⭐ **5g black peppercorns** ⭐ **1 sprig of fresh thyme** ⭐ **1 bay leaf** ⭐ **5 cloves** ⭐ **50g English mustard powder** ⭐ **200g muscovado sugar**

1. Put the gammon joint into a pan, cover with cold water, and add the onion, leek, celery, carrot, peppercorns, thyme and bay leaf. You can vary these aromatics to suit your own taste.

2. After 2 hours of simmering, remove the meat and allow it to cool. The stock makes great soup.

3. Preheat the oven to 200°C. Carefully remove the rind from the ham. It should come away easily, but be ready to help it along with a sharp knife.

4. Cut a criss-cross pattern into the fat, trying to avoid going through to the meat. Stud with a few cloves. Though they're decorative they're really pungent, so go easy.

5. Mix the mustard powder with the dark muscovado sugar and let down to a gritty paste with some hot water.

6. Paint the treacly mess on to the ham, working it well into the cuts on the surface. Foil-line your oven dish if you don't want it glued up with epoxy-strength toffee, then bang the whole lot into the oven for half an hour, basting occasionally. Watch for burning.

7. Allow to cool before slicing and serve with homemade piccalilli (see page 68).

This should serve 6 people, though that won't leave enough of the essential sandwich leftovers. Let's say 4 instead, and be sure you have some good mustard in the fridge and a fresh white loaf for the following day.

BEEF

If you want to know about delis, ask a New Yorker. They'll get all misty-eyed and talk about the glory days of Katz's and the Carnegie, but ask them the last time they ate in one and they'll mumble an excuse and head to the gym. The first delis in Manhattan began as simple cookshops, serving kosher food to young immigrant men living away from their supportive families. As urban Jewish communities grew, they became secular cultural centres and even as later generations moved their homes from the inner city to more prosperous suburbs, the deli still served the traditionally Jewish workplaces, rag trade, diamond-dealing or theatre districts. Deli food was too good, too cheap and filling to remain a secret and it wasn't long before the giant delis so dear to the memory of New Yorkers began serving a wider audience, varying the menu to suit.

Today the New York delis that survive are a sad shadow of their former selves. The trade-specific districts that lent them relevance are dispersing. Their traditional customers are ageing, watching their diets or retiring to the 'burbs, so the delis have become tourist attractions where out-of-towners come to marvel at the rudeness of the waiters and the stupendous proportions of the sandwiches. The prognosis is not good.

London, which has had a settled Jewish community for much longer than Manhattan, used to boast hundreds of salt beef bars. Once they seemed a fixture on every other street corner, yet today there are around half a dozen.

I write as nothing more than a greedy Gentile, but it seems to me that salt beef, though originating in Ashkenazi cuisine and firmly rooted in urban Jewish tradition, is going to be a tremendous loss to all of us; it's part of a wider picture of city eating. I regard the preservation and evangelism of proper salt beef in the UK as a duty as well as an honour.

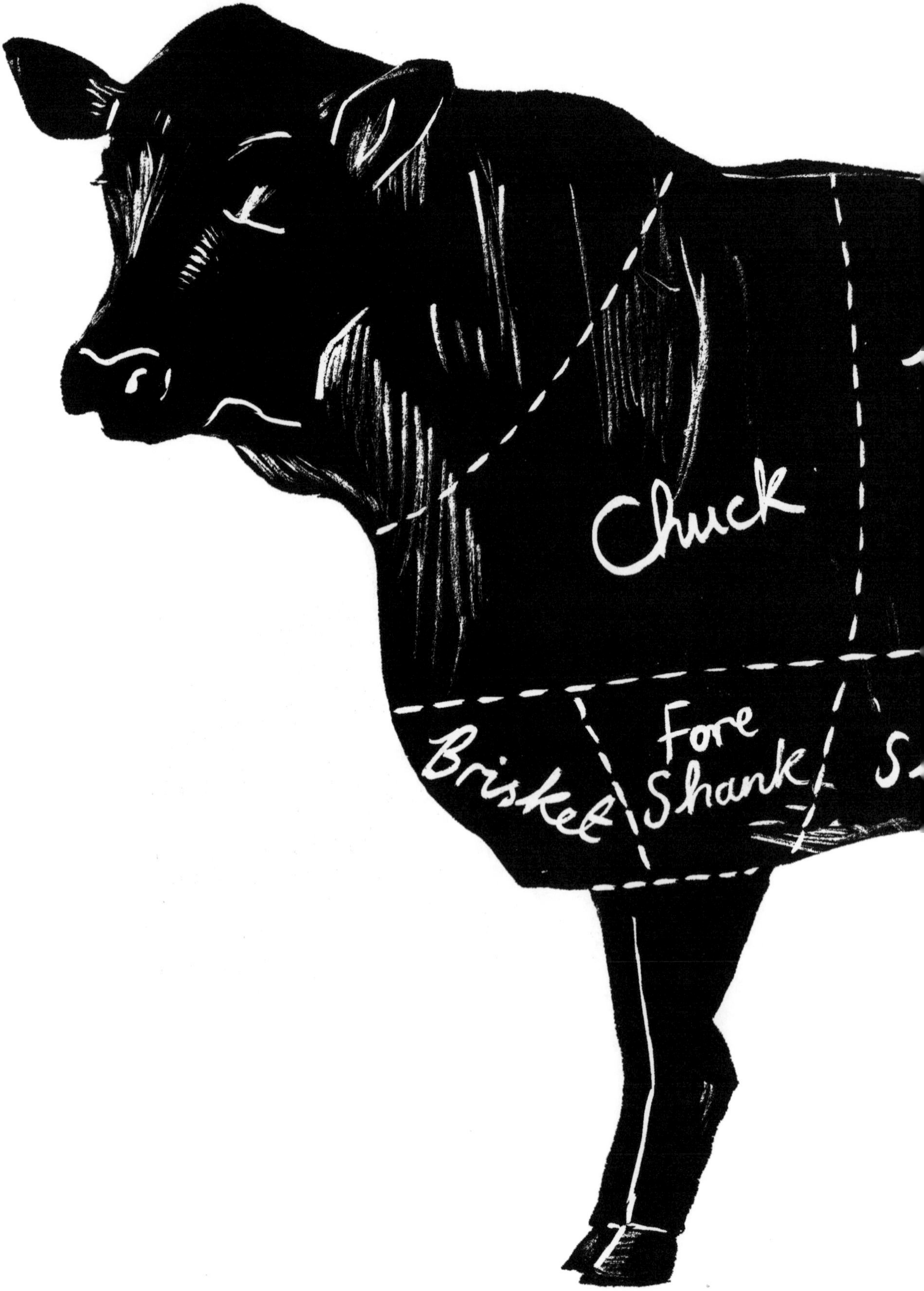
Chuck
Brisket
Fore Shank

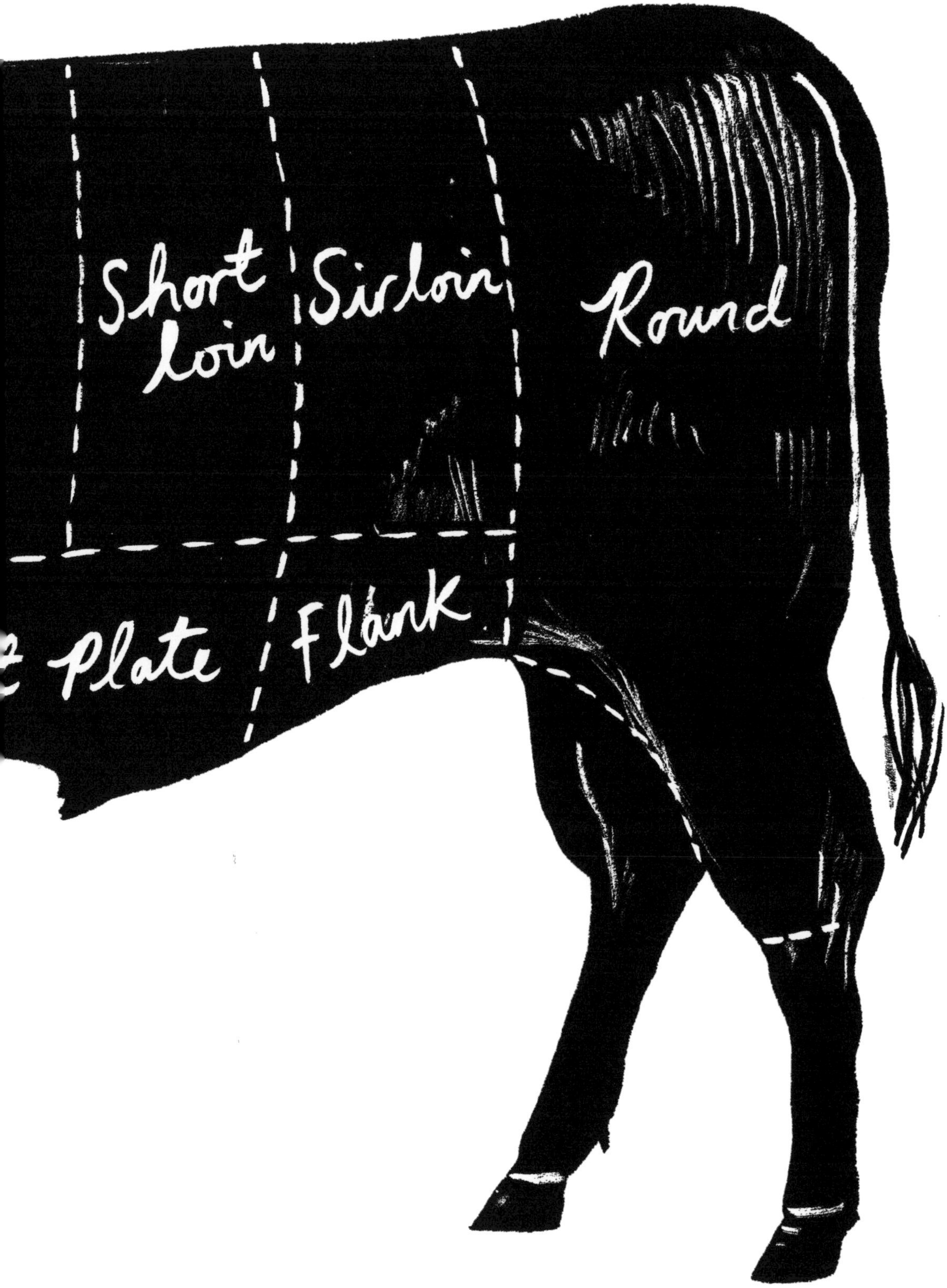
Short loin
Sirloin
Round
Plate
Flank

SALTING BRISKET

Both salt beef and pastrami are made from brisket, a fatty, flavourful and cheap cut from the front/underside of the cow. Brisket usually comes boned and rolled and should be cured in a wet brine.

For salt beef, leave the brisket tied into a roll; if brining for pastrami, untie the piece and trim it to a neat, flat slab.

For the basic brine use 2 litres of water and add 200g of salt, 75g of sugar, 15g of Prague Powder #1 (optional), 2 bay leaves, 2 cloves of garlic and 15g of pickling spice (I use a mixture of mace, allspice, juniper, coriander, ginger, dried chillies and just a couple of cloves, but you can go wherever you fancy with this). The cure for pastrami is traditionally just slightly sweeter, so add 50g of honey if necessary. Bring to the boil and allow to cool.

Pack the brisket into doubled, heavy-duty resealable freezer bags. Ladle in the brine, exclude as much air as you can, then seal both bags. Place in the fridge and turn daily.

PASTRAMI

After 5 days in the brine, remove the brisket and pat it dry with kitchen roll. Crush 10g each of black peppercorns and coriander seed. Massage hard into the surface of the brisket, trying to get as much to adhere as possible.

Hot-smoke to an internal temperature of 70°C. You can do this in any covered barbecue. Try to keep the temperature low and steady so the cooking takes as long as possible, and keep chucking handfuls of wood or woodchips on to the fire to keep it good and smoky.

Put your smoked pieces on a rack over a few centimetres of boiling water, then build a foil tent around it and seal it up. Try to keep as much free space around the meat as possible, for the steam to circulate.

Put it into the oven at 120°C and give it at least 3 hours. A fork should slide into it like butter.

Slice thinly while still hot. Serve hot, in epic quantities on rye bread (see page 168). You won't need butter, and mayonnaise would be a dangerous error. The pickle is a legal requirement.

SALT BEEF

Brisket for salt beef can stay in the brine for at least 10 days before being removed, rinsed and patted dry.

Put into a lidded pot, cover with water and add your favourite aromatics. I like to keep things simple with carrots, onions and a bay leaf. You can, if you wish, add more of your pickling spice … but I'm not sure it adds anything. Simmer on top of the stove for between 2 and 4 hours. Keep the water topped up so the meat is covered. It will be done when a skewer runs through it with alarmingly little resistance.

Carve brutally into inelegant slabs while still hot. You can serve the salt beef on a plate with some simply boiled potatoes and some of the veg from the boiling process. Don't, whatever you do, serve the original ones – dredge them out with a ladle and replace with fresh carrots and onions around 20 minutes before serving time. That way you'll have something that tastes authentic but offers at least the possibility of not collapsing into a slurry on the plate.[9] Alternatively, you can use your hot salt beef to build a Reuben.

BUILDING A REUBEN

Smear two slices of rye bread (see page 168) with a thick layer of thousand island dressing. On one slice mound a pile of salt beef.

Stack a layer of sauerkraut (see page 87) on top of the meat, then get three or more slices of Emmenthal to sit on its chest and hold it down while you slide the lot under a hot grill.

Reunite the sandwich with its besmeared lid and serve forth with the statutory pickle. Do not expect to finish the sandwich in a single sitting. That is NOT the point.

---

9 There's a terrific and rather forgotten condiment in Ashkenazi Jewish cuisine called chrain that goes extremely well with salt beef. To make a quick and dirty version, finely grate a couple of cooked beetroot and add to an equal quantity of bought horseradish sauce. Good chrain has a sweet edge that balances the horseradish, so if your beets aren't sweet enough add a little sugar.

PROPER CORNED BEEF

Americans call salt beef 'corned beef', which is clearly wrong. The original canned corned beef of our childhoods was chippings of salted beef trimming set in its own fat. In the years before refrigeration, settlers discovered it was possible to breed excellent cattle at minimal cost on the vast Argentine pampas, but couldn't ship the meat back to Europe without a method of preservation. Dried and salted beef were both successfully exported, but the most popular product was corned beef, most of which was produced in and exported from the small Uruguayan port town of Fray Bentos. With the advent of efficient canning, corned beef became the best preserved product with which to sustain soldiers, sailors and explorers on long expeditions.[10] French soldiers in the Napoleonic wars are thought to have given it the grand title of 'boeuf boillu' (boiled beef), which the Brits naturally corrupted into 'bully beef'.

In the unlikely event that you have any salt beef left over, chill it and then slice it extremely thinly across the grain of the meat. Having been cooked to rags, it will be simple to break the slices down between your fingers into short shreds which can be bound with melted butter and set into a terrine: an elegant and infinitely more tasty 'homage' to bully beef.

---

10 See also pemmican, page 112.

FISH

Probably the product that's been salted by man for longest is fish. Picturing the environment where sea fishermen operate, it's easy to imagine the discovery that salting and wind- or sun-drying could preserve the catch. Once organized fishing from offshore boats became common, the cod, large, plentiful and easy to catch in quantity, became the fish of choice for salting and drying. Cod could be salted until it was as hard as wood, kept for years and then reconstituted quickly in clear water. Dried cod became a traded commodity and a lifeline for populations with little access to animal protein in the winter months.

Cod caught from Newfoundland to Finland, from the Bay of Biscay to the Arctic Circle, could be gutted, filleted and cured in cheap salt until it could be hung out to dry. In places like the Lofoten islands or the Basque region of Spain, acres of racks would dry thousands of tons of salted cod sides in the frozen, desiccating winds or hot sun. The dried fish could be traded wherever boats could move it, on the coasts and far inland, eventually appearing in African, Caribbean, Indian, Mediterranean and Scandinavian cuisine.

Salt white fish, once properly reconstituted, is not very salty at all. Drying concentrates the flavours beautifully, so, though it will never have the texture of freshly caught fish, it works brilliantly when cooked with other flavourings or, like bacon, with more bland starches.

SALTING WHITE FISH

You'll need: a large pollack, whiting, haddock or ling (have it filleted if you don't fancy doing it yourself, but leave the skin on) ✯ your favoured salting arrangement (see page 25) ✯ 1kg coarse sea salt

Wash the fish clear of any slime, fillet it – unless you've had it done for you – and then bury the two sides in the salt.

Keep the whole arrangement well drained. This is a ferocious dry cure and nothing smells good if it's been lying around in fish juice for a week. Turn the fish regularly and after 7–10 days you should have a convincingly rigid plank of fishleather for your pains. Hang this somewhere cool and dry and you should be able to forget about it until the depths of the next winter famine or until your ship is becalmed off the Dry Tortugas.

SALT FISH CROQUETAS

300g salt fish, well soaked (see page 59) ★ 500g whole milk ★ 100g butter ★ 100g plain flour, plus extra for dusting ★ salt and freshly ground black pepper ★ 2 eggs ★ 200g fresh breadcrumbs ★ vegetable oil (for frying)

1. Poach the soaked salt fish in the milk for 15–20 minutes. Once it starts to flake, lift it out and shred it with two forks. Save the poaching milk.

2. Melt the butter in a small saucepan and add the flour. Cook until it smells biscuity, then remove from the heat and slowly strain in the poaching milk, whisking vigorously. Cook for a couple more minutes. This should create an extremely thick and gloopy white sauce.

3. Stir in the flaked fish, taste and adjust the seasoning. You probably won't need any extra salt, just add pepper.

4. Once the mixture has cooled, take small handfuls and roll each one into a short log shape, about 2cm thick. Lay these on a floured sheet of clingfilm and refrigerate for an hour or so, until set.

5. Beat the eggs in a shallow bowl and put the breadcrumbs into another. Roll the croquetas in flour, then individually dip them in the egg and then in the breadcrumbs. You can, if you like a thick coating, do this twice.

6. Heat about 2cm of oil to around 175°C and fry a couple of croquetas at a time until tanned and crisp.

7. Serve with romesco sauce (see page 58).

ROMESCO SAUCE

1 bulb of garlic ✴ 25g stale bread ✴ 100g blanched almonds ✴ 2 tomatoes, halved and deseeded ✴ 2 roasted red peppers (the ones from a jar are far less fuss) ✴ 100g extra virgin olive oil ✴ 30g sherry vinegar ✴ 2.5g pimentón (smoked paprika) ✴ salt

1. Preheat the oven to 180°C and roast the bulb of garlic for 30–40 minutes, or until the cloves feel soft when squeezed.

2. Tear up the bread and toast it in a hot dry pan. Toast the almonds the same way.

3. Put the tomatoes, almonds, bread and red peppers into a blender and pulse. It's good to keep a little bit of crunch from the nuts.

4. Pour in the olive oil, then squeeze out the roasted garlic from its skins and add. Pulse again, lightly.

5. Transfer the sauce to a bowl and whisk in the sherry vinegar and smoked paprika. Add some salt, if it needs it.

6. Romesco sauce will keep for a week or so in the fridge under a layer of olive oil and also freezes well. It's traditionally used as a sauce with calçots, a leek-like spring vegetable from Spain, but it's fantastic with all kinds of meat and fish, and even, God help me for admitting this, on pasta in an emergency.

If you buy your salt in fashionable little boxes of flakes, then salting will bankrupt you extremely quickly. There are other ways. A couple of varieties of French sea salt are sold at health food shops in kilo bags for only a few pounds. I'm not sure if they're intended for curing or for bathing in, but as they contain no additives at all, they are great for the job. Salt for dishwashers or for melting ice on garden paths looks very tempting but is usually either rock salt or contains anti-caking agents – not in themselves dangerous but not something you want in contact with your meat or fish for weeks at a time.

BRANDADE

Cut off a piece of salted white fish and soak it in clear fresh water for 3 days, keeping the bowl covered, in the fridge, and changing the water twice a day.

After 3 days you can tear off a small piece and taste it. You should find it's not too salty, but if it is, give it another day or two of soaking.

It's possible at this stage to treat salt fish as if it's fresh. In the Jamaican dish saltfish and ackee, for example, the reconstituted fish is fried in big flakes with peppers and onions; it would certainly work well in a kedgeree, and the Portuguese pride themselves on hundreds of ways of preparing bacalao in stews, tarts and tapas. The drying process also develops another odd quality in the fish: it can be used as a base for an emulsion of an almost mayonnaise-like quality. This is brandade de morue, a recipe that always feels to me like a doubly lethal French taramasalata. Start with around 500g of soaked cod. Pat dry, put it into a saucepan and cover it with olive oil. Gently raise the temperature of the oil until it's barely shimmering, then turn off the heat and let the fish poach for 10 minutes.

Peel a medium potato, slice it coarsely and simmer it in 250g of milk along with a peeled clove of garlic. Remove the fish from the oil and strip away any skin or bone while it's still hot (it's the devil of a job once it's gone cold). Flake the fish into a large pestle and mortar or, if you're feeling weak, a food processor. Once you've worked it to a smooth paste, begin drizzling in the oil and the milk – still warm – in alternate bursts. By this point you should be producing a marvellously thick emulsion. Mash the garlic and potatoes together and fold them quickly through the paste with a rubber spatula.

Serve with toasted bread.

GRAVADLAX

'Gravad lax' is Swedish for 'buried fish', which harks back to the time when fishermen would save part of their catch by burying it in the beach. Presumably the salt in the sand had a preservative effect and a degree of fermentation held off decomposition for a while. Today, things are a little better organized. Nobody's suggesting you should bury your salmon in the garden, but you can entomb it in a salty rub, some clingfilm and a fridge for a couple of days and produce something magical. I've no idea what the Swedish for 'sublime' is, but it's le mot juste for this stuff. Because the cure imparts a good flavour and changes the texture, this is a great use for the farmed salmon which might not ordinarily stand your scrutiny. Get your fishmonger to cut two matching fillet pieces, one from either side of the same fish. It's better if they can be cut square, for reasons of neatness and economy. In order to kill any parasites present in the fish, freeze it for 24 hours and then defrost in the fridge.

Grind together 150g of sea salt, 150g of caster sugar, 30g of coriander seed and 50g of black peppercorns in a pestle and mortar and lay the two salmon fillets skin side down on a sheet of clingfilm. Chop 200g of dill finely and spread a thick layer on each fillet. Add a thick layer of the dry cure, pressing it on, vigorously, then lay over 10 whole sprigs of dill to create a retaining layer on the side you're going to flip over.

Turn over one fillet and fit it on top of the other, cut side to cut side, rotating it so the thick edge of one fillet fits on top of the thin edge of the other, then wrap the whole sandwich tightly in several layers of clingfilm. Store in a bowl, in the fridge, for 48 hours.

Unwrap the cured fish, pat it dry, and scrape off most of the cure and the chopped dill. Now lay it skin side down and take thin diagonal slices which include a lovely green layer of the cure along one edge. Serve with bread or boiled potatoes, 'fox sauce' and shots of icy vodka.

FOX SAUCE

The traditional sauce to accompany gravadlax translates from the Danish as 'fox sauce'. I'm not sure exactly why that is, but it sounds more mysterious and interesting than honey, mustard and dill sauce, which is effectively what it is.

Put 50g of cider vinegar, 50g of muscovado sugar, 50g of honey, 50g of Dijon mustard and 30g of vegetable oil into a blender and blitz.

Chop a hefty bunch of fresh dill, discarding any woody stems, bruise a little with the end of a rolling pin or the handle of your knife and stir it in.

If you want to be really authentic you can stir in a spoonful or so of any curing liquid remaining from the fish too.

Pickling

CHAPTER TWO

Pickling, like baking, is one of those cooking processes laden with emotion and significance. There are few things as fulfilling as gazing at a shelf full of jars at the end of a long day's work, knowing you've turned a wasteful glut into a season's worth of stored food. Unlike baking, though, pickling is dreadfully simple. The pickle is usually vinegar or a strong brine, or sometimes alcohol, and is itself lethal to bacteria. The fruit or veg to be preserved are usually salted first to draw out moisture and are then fully immersed in the pickle, which excludes both bacteria and air. Perhaps historically the single most important benefit of pickling is that the food doesn't necessarily need to be sterile before being placed in the pickle – unlike, for example, canning or sugar preserving, which require high levels of cleanliness. Nothing in the kitchen is foolproof, but pickling's well on the way.

When working with something as strongly flavoured as vinegar, it takes a lot of robust flavouring to register at all. As a result, pickling spice mixes are rarely shy or subtle. As pickles are eventually served in small amounts as a relish to other, more bland-flavoured foods, this is almost never a problem.

No discussion of pickling could be complete without mention of Lord Nelson, whose body was brought back from the Battle of Trafalgar in a state we can only describe as 'pickled'. William Beatty, ship's surgeon aboard the *Victory*, having decided that a national hero needed something more elaborate than the traditional burial at sea, had the body stripped, cleaned and carefully packed into a cask full of brandy, fortified with 'spirits of wine' (ethanol). The barrel was lashed to the deck of the ship and heavily guarded.

There was much discussion back in England as to whether Beatty should have used brandy rather than the more common rum. Some of which seems to have revolved around the purported preservative qualities, some around the fact that brandy was French.

PICKLED ONIONS

Could anything be as completely heartening to an Englishman as a pickled onion? After years of neglect, our traditions of cheese-making have come roaring back and these days a fashionably British cheeseboard can be found in creditable homes and restaurants. But British cheeses, particularly towards the Cheddary end of the spectrum, do well with a counterbalance. Like a music-hall double act, the big, fatty, solid straight man needs a cheeky, lovable sidekick with a sharp edge.

Pickled onions are a joy on so many sensory levels. There's something transgressive about putting a whole onion into your mouth anyway, it just shouldn't be right. There's a kind of 'Russian Roulette' frisson as you wonder whether this is going to be one of the fiercely vinegary jobs that catch on the glottis and reduce you to a coughing wreck, and then your teeth close. If it's a good 'un, you'll experience a crunch that transmits through the jawbone at exactly the point that the wave of sweet sharp juice crashes over your tongue. Molecular gastronomists can only dream of creating such a comprehensive oral going-over as that administered by a simple pickled onion, and best of all it leaves you drooling for another helping of cheese.

Creating pickled onions is not a complicated process. By the time you've finished each logical step you'll see how it contributes to that final experience in the mouth.

It's important to pick the right onions. Pretty much any kind of onion can be pickled – shallots are great, particularly in a balsamicky sweet pickle, wild garlic works a treat, as do spring onions, but a proper pickled onion that can stand up to saloon bar scrutiny was grown for the job. Pickling onions are small, tightly packed, absolute buggers to peel but stand up well to the treatment they're bred to receive.

As with most pickling of vegetables, the initial salting draws out some of the water by osmosis.

1kg small pickling onions or shallots ✱ 50g salt ✱ 1 small fresh chilli ✱ 1 clove of garlic (optional) ✱ 5g coriander seed ✱ 5g mustard seed ✱ 10 black peppercorns ✱ 180g granulated sugar ✱ 1 litre vinegar

1. Top and tail the onions with care. There should be no brown skin at the top or roots left at the bottom but there needs to be enough at the base to hold each onion together. Place the onions in a colander and pour over boiling water from a kettle. This will loosen the skins.

2. Peel the onions, dry them in a tea towel, then put them into a large bowl and toss them with the salt. Cover the bowl and allow to stand overnight.

3. Rinse the onions in cold water, dry again with a clean tea towel and pack them into jars that you've sterilized (see page 68). Pack the sliced chilli, and the sliced garlic if you're using it, between the layers.

4. Give the spices and peppercorns a rough scrunch with the handle of your knife, then put them into a saucepan with the sugar and the vinegar. Bring the vinegar to the boil, then pour the lot over the onions and quickly seal the jar, ensuring that all the onions are covered.

5. Store in a cool, dark place for at least a month before even considering trying one. I've had really good onions that have been pickled for up to a year.

STERILIZING JARS

There's all manner of panicky nonsense talked about sterilizing jars and it gets people into a right old state. A good strong vinegar pickle is pretty much guaranteed to slaughter any bacteria left in an unclean jar, but sugar-based preserves, light brines and even some alcohols will allow growth of moulds and other unpleasantnesses if the jar and its seal aren't scrupulously clean. Your grandma probably had a regime of boiling the jars, drying them in the oven, carrying them hot to the table on the handle of a recently boiled wooden spoon, filling and sealing them in a flurry of activity seemingly designed to scald the cook as efficiently as any 'germs'.

Fortunately, we have evolved. The best way to sterilize jars these days is to disassemble them and put them through the hottest cycle on a dishwasher – which is, after all, designed to clean all the unhealthy gunk off stuff – and try to time things so you're ready to pour in the hot brine and ingredients while the jars are still steaming in the racks. If you don't have a dishwasher, then it's back to boiling the jars for 10 minutes, making sure they remain submerged.

PICCALILLI

No one's really sure where piccalilli came from – there are various half-baked stabs at histories involving colonial India or even the Pennsylvania Dutch, but, to most of us, it's as British as it's possible to be. Redolent of popping gas-fires, knitted balaclavas and dried-out seed cake, if piccalilli could pull the nation through rationing, post-war depression, damp fogs and the Festival of Britain, it might even work for three days of Christmas leftovers.

1 cauliflower (about 500g) ★ 2 white onions ★ 1 small vegetable marrow (or a large courgette) ★ 100g French beans ★ 100g salt ★ 1 litre distilled malt vinegar ★ 5g mustard seed ★ 200g sugar ★ 2 cloves of garlic ★ 1 large 'thumb' of fresh ginger ★ 50g plain flour ★ 5g English mustard powder ★ 10g ground turmeric

1. Separate the cauli into small florets, chop the onions coarsely and cut the marrow into 1cm dice.

2. Put the cauli and onions into one bowl and the marrow and French beans into another. Add 50g of salt to each, mix thoroughly and allow to stand overnight.

3. In the morning, drain off any liquid, rinse the vegetables quickly to remove any excess salt and pat dry with a cloth.

4. Bring 750g of the vinegar to a simmer. Add the cauliflower, onions and mustard seed and allow to simmer for 5 minutes. Add the remaining vegetables and the sugar and simmer for a further 3 minutes. Grate the garlic and ginger into the mixture.

5. Drain the vegetables through a sieve, saving the hot vinegar. Try to avoid getting your head in the vinegar steam – it's not dangerous but it will certainly make your eyes water.

6. Working quickly – the vegetables are continuing to cook in their own heat and we don't want them to go soggy – combine the flour, mustard powder and turmeric in a pan and work up to a thin cream with the last 250g of vinegar.

7. Bring to the boil, then whisk in the reserved hot vinegar. The mixture should thicken, a bit like custard or Béchamel. Simmer for 10 minutes to cook out any floury taste.

8. Put the vegetables into a bowl and pour over the sauce. Mix gently and spoon into sterilized preserving jars (see page 68).

9. Store in the fridge for at least a month to allow the flavours to develop.

The nice thing about piccalilli is that it looks great next to pretty much anything and tastes sensational. I find a big slice of cold-cutting pie daunting without a piquant lift but ... and you're going to have to forgive me for this ... there's something about it that's just right with quite egregious leftovers. Once ham or turkey get that over-fridged dullness about them they become the ideal palette for the oral gymnastics of piccalilli. I'm firmly convinced it's this last happy quality that so endears it to the British soul.

PICKLED SHALLOTS

Good pickling takes a while. Onions, particularly, have an aggressive flavour which needs to be introduced to the equally powerful vinegar so that they can settle their differences over time. It takes a good few months in the jar before everything has mellowed to the extent that we can dive in there and enjoy one. Shallots, on the other hand, are a much milder form of onion, and balsamic vinegar is a much kinder vinegar. In this recipe we bring the two together, hurry the process along with a little heat and produce a 'pickled' onion as an elegant side dish to a roast in just an hour or so.

12 large 'banana' shallots ★ 20g unsalted butter ★ 150g balsamic vinegar ★ 100g red wine ★ a pinch of dried chilli flakes ★ a pinch of thyme ★ 100g chicken stock or water

1. Top and tail the shallots carefully, leaving enough at the root end to hold them together during cooking. Peel them and rub them with a little salt.

2. Heat the butter in the bottom of a small casserole or lidded saucepan that can go into the oven. Roll the shallots in the hot butter until they begin to brown on the surface.

3. Pour over the balsamic vinegar and cook aggressively until any throat-catching, tear-gassy whiff of vinegar has subsided.

4. Add the wine and reduce to half. You can also use port, sherry or my favourite, Madeira, all of which add their own distinctive flavours and bump up the sweetness.

5. Add pepper, salt, chilli flakes, thyme and enough stock or water to come halfway up the shallots in the pan.

6. Cover with a layer of foil and the pan lid, then place in the oven for as long as the meat is taking to roast.

7. Just before serving, lift the shallots into a serving dish and, if necessary, reduce the braising liquid over a high heat before pouring back over.

This has a lovely sharp tang to it, so consider it as halfway between a vegetable and a relish. A little goes a long way, so this will serve 4.

PICKLED WILD GARLIC

Wild garlic is one of our more infuriating native species. Wander along any waterway in early spring and you'll spot its deep green leaves poking out of the ground in profusion. You'll know it's wild garlic and not the quite similar-looking bluebell because of the overpowering, knock-you-over honk.

For something that yields such an incredible smell in the wild, it's a surprising under-performer in the kitchen. Almost any heat causes it to lose its flavour altogether, so it's probably best torn up and strewn cold over a plain risotto or used to flavour a plain potato soup. The bulbs, though, can be pickled in a similar way to onions and make a lovely subtle relish for all sorts of food in the months after the short season has passed.

You can pick wild garlic in some places, though there are restrictions in many parks and protected areas of public land. If you can find a reasonable-sized stand of it and it's legal to do so, you can dig up a substantial cube of the damp earth, containing hundreds of the bulbs, tightly packed, and transplant it to your own garden so you can have wild garlic easily to hand. Gardeners will tell you that it takes off like a weed and spreads vigorously in the right conditions, which makes it all the more galling that I tried and failed to start my own patch for five consecutive years. It was only after we'd sold the house and moved to another town that the new owners mentioned, in passing, the appalling infestation of wild garlic ruining their beds. I hope they read this. If they do, maybe they could send me a couple of jars in acknowledgement of five years of persistence in the face of bitter disappointment.

1kg wild garlic ★ 250g white wine vinegar ★ 250g water ★ 250g sugar ★ 5g mustard seed ★ 5g fennel seed ★ 5g black peppercorns ★ 2 bay leaves

1. Prep the wild garlic the same way you'd do spring onions or small leeks. Cut off the stringy roots and peel off any papery outer layers. Cut off the tops about 2cm into the green.

2. Prepare the pickle by bringing all the other ingredients briefly to the boil, then remove from the heat.

3. Blanch the trimmed garlic in boiling water for 2 minutes. Drain and pack into sterilized jars (see page 68).

4. Pour over the pickle and seal up the jars while everything is still hot. The pickles will be pleasant after a week but will keep for several months if refrigerated.

PICKLED BEETROOT

Pickled beetroot, quietly leaching its purple awfulness into a rapidly congealing pile of potato salad, is one of the truly nauseating memories of my childhood. The potato salad had the claggy spud taste of be-mayoed leftovers and, combined with the dyed malt vinegar, would have choked a goat. It's amazing that I could ever be persuaded to eat pickled beetroot again, but a trip to Norway put me straight. A sweeter pickle can enhance the earthy flavour of the root, and a surprising spice addition lifts it completely out of the mundane. This particular pickle is so light, so unexpectedly fragrant, that I find myself using it in a much more Japanese way – a small dish, served alongside starches or fish as a palate cleanser. This goes brilliantly with the pickled herrings later in this chapter.

1kg beetroot ★ 750g white wine vinegar ★ 450g sugar ★ 2 star anise

1. Cut the thin root and the stem off each beetroot at least a centimetre away from the body. If you trim too closely or pierce the skin, the juice will leak out and you'll lose a lot of the flavour.

2. Carefully rinse any dirt from the skins, then, while they're still damp, gently pat a little salt on to the surface of each root. Wrap tightly and separately in aluminium foil.

3. Put the wrapped beets into an oven dish with about 2.5cm of boiling water, and bake at 180°C for an hour.

4. When the beetroots yield to a bit of a poke, whip them out, unwrap them and, while running them under a cold tap, rub off the skins with your thumb. Cut into pleasing chunks and pack into sterilized jars (see page 68).

5. Put the vinegar into a pan, add the sugar and the star anise, bring quickly to the boil and pour into the jars, covering the beetroot chunks.

6. Seal the jars and store in a cool dark place for at least a month.

HOW PICKLING JARS WORK

Preserving jars of various sorts have been around for aeons – pharaohs stored their viscera in them when they were buried, so they have one of the oldest celebrity endorsements. Most pickling jars, at least since the Victorians, have comprised four main parts:

- A really robust glass jar, able to withstand boiling temperatures and clearly marked with a capacity, so judging quantities is made easier

- A solid lid, usually glass or metal

- A rubber gasket seal

- A mechanism, usually in metal, that can squeeze the lid closed.

The science behind the jar, though simple, is fiendishly clever. When the food and its preserving medium are placed in the jar they are hot and sterile. The clean lid is closed and as the food cools, it, along with any air inside, contracts, lowering the pressure inside the jar. Atmospheric pressure, therefore, squeezes the jar tighter and tighter closed.

In 'canning' recipes, food is actually poached in the jar, so the lid is left loose during the cooking, internal pressure rises and then the lid is sealed down as the heat source is removed. Again, external pressure does the work.

Opening a jar of preserves after a while involves breaking that pressure seal. Don't use a knife to prise if the lid is stubborn, just tug on the 'ear' of the rubber ring to break the seal and, with a brief hiss, the pressures will equalize and the jar will open easily.

If for any reason your pickle doesn't work well and the food begins to degrade, gases will be formed as a by-product of decomposition. If the lid pops open on releasing the metal catch, the pressure in the jar is higher than atmospheric pressure and you'll know something has gone wrong.

Brilliant, huh?

An even simpler indicator that the preserve is still good is that 'pop-up' thing in the middle of the lid on a commercial jam jar. Even in the most hi-tech jam factories, the occasional jar goes awry, so 'popping' of the lid enables the manufacturers to spot it and remove it from a batch before it goes bang on a supermarket shelf somewhere and scares a granny half to death.

PICKLED EGGS

Eggs degrade slowly over time. The whites seem to lose some of their body and the yolks lose some of their richness. For this reason, attempts at preservation have usually involved sealing the slightly porous shell before storage. The traditional method was to oil the shell but they could also be dipped in wax. Isinglass, a natural gelatine derived from the swim bladders of sturgeon, could be used to create an airtight coat, eggs could be stored under water in a solution made antiseptic by the addition of caustic soda or, in a move that has either delighted or nauseated British pubgoers since the first pints were pulled, they can be pickled in malt vinegar and displayed like pathological specimens in a big jar on the bar.

Some flavour and texture combinations are frankly polarizing, and the idea of a hard-boiled egg, rubbery and pale, floating for weeks in the sort of vinegar you chuck on your chips makes many people's stomachs lurch. But a properly pickled egg is a lovesome thing and one that rewards trial.

They say it was a brave man who first tried an oyster, and I'm old enough to still remember the transgressive thrill of eating, for the very first time, a lump of rice topped with a slab of raw fish. Think of the pickled egg as traditional British artisanal sushi, shut your eyes and pop it in. You'll be surprised, but you won't be disappointed.

1 litre distilled malt vinegar ★ 1 bay leaf (optional) ★ 10 black peppercorns ★ 5g mustard seed (optional) ★ 12 large free-range eggs

1. Choose your pickling vinegar. Malt vinegar is traditionally pubby and will require only a few peppercorns for flavouring. Wine, cider and spirit vinegars have a less pronounced taste, so bay, or even a teaspoonful of mustard seed alongside the pepper, will jolly things up. Allspice, ginger and even garlic appear in eighteenth-century farmhouse recipes for egg pickle.

2. Add the spices to your chosen vinegar and bring to the boil.

3. Hard-boil the eggs and cool them in cold water, then peel them carefully, removing all shell and membrane. Pack the eggs into your sterilized pickling jars (see page 68). Allow the pickling liquid to cool, then pour over the eggs. Store in a cool, dark place for at least 6 weeks before tasting.

PONTACK KETCHUP

Pontack is a sauce based on elderberries and vinegar which is an excellent accompaniment to meat and game. It's reputed to have been invented at the Pontack Arms,[11] 'a fashionable, genteel eating house' in Georgian London where Defoe, Swift, Locke and Hogarth ate along with the Fellows of the Royal Society. It has the texture and some of the alarmingly perky qualities of Worcestershire sauce.

500g elderberries ★ 500g cider or white wine vinegar ★ 200g shallots ★ 3 cloves ★ 4 allspice berries ★ 1 blade of mace ★ 15g peppercorns ★ 15g grated fresh ginger ★ 15g salt ★ 20g vinegar from pickled walnuts

1. Preheat the oven to 120°C. Strip the elderberries from their stems (these are thought to be mildly toxic), weigh them, and put them into a non-reactive casserole with a close-fitting lid. Pour in a similar weight of vinegar, heated to boiling. Cover the top with foil and then put the lid on, creating as tight a seal as you can.

2. Put the casserole into the oven for 4–6 hours.

3. Mash the berries in the casserole with the end of a rolling pin, or blitz roughly in a blender.

4. Chop the shallots finely and add to the berries, along with the rest of the ingredients except the walnut vinegar. Bring the liquid back up to the boil and cook for 15 minutes. Strain through muslin, then bring back to the boil again, add the walnut vinegar and bottle while hot.

5. Pontack definitely improves with age, maturing into a kind of fruity, tannic Worcestershire sauce. It's supposed to reach its best after 7 years, which is pretty impressive, because it's stonking after 6 weeks.

---

11 The Pontack Arms was an anglicization of 'Enseigne de Pontac'. François-Auguste de Pontac (1636–94) was the last of his family to own Haut-Brion, and opened the pub in Abchurch Lane to promote his family's Bordeaux. In spite of its French roots, pontack remains one of the most British of sauces.

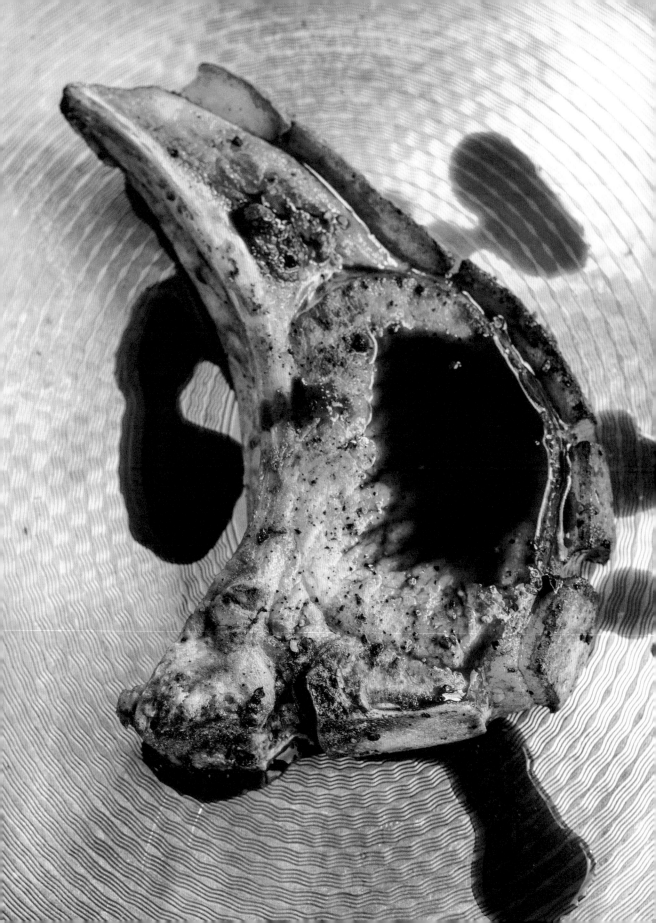

PICKLED HERRING

Pickled herring is like Marmite. Put it out as a starter and half your guests will smack their chops and proclaim their delight in loud, clear voices. The remainder will leave the room and make a silent note never to accept your invitations again. Yes, it's raw oily fish in vinegar and it's probably the kind of thing your old Nan bought in jars before the war, but it's also part of a distinguished history of fish preservation that has hints of sushi, of fashionable ceviche, yet connects us directly with our Viking forebears.

For me, pickled herrings are some of the most complex and delightful pickled food we can produce. In any pickle the acidic liquid preserves and flavours, but with herrings it also marries harmoniously with the oil in the fish. By balancing the oil with the vinegar you're pulling off the same ancient culinary trick as a well-made vinaigrette. You can also see in this recipe how, once an aggressive salting has been used to preserve the fish, a sweet/sour brine can be used to make it palatable again.

Of course, it affects my personal judgement not one jot, but we're told that eating oily fish is good for us, so I suppose there's the added bonus of virtuousness, if that's the sort of thing that floats your gustatory longboat.

You can salt your own herrings for this (see page 55) or you can buy them in vacuum packs from Scandinavian, Polish or Jewish delis.

10 salted herring fillets ★ 1 onion ★ 1 carrot ★ a small bunch of fresh dill ★ 500g white wine vinegar ★ 500g water ★ 300g sugar ★ 2 bay leaves ★ 20 black peppercorns ★ 25g mustard seed

1. Soak the herring fillets overnight in cold water.

2. Slice the onion and carrot finely – they form a traditional garnish – and pick out some particularly fetching-looking fronds from the bunch of dill.

3. The rest of the ingredients form the pickle. Put them into a pan, bring to the boil, then reduce the heat, simmer for 20 minutes and allow to cool.

4. Rinse and pat dry the herring fillets, then cut them into bite-sized chunks and pack them loosely into a sterilized preserving jar (see page 68), interlayered with the carrots, onions and dill.

5. Pour over the cooled pickle to cover everything, then seal the jar and tap it firmly on a folded tea towel on the worktop to dislodge any air bubbles.

6. Stored in the fridge, the herrings will be good after a week and increasingly luscious for up to 3 months.

SOUSING FISH

Nobody's quite sure where the idea of 'sousing' fish came from. There are well-researched roots heading back into central Europe and North Africa for this odd combination of cooking and then pickling. It pops up in Venetian cooking during the Renaissance – which basically means it could have come from anywhere and been exported to almost anywhere else, as Venice was the ultimate entrepôt, the Renaissance equivalent of the Mos Eisley Cantina in *Star Wars*.

Certainly with a food as plentiful as oily fish, so prone to spoilage, it makes sense to both cook it quickly and preserve it, and, though the idea of cooking something in a flour coating and then sinking it in vinegar seems screamingly counter-intuitive to modern palates, it still tastes particularly good. Perhaps one way of looking at it is to consider that most methods of preserving fish involve preliminary salting to firm and partially set the fish. Sousing achieves the same effect by cooking.

Note: If you whip out the obviously Venetian ingredients in the recipe that follows (the sardines, balsamic, pinenuts and raisins), replacing them with herring fillets, a smear of mustard before frying and some dill in the marinade, you'll have the Scandinavian version. My food history simply doesn't stretch to connecting the Venetians with the Vikings, which may just indicate that this is such a great idea in itself that it may have occurred spontaneously to different fish-loving cooks.

SARDE IN SAOR

12 fresh sardines ✶ 100g white wine vinegar ✶ 100g balsamic vinegar ✶ 100g white wine ✶ 40g raisins ✶ 400g onions ✶ 100g olive oil ✶ ½ a clove of garlic ✶ 100g sugar ✶ 40g pinenuts ✶ 50g plain flour

1. Have your sardines gutted, beheaded, scaled and boned by your fishmonger unless you're happy to do it yourself.

2. Put the two vinegars and the wine into a bowl and soak the raisins in the mixture.

3. Slice the onions finely and stew them gently in the olive oil until they begin to take on a straw colour. Towards the end of cooking, grate in the garlic.

4. Strain the mixed vinegars over the hot onions in the pan, reserving the raisins. Add the sugar, then bring to the boil and cook gently for 3 minutes. Add the pinenuts and raisins about 30 seconds before the end of cooking, then take the pan off the heat while you cook the fish.

5. Open the sardines out flat, dip them in seasoned flour and fry them in batches, skin side first, in olive oil. Allow 3 minutes on the skin side, 1 minute on the flesh side.

6. Use a slotted spoon to lift about half of the solid stuff out of the vinegar marinade and use it to create a bed in a flat dish. Lay the fried sardines on the bed and spoon over the rest of the marinade.

The sardines will be good after a couple of hours marinating in the fridge and will keep for 3–4 days. Because the idea is so counter-intuitive to many Brits, I usually offer sarde in saor as a starter – that way people feel they can opt out if they fancy and I also get to neck at least one full-size portion on my own the following day. This will serve 8 as a starter and 4 as a main.

ACIDIC MARINATION

Way out there on the outer frontiers of pickling and fish cookery comes acidic marination. Immersing fish in an acidic pickle (usually citrus juice) denatures and coagulates the proteins in the tissue – the same changes that heat creates, with none of the damage. It's not completely inaccurate to say that marinating fresh seafish in fruit juice actually 'cooks' it.

Of course, a few years ago this idea would have seemed outrageously dangerous to most westerners, but now, in the age of supermarket sashimi, we're all as happy as little sharks to chuck down quantities of raw fish. So perhaps it's time to revisit the ceviche, a South American preparation of 'citrus-pickled' fish.

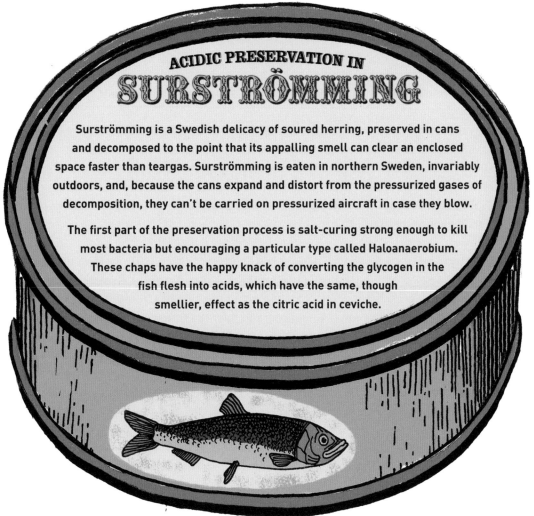

ACIDIC PRESERVATION IN
SURSTRÖMMING

Surströmming is a Swedish delicacy of soured herring, preserved in cans and decomposed to the point that its appalling smell can clear an enclosed space faster than teargas. Surströmming is eaten in northern Sweden, invariably outdoors, and, because the cans expand and distort from the pressurized gases of decomposition, they can't be carried on pressurized aircraft in case they blow.

The first part of the preservation process is salt-curing strong enough to kill most bacteria but encouraging a particular type called Haloanaerobium. These chaps have the happy knack of converting the glycogen in the fish flesh into acids, which have the same, though smellier, effect as the citric acid in ceviche.

CEVICHE

500g white seafish, or mixture of white fish with peeled raw prawns ★ 6 fresh limes ★ 1 fresh red chilli ★ salt and freshly ground black pepper ★ 1 sweet red 'romano' pepper ★ 1 medium red onion ★ 50g tomatoes ★ chopped fresh flat-leaf parsley

1. Depending on how you want to lay your finished dish out, either dice or slice your fish finely: 1cm dice makes an easy-to-eat salad, while thin, carpaccio-like slices look superb on the plate. If you're using prawns, cut them so that each piece is roughly the same thickness as your fish so the marinade penetrates at the same speed.

2. Warm the limes for 20 seconds in the microwave, then roll them about on your worktop, applying pressure with the flat of your hand. This helps the limes give up more juice, more easily. There seem to be two kinds of limes: plump, ludicrously green ones that yield an embarrassment of mouth-watering juice, and tough little leathery numbers looking not unlike an alligator testicle and yielding about as much useful fluid. Go for the flash ones or you'll be squeezing for ever. Squeeze the juice into a bowl and add the chilli, finely chopped.

3. Lightly season the fish with pepper and salt, then add it to the marinade and work it through with clean hands. Cover with clingfilm and refrigerate while the citrus does its work. The fish will become cloudy in a few minutes as the proteins begin to denature and the flavours of the marinade begin to penetrate. I'm very happy with ceviche that's marinated for minutes, but some people like to keep it in the liquid for hours or even overnight to ensure it's 'properly cooked through'.

4. Drain away most of the lime juice, then mix with the rest of the ingredients. I like to chop the sweet red pepper into fantastically show-off tiny brunoise, and I also shred the onion into fine strips and blanch it quickly in boiling water to remove just a little of its heat. For maximum cheffy impact you can also deseed and peel the tomatoes. In almost all cases I disagree violently with poncy presentation of food, but ceviche can look quite challenging unless you make an effort on the plate. Keep to one side some particularly attractive shreds of lime, chilli and onion to decorate the top, along with the chopped flat-leaf parsley, which should be sprinkled over at the last minute. For an authentically 1980s touch, substitute coriander leaves for the parsley.

5. Toss all the ingredients together in the bowl and allow them to stand for a while in the fridge. Most people assume that fish, coming from the sea, needs little salt. This would be a huge mistake with ceviche, which needs a generous hand.

FERMENTATION PICKLING

Pickling in vinegar produces 'directly acidified' pickles. Some foods, though, contain bacteria which create their own acids by fermentation as they begin to decompose. When the pH reaches less than 4.6, bacteria cannot survive and the food has produced its own acid pickle.

This simple, ancient and rather elegant process creates kosher pickled cucumbers and most of the fresh-tasting pickles that accompany Japanese food. Pickling with the food's own naturally occurring acids produces subtle results which enhance rather than overwhelm the original flavours of the produce.

For most fermentation pickling, the 'brine' is salty enough to prevent bacteria multiplying on the surface of the fruit but mainly exists to seal the fruit or vegetable in an airless environment. It's vital that the pickles stay entirely immersed in the brine. In traditional Japanese pickling, this was achieved in a wooden barrel by weighting down the food with clean pebbles. Today, neat little plastic pickling boxes are available with a spring-loaded plate to prevent the food floating up (see stockists, pages 370-71). It's easy to rig up something similar in your own kitchen, perhaps using a drying rack and a clean weight, or – and be warned that this is a bit fiddly – you can use zipped freezer bags and carefully exclude all air bubbles before sealing.

PICKLED CUCUMBERS

1.5 litres water ★ 15g white wine vinegar ★ 45g sea salt ★ 1kg small cucumbers ★ 15g black peppercorns ★ 3 cloves of garlic ★ a bunch of fresh dill ★ chillies (optional) ★ coriander seed (optional) ★ juniper berries (optional)

1. Put the water, wine vinegar and salt into a pan and bring to the boil, then set aside and allow to cool completely.

2. Wash the cucumbers carefully, then dry them and pack them into sterilized jars (see page 68) with the aromatics distributed between them. Pour over the cold brine, ensuring that everything stays completely immersed (this is why commercial pickles are packed tight into their jars. It prevents them floating out of the brine cover before they're properly pickled).

3. The cucumbers will be ready after 7 days, but develop better flavour as they age further.

1910

DILL PICKLES

SONG

·A·RAG

Words by
ALFRED BRYAN

5

Music by
CHAS. E. JOHNSON

JEROME H. REMICK & CO., NEW YORK - DETROIT.

JAPANESE QUICK PICKLING

In Japanese home cooking, lightly pickled vegetables form a part of most meals. Families often have a large repertoire of favourite recipes using seasonal vegetables and adding a variety of flavourings to the basic pickling medium. Chilli, garlic, soy, yuzu,[12] shiso leaf[13] and kelp[14] can all tweak the flavours, but it is the beginning of lactic fermentation that adds the crucial umami element to the raw vegetable.

Pickles are usually served alongside the main courses. Like many elements of Japanese cuisine it can take years to get really good at pickling, but when they're done just right, served simply with rice, they can make a whole meal.

JAPANESE-STYLE PICKLED VEGETABLES

500g carrot, turnip, daikon, Chinese cabbage ★ a 5cm piece of kombu ★ ½ a red chilli ★ 5g salt ★ 15g yuzu or lemon juice

1. Peel the root vegetables and slice them, and the Chinese cabbage, extremely thinly. If you don't have the knife skills of a ninja, use a mandoline slicer or even, at a pinch, a veg peeler.

2. Cut the kombu into thin strips. Deseed the chilli.

3. Put the sliced veg along with all the rest of the ingredients into a strong ziplock freezer bag. Exclude as much air as possible, then vigorously massage and squeeze the contents.

4. Refrigerate the bag for a day or two, by which time you may begin to see tiny bubbles produced by the lactic fermentation.

---

12 Yuzu: a Japanese citrus fruit that tastes somewhere between grapefruit and mandarin. Available in small bottles of juice or as a flavoured vinegar.

13 Shiso: the leaves of the perilla plant, a relative of mint. It has a distinctive herby fragrance, quite sharp, and is used in much the same way we might use basil.

14 Kombu: or kelp, a thick, leathery culinary seaweed that's the main source of umami flavour in Japanese cooking. For suppliers of all the above, see pages 370–71.

SAUERKRAUT

Sauerkraut and kimchi take fermentation pickling on to another level altogether. The mid-European version of 'pickled cabbage' uses enough salt to keep noxious elements at bay, but the vegetable itself is allowed to ferment a good way towards putrefaction using naturally occurring bacteria. Because cabbage is such an unbelievably tough vegetable – think how long its leaves can survive in a compost heap – it retains a shape, a structure and even a crunch as it breaks down, so it remains appetizing.

The internet is awash with sites attributing health benefits to sauerkraut, and it's true that the process can be so 'natural' that it seems inherently virtuous. I always consume my sauerkraut with a big old pile of smoked pork product in an ostentatious 'grande choucroute' blowout or packed generously into a Reuben sandwich (see page 53) the size of my forearm, to ensure that any presumed health benefits are, to some degree, mitigated.

1 head of white cabbage ★ 50g salt ★ 10g caraway seed (optional)

1. Slice the base off the cabbage, creating a circle that will just fit into the neck of your preserving jar. Shred the rest of the cabbage finely. Many food processors have excellent slicing attachments which are just great for this sort of project.

2. Toss the cabbage in the salt, working it in hard with clean hands. Add the caraway seed here if you like the flavour, but they're not essential.

3. Pack the salty cabbage into a sterilized jar (see page 68), leaving a good 5cm of expansion space at the top. Pour over boiled and cooled water until it rises above the level of the cabbage. Use the cabbage stem disc to create a floating lid that will keep the shredded cabbage submerged.

4. Fermentation needs cool temperatures to begin, but not as cool as a fridge – which is, after all, designed to stop bacteria breeding. Keep the jar in a cool, dark place with the lid just askew and after 3 or 4 days there will be a bubbling from the liquid.

5. Check the jar daily, skimming off any scum or the beginnings of mould. If the liquid is in danger of drying out and exposing the cabbage, top it up or use a clean spoon to discipline it back under the surface. After about a month, the fermentation will have died down and the sauerkraut is ready. If the whole process has made you a little nervous you can always bring it to the boil in a small pan before serving it hot, but I prefer it cold and raw.

KIMCHI

Korean kimchi adds garlic and chillies to the mix, both ingredients with further preservative properties as well as ludicrously strong flavour. Aficionados believe that kimchi can only improve with age and never degrades. A good kimchi is effervescent with the gases given off by breeding bacteria, so it's stored in sealed vessels which can actually explode under the pressure. Many Korean families keep a separate fridge for their kimchi, just in case. This is the modern equivalent of the original technique, which involved burying it in a specially constructed pit under the house.

On the face of it, preparations involving decomposition, strong smells and explosive results might seem a cultural step too far for a western cook, yet we're entirely happy to pay a fortune for something like a well-affined Époisses, which, as it sits on the table at our fashionable dinner party, smells like a slurry tanker.

In the same way as many of the more disturbingly stinky western foods add remarkably complex and subtle flavours, kimchi, particularly when added as a condiment or cooking ingredient, can be as effective as a trace of anchovy with lamb or nam pla fish sauce in a Thai curry.

1 Chinese cabbage ★ 200g salt ★ 1 medium carrot ★ 6 spring onions ★ 120g Korean chilli powder – kochugaru[15] ★ ¼ of an onion ★ 75g fish sauce ★ 30g sugar ★ 5 cloves of garlic ★ 1 knob of fresh ginger

1. Quarter the cabbage lengthways and remove most of the solid core or stem.

2. Bring a large pan of salted water to the boil and blanch the quarters for a couple of seconds.

3. Drain the cabbage chunks, then layer them into a bowl, sprinkling them generously with more salt and working it down between the leaves. Leave the bowl covered for up to 6 hours, until the leaves are floppy but the stem still 'snaps' when broken.

---

15 Kochugaru (or gochgaru) is dried and flaked chillies. Aficionados of Korean food say that you can't substitute directly with any other kind of chilli and expect the same effects, so be sure to grab some if you see it at an Asian grocery or supermarket. It is milder than many Mexican chillies and as fragrant as some of the mild paprikas. I find it closest to the flaked red peppers available in Turkish supermarkets but I've never met a Korean who agrees with me. Whatever happens, if you substitute regular chilli powder, please moderate the quantities or you'll blow your head off.

4. Rinse the cabbage in a couple of changes of cold water, then wring out vigorously and leave to stand in a colander for half an hour.

5. Julienne the carrot. Clean the spring onions and cut them into 1cm lengths.

6. Cut across the cabbage quarters at about 5cm intervals, making roughly square blocks. Stir in the carrot and spring onions with your hands.

7. Blitz the remaining ingredients in a blender, pour over the vegetables and work through thoroughly with your hands. You might want to wear latex gloves for this stage. You might even want to wear two pairs.

8. Once everything's been coated, pack it down carefully into an airtight container. A glass jar might be a little risky unless it's the kind with a clip-down top and a rubber seal – they can actually blow off excess pressure instead of exploding. I use a 2 litre plastic pot, the type where the lid locks on with clickable 'ears'. Store in a cool dark place – I use a covered bucket in the larder. That way if anything goes bang, I'll have limited the collateral damage. Allow 'headspace', no matter how you pack the ingredients, so there's room for expansion.

9. After 3 days, taste the kimchi, which will be spicy but you should be able to detect the tang of the beginning of fermentation.

10. Store in the fridge for up to 3 months. I like to 'burp' my kimchi regularly to relieve pressure, but the real experts leave it sealed so the gases are forced back into the mixture and cause a 'fizz'.

WHEN SMELL and TASTE DON'T AGREE

Kimchi, Époisses, nam pla, truffles[16] – they smell so revolting yet they taste so good. We know that smell is a big part of our experience of flavour, so how is it that something that smells like a pile of sweatsocks can be sublime in the mouth?

It seems that it's all to do with the direction you're breathing. When you breathe in, with your mouth empty, your brain is using the nose as a sensor for threats. It's highly attuned to those smells that warn us away...the feral smell of predators, the bodily wastes of our own or other species, and decomposing food. Smells coming in via your nose are referred to as 'orthonasal'.

When we chew, we're breathing the smell of the food outwards from the oral cavity, over different 'retronasal' receptors, and our brains respond in a different way: in the case of most of the smelly foods we lovey...with sheer joy.

Now of course this doesn't mean that if you nosh in to the next dead badger you smell, rotting at the roadside, it will actually taste like foie gras...but the rather worrying thought is that it just might.

---

16 Asafoetida, natto, garum, dried shrimp, bacalao, durian, bumalo, chitterlins, andouillette, surströmming and even Parmesan cheese.

DRYING

CHAPTER THREE

We used to have a fantastic tradition of salting meat in the UK, though not perhaps with the self-publicizing elan of other nations (York, Wiltshire and Bradenham have been names associated with various hams and our bacon was ever legendary, but they were never really star players on the international platter of cold meats), but, perhaps because we like our bangers fresh and our bacon salty, we've never quite got round to drying stuff.

It's a shame really, because everyone else has got something hanging out the back: bresaola, jerky, droëwors, Bündnerfleisch, biltong, salami, kabanosy, lap cheung, chorizo, saucisson sec and innumerable others. We Brits, on the other hand, have even had to nick the word 'charcuterie' from the French so we'd have something to call the stuff.

There's a common belief that we don't 'do charcuterie' in this country because our humid climate makes meat 'go off' rather than dry; that's a complete myth. You actually need a cool, moist environment for curing, preferably with a decent breeze. If a sausage or piece of meat dries quickly in dry air the outside becomes hard too quickly – 'case hardened' – preventing the moisture from escaping from the centre. In moist air the outer surface remains pliable as the meat dries evenly throughout. Most of the best charcuterie in the world is cured in moist temperate climates, often in mountains or where a good clean sea-breeze can promote drying through evaporation.

This is obviously not an accurate description of conditions in my backyard, but I've had great success drying meat in my kitchen, hanging it close to a north-facing window for maximum chill and breeze through the knackered sashes. I also tend to hang it over the sink to keep the humidity up. If things get too hot I move it to the shade. In fact the more you can keep an eye on your meat, checking it daily, the better result you're likely to get.

Many home-curers starting out get jumpy when mould appears. Actually a chalk white bloom on the surface is healthy, and any spots of slimy or black mould can be quickly removed with plain vinegar – another good reason for a daily check. The best reassurance, though, is a good deep sniff. If your meat is going off you'll definitely know by the smell – in fact, in Italy this is still considered the only sure way to check. Testers use a long needle made from horse bone which can be slid into the ham or salami and sniffed to ensure there's no trace of putrescence.

I've been forced to the conclusion that, love as we do our hams, bangers, bacons and chops, we Brits are funny about pork. Nominally sane people who'll happily wolf street food in the most 'authentic' of milieus, who harbour an ambition to try fugu and will cheerfully eat takeaway sushi from a convenience store, will blanch, gag and retch if served pork properly pink near the bone. They'll reel off a scad of ill-informed guff about trichinosis, some vague superstition about how it 'tastes a bit like human flesh' and then go off into a load of ranting cobblers about worms. Then you offer them a bit of home-cured salami and they go right off the rails. Come on. That half of the population of the world who don't reject pork out of hand have been salting and air-drying pork for as long as they've domesticated the pig. What can be the problem?

Once chopped meat has been salted and packed in a robust natural skin, it's proof against most that the elements can throw at it and creates an environment hostile to bacteria. Once that's sorted, time and the free flow of air will dry it out, making any kind of spoilage even more unlikely. That, as they say, is the science bit. So simple that millions of illiterate peasants have been doing it, all over the world, every year for countless centuries, feeding it to their beloved and treasured families throughout the winter and not just surviving but apparently enjoying the results.

Some of the most highly refined connoisseur snobbery in the food world is reserved for air-dried pork in the form of jamón ibérico or prosciutto di Parma, and it is true that curing and air-drying a whole leg is technically challenging. Maintaining conditions under which the curing salt can penetrate the dense muscular flesh of a whole ham is not something you can easily achieve in the average garden shed, but thinner cuts – belly for pancetta, for example – or roughly chopped meat allow the salt to penetrate more surely.

After the first couple of tries, pride and greed overcome any lurking superstitious worries or general mimsy gutlessness.

'You mean you chop up a load of pork, stuff it in a pig gut and hang it outside for a month . . . in England?'

Damn right I do . . . and so should you.

BRESAOLA

Call it bresaola, call it spiced, air-dried beef, but it's one of the simplest bits of charcuterie to do at home and makes a great introduction to doing it yourself. Bresaola is salted and dried just like a salami but it's made from a single muscle of beef. This means that, though the surface might develop a healthy bloom of mould while it dries, the inside of the meat is never exposed to the air, making any kind of unhelpful bacterial development much less likely. This kind of 'single muscle' charcuterie is the easiest to carry off successfully, so it makes a great first project if you're just dipping your toe in the water.

single muscle from beef 'top round' (usually around 500g–1kg) ★ 1 glass of red wine ★ 100g coarse sea salt ★ 100g sugar ★ 20g fresh or dried rosemary ★ 5g black peppercorns ★ 2.5g Prague Powder #2 per kg of meat ★ butcher's string

1. Ask your butcher for the main muscle in the top round. This is from the top of the leg, usually regarded as a second-class roast but excellently lean and close-textured for our purposes. Trim off all the surface fat and silverskin. Be merciless, it all makes for great stock. Don't, however, try to remove the single vein of silverskin running through the centre of the muscle – your meat will fall apart if you do.

2. Put the meat into a bowl, pour over the red wine and leave to marinate overnight.

3. Make up your cure by putting the dry ingredients through a grinder, then put half the cure into an airtight jar and set aside.

4. Take the meat out of the wine marinade, dry it with kitchen paper, then rub the other half of the cure into the surface and seal it in a freezer bag. Place in the fridge and allow to marinate, turning daily. After a week, take the meat out of the bag, dry it with kitchen paper again, then rub with the second half of the cure. Reseal and marinate for a second week.

5. Remove any remaining cure from the meat and pat dry with paper towels. Tie two pieces of string vertically around the meat, then tie a series of butcher's knots (see page 278) horizontally around and wrap it in clean muslin.

6. Label clearly with date and weight and hang in a cool place, not too dry. Check regularly by sniffing for unpleasantnesses and weighing carefully. Your bresaola will be ready after around 3 weeks, when it's lost 30% of its weight. I usually remove the muslin for the last week.

7. Slice the bresaola paper thin and serve either as it comes or with olive oil and lemon.

MOULD

Home-curers have a complex relationship with mould. It can be the first sign of spoilage or the vital ingredient in successful preservation. Gardeners define a weed as any plant that's growing in the wrong place and we could probably look at moulds the same way.

Moulds are fungi and come in two forms. Some grow as multi-cellular strings or hyphae, which gives the characteristic 'furry' appearance. Others are single-cell types which we call yeasts – so we couldn't have bread, beer, cheese, soy sauce or any one of a million other food products without mould. That doesn't help, though, when your bacon has grown fur and you're wondering whether it's safe to eat.

Perhaps the most widely known food mould is the genus *Penicillium*, which has the ability to kill a variety of unpleasant bacteria. Species of penicillium crop up throughout the food world: their names, *P. camemberti* or *P. roqueforti*. The wonderfully evocative *P. nalgiovense* forms the white 'chalky' coating you'll have seen on the surface of a good salami, which not only protects it from bacterial growth but adds subtly to the development of flavour.

It was from *P. chrysogenum* that Alexander Fleming extracted penicillin, the life-saving antibiotic, in 1929.

THE ECOSYSTEM IN YOUR LUNCH

Good preservation is often a matter of understanding the relationships between the things that want to live on your food and balancing them against each other. Bacteria like lactobacilli turn the lactose in food into lactic acid, thereby creating a hostile environment for other organisms. A surface coating of penicillium mould kills other bacteria. In baking, a symbiotic relationship between naturally occurring yeasts and lactobacilli forms the living 'mother' which gives sourdough its flavour and texture.

These combinations of life-forms, tiny ecologies, if you will, are often subtly different from place to place. A natural sourdough varies depending on the environment of the kitchen or bakery in which it's grown. In a bakery that's been used for the purpose for, say, 100 years, the combination of airborne wildlife is as unique as that in French cheese 'caves', and may be as worthy of careful conservation.

JERKY/BILTONG

In both South Africa and in parts of the USA there's a strong tradition of rapid drying of meat. Both pioneer cultures were reliant on hunting, which meant a large-sized kill often had to be preserved quickly. Lean meat was cut into thin strips and dried on gratings over a low fire, or perhaps hung in direct sunlight to drive off all moisture. Here, though, the difference ends. If you ever want to start a large punch-up, walk into any bar full of backpackers and assert that jerky and biltong are the same thing. Both cultures swear that theirs is the best and the alternative nothing better than meaty shoe leather.

BILTONG

Try making biltong with venison or ostrich meat, if you can get it. The important thing to remember is that the meat should be a lean single muscle. That way it remains impervious to bacteria until it's cut.

The vinegar has a very important role to play in killing surface bacteria on the cut meat, but, if you wish, you can experiment with other 'washes' after the vinegar has been applied. Worcestershire sauce, whisky and even barbecue sauce are popular.

1kg beef sirloin, silverside or top round ★ 100g salt ★ 100g cider vinegar ★ 100g black peppercorns ★ 100g coriander seed

1. Slice the meat along the grain into 1cm thick strips.

2. Lay the meat strips in a non-reactive dish, strew with the salt and mix thoroughly with your hands to ensure good coverage. Store covered in the fridge for 2 hours.

3. Pat the meat dry with kitchen paper, carefully removing any remaining salt. Paint the meat with the vinegar, using a pastry brush.

4. Crush the pepper and coriander seed or blitz them momentarily in a grinder, then lay the vinegar-coated meat on them and press down so the ingredients adhere.

5. You can arrange the strips on the grating of your desiccator or an oven cooling rack or hang them in your drying box.

6. The biltong is done when it's almost black on the outside and has a tight, rubbery consistency inside. It will keep in the refrigerator in an airtight box for up to 2 months, and much longer if frozen in small batches.

BUILDING A DRYING BOX

Jerky and biltong both require dry heat, as they'd have received in their traditional outdoor preparation. There are commercial desiccators for the process, and people with an Aga often swear by the bottom oven, but a drying box is easy to build and allows much more control over the process.

The heat source is one of those horribly old-fashioned and inefficient incandescent light bulbs. They're not terribly green because of the enormous amount of energy they put out as heat rather than light – though in this case it works to our advantage. This might be the only remaining ethical use for such out-of-date technology.

Because not much heat is involved, the enclosure can be something as simple as a cardboard box or something more elaborate in wood or metal if you feel like going into mass production – however you tackle it, though, the principles are the same. You're just creating a chimney so that the hot dry air can flow up and over the hanging meat.

You can use the box for jerky, biltong or droëwors (see page 307), but remember that things like bresaola, ham, salami, etc. need a longer, more gentle process to retain their texture, so don't be tempted to hurry them along in your box.

REDNECK JERKY

The simplest jerky would be prepared from beef or venison in much the same way as biltong, only without the vinegar or coriander. Modern jerky, though, is a very different thing. It's popular with guys who hunt, shoot, drive big trucks and like to barbecue, so many recipes today contain incredibly complex mixtures of suitably manly ingredients. This recipe is homage to my time living in the Deep South and throws in pretty much every cliché available. I suggest that in this case, you subtract to your own personal taste.

1kg sirloin, silverside or top round of beef, or any single muscle of something you've shot ★ 100g salt ★ 100g Worcestershire, soy or teriyaki sauce ★ 100g bourbon, tequila or beer ★ 30g dried herbs – including thyme, sage and oregano ★ 20g mixed chilli powder, onion powder and garlic powder ★ 25g black peppercorns ★ plus your own mystery ingredient?

1. Cut the meat into strips along the grain of the muscle and put them into a non-reactive dish.

2. Salt the meat for a couple of hours to draw out the moisture.

3. Combine the ingredients for your wet marinade – that's your main liquid plus the herbs, chilli, onion powder, garlic, etc. – and soak the strips in it overnight.

4. Dry the strips carefully with kitchen paper and roll them in any dry ingredients that you'd like to form a crust – I particularly like roughly cracked peppercorns.

5. Lay or hang the strips in your desiccator, slow oven or drying box.

6. The jerky will be done when it's still soft enough to tear at manfully with your teeth but before it's hard enough to snap, which, depending on your drying conditions, may take either a few days or a couple of weeks.

SALAMI

The only thing vaguely disturbing about making salami at home is how easy it is, and the result is an entirely different animal to the dried-out and leathery staple of the supermarket deli. The texture is softer, fudgier, the flavours clearer, the fat and meat taste cleaner, with none of the rancid edge of long-stored 'products'. In fact the only downside I can find in staring at a length of home-cured salami is knowing I probably won't be able to stop until I've finished it.

Note that in this recipe we're departing from the territory of single-muscle curing and working with minced and chopped meats, which have a much larger surface area and are, therefore, an easier target for bacteria. When making salami for air-drying I'm even more careful than usual about cleanliness in the kitchen, and I don't recommend trying the recipe without using the Prague Powder.

1kg pork shoulder ★ 200g pork backfat ★ 30g salt ★ 2.5g Prague Powder #2 per kg of meat ★ 1 clove of garlic ★ 2.5g fennel seed ★ 2.5g cracked black peppercorns ★ sausage casings ★ butcher's string

1. Half an hour in the freezer will make the meat easier to handle.

2. Remove bones, skin and any stringy connective tissue from the shoulder and slice the meat around 1cm thick. Cut each slice into batons, then across into dice.

3. Go over the pile roughly with a big chopping knife so that part of the meat is more finely and irregularly cut. Skip this phase if you like your salami chunky, spend ages on it if you like it smoother.

4. Cut the backfat into 1cm dice.

5. Combine the chopped shoulder meat (should be around 800g) with the cubed fat (200g) and weigh accurately. The proportion for curing is at least 25g of salt for every kilogram of meat. Add your Prague Powder #2 to the salt first and mix it thoroughly.

6. Select your flavourings. You can go all manner of wild here, but I've stayed basic. One clove of garlic and 2.5g each of fennel and black pepper. Grind the flavourings with a pestle and mortar, mix them with your measured salt, then work it all into the meat mixture with your hands. You can also try paprika, rosemary, orange peel or pretty much anything else you fancy. If you're feeling particularly French you can add 150ml of rough red wine.

7. Chill the stuffing mix for a couple of hours while soaking the casings, then stuff away. Twist and cut your salamis to length, then tie off the ends of the casings in a knot and secure with string. Make a loop at one end.

8. Examine the salamis carefully and use a needle to pierce the skin and relieve any air bubbles. As the skins dry and tighten they'll tend to drive out excess air, but it will need an exit point.

9. Weigh each salami and label it with ingredients, date and weight. Calculate what your target weight will be – minus 30% from moisture loss – and write this on the label too.

10. Hang your salamis inside for a couple of days while the skins tighten and become papery. Then move them outside to dry. Choose a place where they're under some cover, in clear circulating air and protected from animals and birds. If you have an outdoor shed or garage it might do, or you can rig up a simple hanging cage. A dry white mould is acceptable on the outside of the skin, but patches of fur or coloured mould should be washed off as they develop with a weak solution of vinegar in water.

11. Your salamis will be ready to eat after a month of hanging. You'll know they're done when they have lost around 30% of their weight. They will be softer in texture than many cheap shop-bought salamis (which have often been quite literally hanging about for years) and infinitely more delicious.

WEIGHT LOSS – THE MAGIC PERCENTAGE

Once most meat products have been effectively sterilized by salting, the drying process is a continuous one that depends on airflow, temperature and humidity. Left too long, meat will become dry and brittle. Not long enough and . . . well, you're effectively just eating old raw meat.

Getting it right is surprisingly simple. As water evaporates the meat naturally loses weight. The optimum state of drying for most preserved products is when they have lost 30% of weight.

Weigh your salami or ham carefully once it's been salted and is ready to hang. Write the date and starting weight on a cardboard swing tag and tie it on. Reweigh weekly at first and then daily as you get closer to your target weight.

It's worth keeping a record of dates and weights on the tag so you begin to get a feel for how drying works; initially a rapid fall-off, slowing gently over time.

Once you hit the target point you can prevent further moisture loss by airtight packing. A vacuum-sealer is ideal if you have access to one, but you can achieve great results with freezer bags or a generous wrapping in clingfilm.

Storing under refrigeration or even freezing stops fats becoming liquid or going rancid and extends potential storage time.

BUILDING A DRYING CAGE

During the autumn and winter, if there's no rain or frost, it's great to dry outdoors. Cold winds speed up evaporation while the generally moister air stops the outer surface of the meat from becoming hard and impermeable, so the meat dries at an equal speed throughout. Both Parma and Appalachian 'country' ham rely on the cold/moist/windy climate combination and that's some of the finest ham in the world. It's possible to do it in the UK but you'll need to keep a close eye on the weather and to keep inquisitive animals off the project.

A drying cage looks not unlike a giant bird-feeder. The one on page 106 is made from two sheets of 1cm steel mesh, laid on top of each other at a 0.5cm offset and stitched into a tube with galvanized wire. I used two discs, snipped from the same material, as a floor and a lid stolen from a small-sized galvanized dustbin. The hanging frame inside is made from a couple of pieces of scrap timber and some stainless steel cuphooks.

I usually dry salami or bresaola indoors for the first few days, by which point it's stopped dripping and is beginning to tighten up enough to be of less interest to bugs.

These days I hang the drying cage from a tree in the garden, where I can see it from the kitchen window, but I've lent it to friends who've used it inside a garage and hanging off the balcony of a city high-rise. Wherever you site it, it needs to be out of direct sunlight, with a clear flow of air around and through it and high enough that it won't be troubled by dogs or foxes. Squirrels and birds are welcome to have a go, but they can't reach far enough through the bars to get to the food and the lid ensures they can't climb up above it and take revenge the natural way.

I've never had a problem with flies, as I usually find elements like vinegar and pepper in the marinades keep them off, but it might well be possible to build the whole project in perforated zinc which is also flyproof. If flies do become an issue you're probably trying this too late in the season.

In the past, I've left meat in my hanging cage through light rain and very heavy snow without losing so much as a sausage, but if at any point you're worried, just unhook it and keep it inside, somewhere cool, until the weather improves.

HAM (AIR-DRIED)

Air-dried ham is 'the big one' in the world of charcuterie. All the really aspirational brands, the Parmas, Pata Negras, Bayonnes and Westphalias, are made from whole legs of carefully reared pigs, salted and hung so that those busy lactobacilli can develop their complex flavours. There's a very good reason why a few ounces of the best air-dried stuff will set you back a small fortune: it's still unbelievably expensive to produce. Feeding pigs on specialist diets – beechmast, acorns, chestnuts, etc. – rather than commercial pig feeds is old-fashioned, costly and labour-intensive. The skills involved in correctly curing such large pieces of meat are increasingly hard to find. Big slabs of pork can take years to dry properly and when a cure doesn't take – which in most processes is calculated at around one leg in twelve – a lot goes to waste at once.

Doing a whole leg as an air-dried ham is certainly possible for a home cook; the process is exactly the same as for the simpler, small pieces, but, like the big producer, you'll need to invest quite a lot of money up front, plus an enormous amount of time and care, and if you do

absolutely everything right there's still that one-in-twelve chance of things going awry and having to junk the project. Perhaps those odds are just too risky or outright heartbreaking for most of us, so here are a string of smaller ham projects with which to build up your experience before taking your chances with the Big One.

Duck and rabbit take well to a 'prosciutto' style cure with gorgeous, safe and sure results. Spanish lomo is a simple development which adds up to a pretty stunning platter of homemade charcuterie. In each case be sure to trim the breast or loin fully. Remove the tenderloin if it's present – that's the tasty little secondary muscle that sometimes comes attached. The important thing about these simple 'hams' is that they're comprised of single muscles, so there are no intramuscular surfaces where bacteria can hang out.

DUCK HAM

Farmed duck breasts are easily available in supermarkets. The meat is full of flavour and the thick fat layer is wonderfully tasty when cured. It's a smaller piece of meat, so salt quickly extracts the first moisture and hanging and drying completes the process in just a few days. Duck is also a great starting place for air-drying experiments because it tastes equally good when dried to a tight, hammy texture at 30% moisture loss or when taken on to a more leathery 'jerky' style.

If you'd like to experiment with flavourings, choose aromatic compounds that are oil-based. Thyme, rosemary and juniper are useful herbs, and dried orange peel can add a twang.

10g fresh or dried thyme, rosemary or juniper ★ 5g cracked black peppercorns ★ 200g coarse sea salt ★ 1 duck breast ★ butcher's string

1. Mix the aromatic component with the peppercorns and salt to create a cure. Coat the duck breast with a thick layer, then place in a freezer bag or a non-reactive dish and cover with any remaining cure. Refrigerate for 24 hours.

2. Wash off the cure. Pat the breast dry, season it with a little ground pepper and wrap it in muslin.

3. Tie the breast tightly with butcher's string in several places. This holds the breast in a pleasant shape and allows you to hang it without penetrating the meat with a hook.

4. Hang in a cool airy place for a week.

5. Slice and serve.

Rabbit loin can be cured in exactly the same way, though it will lose weight quicker as it doesn't have the same flavourful layer of fat and skin.

LOMO (SPANISH CURED PORK LOIN)

There are many different types of lomo. Most don't use sugar in the cure, but I like the robust extra kick of the hot paprika so a little sweetness helps balance things out.

200g salt ★ 20g pimentón (smoked paprika – the hot type) ★ 1 whole pork loin (tenderloin and silverskin removed) ★ 100g sugar ★ butcher's string

1. Mix the salt and pimentón to form the cure.

2. Put the cure into a bag or a non-reactive dish and pack in the trimmed pork loin. Put it into the fridge. I usually salt a 1kg loin for 3 days, but vary this time depending on the weight and thickness of your loin.

3. Rinse off the cure, pat the loin dry, then powder it lightly with more of the smoked paprika.

4. Tie the loin with butcher's string at four or five places along its length.

5. Weigh the loin and mark the weight and date on a label before hanging.

6. Hang in a cool, airy place until 30% weight loss is achieved.

PEMMICAN

Like many small boys I was fascinated by polar explorers and read avidly of their insanely heroic exploits. Particularly thrilling were the reports of what they ate. Today, both Scott's and Shackleton's huts still stand in the Antarctic, stocked with the stores they took, bottles of whisky, jars of beef extract and tins of corned beef. Many of the Edwardian prepared foods that later became household names still fill the shelves – preserved by the freezing temperatures. It wasn't the tinned goods that seized my imagination, though, nor the stories of dried sealmeat, nor considering eating the dogs and horses in extremis, it was pemmican, an impossibly exotic-sounding foodstuff to which the explorers attached an almost supernatural faith.

Pemmican was first adopted as a travelling ration by trappers in North America and Canada, who learned the recipes from the Native American Cree. Pemmican was made by slow-drying lean game meat over a fire, much like biltong or jerky, then pounding it to a powder with rocks and adding it to an equal quantity of animal fat – for preference the marrow extracted from the large bones. Dried berries added to the high nutritional content and, being mildly acidic, may also have helped with preservation. Pemmican was sewn into skin bags for travel and had an effectively indefinite 'shelf-life'.

Both Scott and Shackleton served the pemmican mixed with equally long-lasting dried ship's biscuit and hot water to create a stew they called 'hoosh' – a sort of portable corned beef hash.

Scott's expedition developed a special form of pemmican to feed their dogs. The 1914–16 Shackleton expedition, I noted with boyish glee, ate the dog pemmican when stranded on an ice floe.

DRIED FRUIT SALAMI

Not a salami in the strictest sense, but this useful dried fruit preparation sits well on the cheeseboard; and though drying is the main method of preservation, it's also the resulting high levels of sugar in the finished 'salami' that prevent bacterial growth.

500g dried prunes ★ 500g dried figs ★ 250g shelled walnuts or almonds ★ 10g ground black pepper ★ rice paper

1. Remove the stones from all the fruit and any woody bits from the figs.

2. Put the fruit into a food processor and blend to a pulp. You can leave any portion of the fruit chunkier if you'd like extra texture in the salami.

3. Chop the nuts coarsely and mix into the fruit pulp along with the black pepper.

4. Form the paste into a sausage shape on a sheet of clingfilm. If you have one, you can use a sushi-rolling mat to get a really regular shape.

5. Roll the sausage off the film and on to a sheet of rice paper. Roll it tightly around the sausage.

6. Roll the finished sausage in greaseproof paper, tie with string and hang to dry for a couple of weeks in a cool, dry place.

7. Slice and serve with cheese – and you can, of course, eat the rice paper.

BADGER HAM

In 1952 Florence White published *Good Food in England*, a collection of traditional recipes she'd collected from all over the country. The book was the last gasp of her attempt to create a British 'folk food' movement that would be as popular as the folk tale, craft, song and dance movements that were then taking place. It's a huge loss to us today, as we attempt to reconnect with our food culture, that her efforts never really came to fruition, but the books she left still contain some gems. One particular favourite is a recipe for badger ham which she attributes to a ferocious-sounding Colonel Cameron, writing during the First World War.[17]

---

[17] He also recorded that '... the badger's fat is used by the peasants in Gloucestershire for cooking, and also as a cure for colds and rheumatism applied externally'. History doesn't record what happened to Colonel Cameron but for his use of the Oxford comma, his heroic snobbery, and his ability to punch out badgers, he is my personal Food Hero, and I for one will always remember him with awe.

"Though formidable to encounter at close quarters,

A SMART BLOW ON THE SNOUT

WILL KILL

or
STUN

A BADGER SUFFICIENTLY TO

allow of the knife being brought into play to

dispatch it finally.

THE HAMS, WHEN CURED BY SMOKING

over a fire of birch wood for preference after
the manner used in curing bacon, are

A DECIDED DELICACY,

and may be cooked and eaten either hot or cold."

CAMERON, *Colonel.*

CHAPTER FOUR

Imagine yourself for a moment in a nomad's tent, a small twelfth-century peasant's cottage, a mud hut or a cave. Any enclosed shelter with a fire to keep warm is basically a smokehouse. If an Inuit or Maori brought meat into their home and hung it up for a couple of days it was effectively smoked – in fact it would be an interesting anthropological exercise to work out not when man began to smoke his meat but at what point in our evolution he realized that there was any alternative.

As buildings evolved with chimneys to carry away smoke, places were found to hang meat – hooks inside the chimney, sometimes smoke cupboards accessible through a door on an upper floor or the outside of the house. Salted meat could be hung here, as the smoke would keep away flies and slowly flavour the cured meat.

BUILDING A SMOKE GENERATOR

A quick and convenient way to generate smoke is in an adapted garden incinerator. These are available from hardware stores and look like a galvanized dustbin with a short chimney pipe in the lid. Some have small legs, some are pierced with airholes around the sides. The legs raise the working height, which you may find convenient, but the airholes allow smoke to escape so, if you can find one without, it will save you having to find a way to block them.

You won't need a huge, raging conflagration to produce smoke; something like a biscuit tin half filled with sawdust will burn with little heat and loads of smoke for several hours. The large size of the incinerator just gives the smoke more space to cool. Suppliers of ducting also sell adapter plates, joining clamps, angles and elbows, so you should be able to find parts to fit the other end of your duct to almost any smoking chamber. Remember that by the time the smoke gets to the food it should be completely cold, so you might even get away with something as simple as duct tape.

It's also possible to build a small fireplace out of bricks or cement blocks, place a paving slab over the top and bank it over with earth. A length of cast-iron drainpipe let into the side of this 'hearth' will divert the cool smoke where you need it.

Either of these smoke generators could be used to pipe cold smoke into the bottom of a standard barbecue, which can be used as a cold smoke chamber or, when switched on low, can fake the conditions in an 'offset style' American barbecue.

For cold-smoking, any wooden or metal enclosure from a tea chest to an old filing cabinet can be used.

ANIMAL-PROOFING

Long overnight smokes and any outdoor drying means leaving food unattended where bugs, pests or larger animals will be tempted to get at it. A drying cage keeps birds and squirrels away (see page 104), but be aware that your smoker may incite foxes, rats, badgers, etc. to trespass. Make sure that lids and doors are secured, and be aware that larger animals are often prepared to knock over something quite substantial to get at food inside – so anchor things securely to the ground too.

HOT-SMOKE IN A BARBECUE

The easiest way to hot-smoke controllably is in a domestic barbecue, provided it's large enough that you can confidently cook with 'indirect' heat. This means one of the large circular 'kettle style' barbies or something with three or more independently switchable gas elements.

In the kettle barbecue, rake the coals to one side once they're good and hot and dump in some of your favoured wood, either in dust or chip form. This will smoulder nicely, particularly if you've damped it a bit first, so you can cook your meat off the main heat source but bathed in smoke.

In a gas barbie, make a parcel of damp chips or dust out of tinfoil, pierce it on the top in several places and set it on the bars directly over the flames of one of the burners, switching the others off. Keeping the meat out of the direct heat will help to extend the cooking process, giving the smoke longer to do its work.

WOOD FOR SMOKING

Different woods give different smoke flavours. The fruit woods are supposed to have the flavour of the final fruit – which I don't actually believe – but they do have a lovely smell to them. Apple and apricot wood are particularly pleasant. Oak is a traditional rich smoke that works well with meat and fish, while beech, the more traditional smoke flavour of Scandinavia, is lighter and cleaner-tasting. Mesquite would be authentic for US or South American barbecues, and some of the oily herbs – think rosemary or thyme – can be pulled from the garden and thrown into the coals to add their own magic. The only things to avoid are resinous softwoods like pine and fir, and evergreens like holly, ivy or yew. All produce a bitter, unpleasant smoke.

COLD-SMOKE WITH SAWDUST

In a traditional smokehouse, long lines of sawdust are laid out on the stone or concrete floor and lit at one end with a blowlamp. If you have access to any kind of disused outbuilding, outside loo, shed or garage with a fireproof floor you can try the same trick. This will also work in an old water tank or filing cabinet – just scrape the sawdust into Toblerone-like heaps. You can set these up in lengths of metal guttering outside the enclosure and then slide them in when they've been lit. A favourite method of lighting without producing too much flame is a cheap soldering iron – don't expect to be able to use it for anything else, though.[18]

HOT-SMOKING

In 'hot-smoking', food is cooked while it's being smoked, the best examples being traditional kippers or American-style barbecue. Hot-smoking is easier to achieve with ordinary garden barbecue gear – you don't need so much special equipment to keep the smoke cool, but in most cases you'll find yourself working to slow the cooking down; the longer things spend in that wonderful smoke without overcooking, the better.

PULLED PORK (AND A WAY OF CHEATING)

I think it's safe to say that Americans take their barbecue seriously. Get most US food-lovers into conversation about it and they'll bang on for hours about the relative virtues of the different styles. In Texas and Kansas City – cattle country – beef is popular, particularly ribs and brisket, with big, sweet, hot and smoky sauces. The variations between the two

---

18 The ProQ is one of those blindingly simple ideas you wish you'd come up with yourself. It's a small tray made of stainless steel mesh with a labyrinth of metal plates inside. The tray is filled with sawdust and lit with a tealight, and the sawdust then smoulders, meandering along the serpentine line, for up to twelve hours. The ProQ is by far the cheapest and most efficient way to get into home-smoking and, as it means you don't have to get up in the night to reload it during a 12-hour smoke, it's an immeasurable boon to mankind. ProQ also manufacture a cardboard box smoker, which flatpacks and can be mailed to you if you don't feel up to building your own.

can be discussed endlessly and with positively rabbinical precision. In Memphis, the hog is favoured. Great slabs of pork, slathered in enough sauce to satisfy big Kung Fu Elvis at his most unhinged. But for me, the barbecue of the Carolinas is the best.

I was lucky enough to live in North Carolina for a few years and I've never forgotten the experience of driving off the main roads to some grapevine-publicized pit, hidden in a mountain hollow or a coastal backwater, to see a legendary pit-master slaving like a kobold over the coals. Furniture in these places usually stretched to the plastic and folding. Tables were covered with newspaper if you were lucky, and iced tea came in jam jars.

I hope there are still a few of these places around but the last time I visited was twenty years ago, so there are no guarantees. What sticks in the memory, though, is the pulled pork – shoulder in the east of the state, whole hog towards the Appalachians. A thin, vinegar-based sauce towards the coast; sweeter, thicker and with tomatoes west of Raleigh. The meat is cooked as slowly as possible over indirect heat until, at around 85°C (internal temperature), it gives up any structural integrity at all, then it's literally pulled apart, usually by a huge guy wearing thick rubber gloves, and served in an awful cottonwool bun with coleslaw.

It's sublime. Completely, overwhelmingly delicious. As the juices run down into your stubble, they mingle with discreet tears of sheer joy. God's food.

In a normal pit or 'offset' barbecue, the meat is dry-rubbed and then slow-cooked, usually overnight, with indirect heat from burning wood. The air temperature in the closed cooking vessel rarely gets above 100°C and the gentle smoke builds up a tarry layer of flavoursome particles on the surface of the meat which is enhanced by constant mopping with a liquid.

Many barbecuers believe that the smoke flavours actually penetrate the meat during the process, though a more practical cook might argue the point. There is certainly a limited penetration of the marinade and the rub (the legendary 'smoke ring'), but the beauty of pulled pork is that it bypasses all such controversy – before serving, the meat is shredded so that the moist interior, the gorgeous layer of lubricating fat and the charred, tarry exterior 'bark' are thoroughly mixed so the flavours really can marry together. To my mind it's this effect, plus the acidic bite of the special vinegar-based sauce, that makes North Carolina pulled pork the über-'cue.

This recipe is designed to work with any kind of offset barbecue where you can keep the temperature low, but – on account of that shredding, mixing and saucing at the end – you can achieve similar results without.

PULLED PORK

1. For the dry rub I use roughly equal quantities of smoked paprika, chipotle chillies, salt, dried onion flakes and English mustard powder. These are run through a grinder or blender. Using smoked ingredients in the rub helps build up the flavour if you don't have a big smoker.

2. Massage the rub into the surface of a pork shoulder, making sure to cover it completely, then seal it in a heavy plastic bag and refrigerate overnight.

3. If you have a proper smoker (see Chapter 8, Outdoor Cooking), stoke it up and cook the shoulder at around 100°C for at least 6 hours – longer is better. Remember to 'mop' the surface of the meat regularly with a mixture of equal quantities of vinegar and water liberally sweetened with sugar, honey or molasses and flavoured with several big tablespoons of English mustard powder.

4. If you're working with a normal-sized barbecue, set it up for the most indirect heat you can manage. If you're using charcoal, add woodchips. If you're using gas, put a metal box or tray of smoking chips or sawdust on the bars over the direct heat. Close the lid and allow to smoke for 45 minutes. With the charcoal barbecue, put the meat on as the heat is past its peak. With gas, keep the flame to medium. The intention with this 'cheat's method' is not to cook the meat but to build up a healthy smoke deposit on the outside.

5. Make a large wrapper for the meat with a double layer of foil in a roasting pan. Lift the meat in. Pour over your 'mop'. The idea is that this will keep the meat moist while building another layer of flavour.

6. Seal up the foil into an envelope and place in the oven, preheated to 100°C, for 5 or more hours.

7. Remove the meat (the internal temp should be 85°C), open the foil and allow to rest. Crank the oven up to the maximum. Draw off the liquid – a mixture of pork juice, fat, the mop and the rub – with a turkey baster and keep it in a safe place. If you have time to cool it, it will make it easier to de-fat it. When the oven reaches top heat, put the meat back, uncovered, for a 10-minute sear.

8. Whichever method you've chosen, the meat should now be at least tender enough to cut with a spoon. Lift aside the skin layer and, wearing thick rubber gloves, pull the pork apart with your fingers. You can also use forks. Be sure to thoroughly mix the spicy outer crust with the moist, steamy interior (the only downside of the cheat's method here is that the skin may have to be discarded as too rubbery to be good).

9. Heap on to a dreadful white bun and top with coleslaw.

10. The magical liquid you saved from the pan, de-fatted if you so wish, contains not only the ingredients of a rich sauce but also all the juices that would have been lost in a traditional barbecue. Treasure it. Add only a healthy squirt of commercial ketchup or Sriracha hot sauce for the vital hit of MSG before pouring it back over your bun. Do not, I repeat do not, make the mistake of adding any kind of commercial barbecue sauce. You'll miss the whole point if you do.

Consume in a lawn chair with some beans on the side, an ice-cold Pabst Blue Ribbon and try to imagine what the sun would look like if it was going down behind Grandfather Mountain instead of your garden shed and the incinerator chimney on the hospital.

COLESLAW

1 small white cabbage ★ 2 red onions ★ 1 bulb of fennel ★ 1 root of kohlrabi ★ 2 carrots ★ 5g salt ★ 10g celery seed ★ lemon juice ★ 75g plain yoghurt ★ 75g mayonnaise

1. Use a mandoline to slice the cabbage, onions, fennel and kohlrabi as finely as possible. If you have a suitable attachment, julienne the carrots into the thinnest possible shreds.

2. Put all the cut ingredients into the bowl you'll eventually serve them from. Add the salt, celery seed and a good squeeze of lemon juice. This will both keep the vegetables from browning and tighten them up into extra crispness.

3. Just before serving add equal quantities of yoghurt and mayo, a little at a time. The trick is to moisten everything but not to crush the interesting flavours. The fennel in particular can be beaten into submission by too much gloop.

4. Stir vigorously and serve.

BONUS BEANS

Use leftover pork pieces, juices, pan scrapings and sauce to enrich your own baked beans (see page 234). Proper barbecue baked beans are a blessing from the pig gods. Distribute them carefully to your friends and watch them become followers.

THE OFFSET SMOKER

American barbecue in the Southern states is usually cooked either in a purpose-built 'pit' – a kind of brick oven – or some variation of an 'offset' grill/smoker. These can be bought pre-made or more likely are knocked up in a garage by a cousin who's handy with a welding torch and an angle grinder. The base is usually a recycled propane tank (don't try this at home, you'll blow yourself up) into which a door is cut. All that's then needed is a simple metal grating for the meat and a second, smaller tank or box, hung off one end and connected by a simple adjustable baffle.

The fire is located in such a way that its direct heat rises away from the meat (hence 'offset') but can be redirected, along with the smoke, over the meat to create a combination of incredibly slow cooking with gentle smoking.

There's nothing to beat a good offset smoker and they're cheap and simple to build (see pages 248–9). You may well have a local blacksmith, a light engineering company or even an enterprising garage that might be able to make one for you. The main reason they're not common here in the UK is their size. They can be huge – often mounted on trailers – and are possibly more of a space commitment than most of us wannabe urban rednecks can spare.

Set up correctly, an offset smoker can also produce almost cold smoke.

THE 'BULLET' SMOKER

A more manageable alternative is the upright or 'bullet' smoker, now widely available in the UK. This separates the heat from the food a little by distance and also by interposing a wide tray full of water. The burning wood releases smoke but most of the heat is expended in boiling the water, giving a steamy environment which can be controlled down to a usefully low level. If you're prepared to ride the controls for hours, tweaking the heat and drinking cold beers, a bullet smoker will turn out a fantastic shoulder of pork.

Because of its convenient small size and, therefore, the proximity of the food to the fire, a bullet smoker can never successfully cold-smoke.

SMOKED MACKEREL

Mackerel is an ambrosial, cheap oily fish that tastes even better salted and smoked. Because it has a good robust texture and quite tough skin, it will hold up well under even the most rough and ready smoking techniques. In fact it's pretty hard to mess up. All you need is a simple metal box with a firmly closeable lid and a way of suspending the fish inside it. My tin came with some rather fashionable Scandinavian crispbread, but an old-fashioned biscuit tin or even the one the Christmas chocolate assortment comes in will do the job.

You can hang your fish from a skewer as I've done (see page 132) or you can use a cheap cooling rack – bent so it fits inside the tin and creates a shelf a few centimetres off the bottom. You'll also need a couple of handfuls of sawdust or woodchips.

Fillet your mackerel (or ask your fishmonger to do it for you) and cure them quickly in plain salt. I usually lay them skin side up on a layer of salt in a baking tray and then pour a generous layer over the top. Curing time depends on taste and the thickness of the fillet, but it can range between 10 minutes and an hour. Remember that we're not aiming for preservation here, so it's much more important that you balance the saltiness with the smoke than that the cure should necessarily completely penetrate the fish. When you've cured it enough, wash off the remaining salt and pat the fish dry with kitchen paper.

Put a layer of woodchips or sawdust in the bottom of the tin, and arrange the fish, allowing space around them for the smoke to circulate. If you're using a wire rack, laying them skin side down means that the flesh is protected from the direct heat.

Close the lid of the tin and put it on top of the stove or barbecue. The wood will smoke but, lacking much air, won't actually burst into flames. The fish will cook beautifully in around 10 minutes.

Hot-smoked mackerel is delicious cold and makes an amazingly good simple pâté when mashed with a little cream cheese. Lemon and horseradish make excellent tweaks to the flavour, but probably the best way is to lift the fish straight out of the smokebox and into a soft bread roll, thickly spread with unsalted butter, or serve flaked with a creamy potato salad.

ARBROATH SMOKIES

Arbroath smokies were originally prepared by hanging gutted and salted haddock over a small smoky fire in a whisky barrel, partially buried in the ground. This is a hot-smoking process which cooks the fish as it deposits a strong smoky coat. Original smokers controlled the heat and smoke in their barrel by draping wet sacking over the top. If you feel confident about controlling temperature and smoke in an incinerator-style smoke generator, you can do the same – though remember to block the chimney to retain heat and smoke.

Cut a short piece of timber to fit across the top of your bin and hang two sides of haddock over it, tied together by their tails. A heavier smoking means you can up the level of salt-curing, which, in this case, tightens and firms the flesh before cooking/smoking. A brilliant way to eat smokies is grilled with cream or as the base of a classic cullen skink.

ARBROATH SMOKIES AND CREAM

4 Arbroath smokies ★ 5g Dijon mustard (optional) ★ 150g single cream ★ freshly ground black pepper

1. Choose a low-sided frying pan with a lid into which all the smokies will fit. Add enough water to come halfway up the fish and put on the lid. Simmer gently for 5 minutes, then lift out the fish on to heatproof plates.

2. Crank the heat up under the pan as far as you can and ferociously reduce the cooking liquid. If you like the idea of mustard working with the smoky flavour of the fish, drop in a spoonful here.

3. Pour in the cream and keep the heat high so it also reduces. This will take up to 3 minutes. Season with black pepper just at the end of cooking – you probably won't need salt, as there's plenty in the reduced poaching liquid.

4. Pour the sauce over the fish and flash under a hot grill or with a blowtorch before serving. There are usually two sides - or one whole smokie - to a serving, as commercial smokies are generally of a pretty standard size. If you're doing your own you'll need to make a judgement based on the size of your own fish.

CULLEN SKINK

500g Arbroath smokies ★ 1 bay leaf ★ 1 onion ★ 1 leek ★ 15g butter ★ 2 medium potatoes ★ 500g whole milk ★ freshly ground black pepper

1. Put the fish into a pan and barely cover with water. Add the bay leaf and bring up to a low simmer, then immediately remove the fish. While the fish is still hot, strip off the skin, remove any bones and return them to the simmering poaching liquid. Flake the fish.

2. Slice the onion and leek finely. Put them into a pan with the butter and stew gently until clear and soft. If you're using fresh potatoes, peel them, slice them thinly and add them to the pan, then cover with the strained fish poaching liquid and simmer until soft.

3. In some recipes, leftover mashed potato is used to thicken the soup. It's a marvellous refinement, so, if you have 100g or so left over, skip the bit about the spuds in the section above and just add the liquid to the sweated onions and leek.

4. Spoon out one-third of the cooked veg and set aside, then add the milk and half the fish to the pan, plus your mashed potato if you're using it. Remove the bay leaf and blitz until smooth.

5. Season with black pepper – you may not need salt. Put the rest of the fish and vegetables back into the pan, heat through gently without allowing it to boil, and serve.

This will serve 4 in delicate bowls and will really seem quite refined. On the other hand, if you feel like you've spent a day crofting or pulling nets and you deserve a little more, serve it larger, with crusty bread on the side. Like many soups and stews, I think cullen skink actually develops an even better taste after a night under refrigeration, where the flavours can get promiscuous with each other.

OMELETTE ARNOLD BENNETT

250g Arbroath smokies ★ 200g milk ★ 1 bay leaf ★ 1 small onion ★ 4 black peppercorns ★ nutmeg ★ 15g plain flour ★ 30g unsalted butter ★ 7 eggs ★ ½ a lemon ★ salt and black pepper ★ 50g double cream ★ a good sprinkling of Parmesan

1. Put the smokies into a pan with the milk, bay leaf, sliced onion, peppercorns and a scrape of nutmeg and poach gently for 3 minutes. Lift out the fish and flake it, returning any skin, bones or other bits to the milk. Leave this to cool and infuse.

2. The original recipe for the Arnold Bennett combines béchamel and hollandaise sauces, both of which would have been at hand in a gentleman's club kitchen. We can achieve a very similar effect with an egg-enriched béchamel. Heat the grill to its highest setting. Combine the flour and 15g of butter in a saucepan and cook, stirring continuously, until it gives off a pleasant biscuity smell and turns a kind of blondish beige. Take the pan off the heat and pour in a little of the cooled poaching milk, catching the bits in a sieve.

3. Whisk the mixture ferociously to avoid lumps. Initially it will seize up into a gooey mass, but as you add more milk and keep whisking it will let down into a smooth sauce. Continue until it's a thick, ketchupy consistency, then separate one egg and beat in the yolk.

4. Now put the pan back on a gentle heat and continue to stir but don't let it boil. It will thicken a little more, at which point you can add a squeeze of lemon juice and some seasoning (you won't need much salt). You've now effectively created a hollandaise-flavoured béchamel into which you can stir half your flakes of smoked fish and your double cream.

5. Lightly beat the 6 remaining eggs – plus that spare white – and add the last of the fish. Swirl another 15g of butter in an omelette pan with a heatproof handle and, as soon as it foams, pour in the egg mixture. As it starts to set on the bottom, lightly 'scramble' your omelette once with a fork and, almost immediately, you should have a fully set bottom with a fluffy, custardy centre.

6. Immediately pour over the haddock béchamel mix, top with a good sprinkling of Parmesan and flash under the grill until the top is bubbling and deliciously brown in spots.

This would have suited a gentleman as a snack after a night at the theatre. The kind of thing his valet might knock up while he was soaking in the bath. Sadly, most of us lack that kind of constitutional grit today, so regretfully I have to say: 'Serves two as a main course.'

TEN TIPS: SMOKING

1. Woodsmoke contains flavour compounds which are deposited on the surface of the food. Most of these are oil-soluble in nature so they seem to penetrate better on fattier foods.

2. Any mechanism that will help separate heat from smoke and make both controllable will enable you to carry out most smoking techniques.

3. Charcoal is wood that has already been burned once. It will already have given up all its interesting smoky flavours long before you buy it, so it should only be used to supply clean heat.

4. Some of the phenolic compounds in smoke are anti-oxidant and prevent fat from going rancid. Some are, to some degree, bactericidal. A thick smoke coating was once used as a partial preservative but today is only used as a flavouring.

5. Smoke particles stick to the surface of the meat during smoking – this is helped by building up a 'pellicle' layer or sticky surface, but the flavours will penetrate as the food is stored after smoking.

6. Cold-smoking is partially an air-drying process. During the long hanging in gentle smoke, meat or fish continues to dry through evaporation.

7. Preliminary curing helps to preserve food through the smoking and maturing process.

8. Cold-smoked food is effectively hung raw. Ensure that your smoke chamber is bug-proof, animal-resistant, weathertight and runs at a temperature that delays spoilage. Hanging fish outdoors in British summer temperatures is often not practical, and, as few of us can afford refrigerated smokesheds, it's sensible to attempt long smokes only during the colder months and then preferably at night. It's a smart move to site your smoking rig in a shady corner.

9. Don't use resinous softwoods for smoking. The heavy sap in conifers, eucalyptus and cedar smells wonderfully fragrant while burning but gives rise to unpleasant acrid tastes in the food. Stick to native hardwoods and fruit tree trimmings if you can get them.

10. Never use any kind of firelighter or accelerant. The petrol taste is impossible to get rid of. If you're impatient, use a kitchen blowtorch.

COLD-SMOKING

Cold-smoking is an entirely different process. It's absolutely imperative that heat should not affect the food – no hint of 'cooking'. Hanging salted food in a smoky but cold environment has two effects. First, the smoke keeps bugs away while the food continues to dry out, and second, it deposits a layer of tarry particles on the food surface. The smoke itself doesn't penetrate the food but the aromatic elements of that surface layer can and do move into the food, particularly if they are left for a while after smoking. It's an odd thought, but the same process that made your dad's sweater smell of pipesmoke is what gives the appetizing flavour to country hams and smoked salmon.

Cold-smoking needs a smoking chamber where the meat or fish can be hung far enough from the source of combustion that there's no element of 'cooking' involved. The traditional smokesheds you might see in small fishing towns were often tall buildings where salt fish could be hung high above small fires in sawdust heaps. As sawdust doesn't tend to flare up, the small amount of heat generated by smouldering wouldn't reach the fish, but great billows of smoke would. Over the years the inside of the shed would become coated with thick deposits of black tar, which added to the developed smoke taste.

The chimney of a cottage or house with a wood fire is a natural 'smokehouse', and some old buildings have a trapdoor into the chimney, equipped with hooks, high up near the top of the building. They are often reached through the attic or up a ladder and through an external hatch.

If you don't happen to have a chimney, all sorts of more sensible arrangements can be made for cold-smoking. Any smoking chamber can be connected to a firebox by a pipe long enough that though the smoke moves through, any heat has dissipated. Many amateurs have success with old fridges, water tanks or filing cabinets, rigged to a small fireplace with a length of air-conditioning duct or metal drainpipe. The only problem with simple rigs like this is keeping the fire going throughout the night if a long smoke is needed.

Food continues to lose moisture throughout the cold-smoking process, effectively continuing to air-dry, so when planning to smoke, try to balance out all the effects. Salmon can be subjected to a brief, intense cold-smoke and then hung for a while to continue drying and to allow the smoky flavours to penetrate. In a different set-up it can undergo long treatment, sometimes overnight in a more gentle smoke which may generate a similar effect. Trial and error is the only way to tune your own particular smoking arrangement. Keep notes of every stage, as you are sure to want to repeat your success and make your own improvements.

Cold-smoking salmon in particular involves many of the preservation techniques, each of which can be varied to change the balance of finished flavours. Personally I favour a short curing in half salt, half sugar, followed by overnight drying under refrigeration, then a 24-hour gentle smoke. The smoked food is sealed into a bag and stored for 4–5 days in the fridge. During this time the smoke flavours deposited on the surface distribute through the food, which – because of the cold – will not deteriorate any further. This is a useful set-up for a side or two in a domestic kitchen, and also leaves you less of a hostage to the weather and season – hot summer days and nights make long smokes difficult – but if I had more space I think I'd probably hang after smoking in a cool, dry place just loosely covered with a 'tent' of greaseproof paper. I'm not sure how much difference it would make to the taste, but I think it would give a drier, tighter texture and it certainly feels more 'authentic'.

COMMERCIAL COLD-SMOKERS

Modern cold-smokers can be expensive, purpose-built machines, like the Bradley, which uses a clever mechanism to move blocks of compressed woodchips on to an electric heating platform where they smoulder for a set time before being automatically replaced. A Bradley can generate consistent smoke for hours without needing any attention from the operator, so they're great for restaurants or small businesses. More recently, as we've come to a better understanding of how smoking works, many home-smokers have been developed that rely on very small amounts of combustion and so scarcely generate heat at all. A ProQ smoker is a small stainless steel mesh tray which is loaded with a few hundred grams of sawdust and lit with a tea light. The clever 'labyrinth' pattern in the tray means that the sawdust can take up to 6 hours to burn through, creating loads of smoke but almost no heat. It's possible to smoke using a ProQ (or two if you want more smoke or more certainty) in a dustbin, a cupboard, a small shed or outbuilding or even a cardboard box – as long as the unit is set inside on a fireproof base like a sheet of metal or a couple of bricks. I've successfully used two ProQs to cold-smoke up to 8 sides of salmon at once in an adapted metal dustbin.

SMOKED SALMON

Smoking a side of salmon is a serious investment of time and effort, but is probably one of the most rewarding bits of DIY cooking there is. Most techniques are fun to try once or twice, but home-smoked salmon is so cheap, so much more tasty than the shop-bought stuff and so much a guaranteed success that you'll probably end up doing it regularly. A smoked side lasts a while in the fridge if you're eating it yourself but I've never managed to keep one more than a few days, as family and friends always demand large chunks. Think about doing a batch before Christmas both for your own immediate needs and as gifts.

CHOOSE YOUR FISH

It would obviously be wonderful to get a chance at smoking a side from a freshly caught wild salmon but that's an increasingly rare opportunity these days and, to be honest, I think I'd prefer to treat something that wonderful more simply. Farmed salmon (and trout or sewin) all cold-smoke beautifully, so, as long as you're happy with the sustainability of your source, farmed is the way to go. Look out for supermarket clearances on farmed salmon. I've had extremely acceptable sides of certified salmon with short sell-by dates for as little as £5, and with premium smoked salmon, of undisclosed provenance, costing up to £40 per kilo in the same supermarket you don't have to do much maths to work out how sensible it is to do it yourself.

Unless you have a cat, salmon head and bones are difficult to find a good use for. It's definitely not cheating to ask your supplier to fillet and scale, just for convenience.

PREP

Salmon skin and flesh are some of the most beautiful textures you'll find in cooking. I really enjoy the prep phase of smoking, so it's one of those occasions for a bit of Radio 3, a glass of wine and hustling everyone else out of the kitchen.

Unpack the side and rinse gently in cold water to remove any slime before patting dry with kitchen paper. Turn flesh side up and, using a sharp knife, trim away the tail, the gill covers and the pectoral or front fins. The fillet is thick towards the fish's spine and thins towards its belly, which is where you'll see a band of fattier, greyish-coloured flesh. On a tuna this would be 'toro', the stuff the Japanese love as sashimi, but on a salmon, particularly a farmed fish, it's unpleasant in texture and colour and, as it's fatty, has a tendency to go rancid and spoil

the side. Locate the line along the fillet where the texture of the belly flesh changes and slice along it at a slight angle, removing it in a single long strip.

The side should now look beautiful; jewel-like with the clear V-shaped grain pattern that's so characteristic of the good smoked stuff. But if you lay your hand flat on the surface and run it from head to tail and back you'll detect a line of sharp little 'pin-bones' buried deep in there. Grab the end of each with a big pair of tweezers (there are specialist tools made just for removing pin-bones but I actually keep a clean pair of needle-nose pliers for the job) and pull smartly up and away. The bones should come out completely cleanly.

Pin-boning is a pain but it's worth doing it well, as it makes slicing so much easier later and stops anyone finding anything unpleasant on their canapés. I do the job when I'm prepping the fish, as I like to get all the rough processes out of the way early on. Some people recommend removing them just before cutting, when the flesh has been firmed up by the cure and the smoke. Either way . . . it's your choice.

Finally, using the sharp tip of your knife, cut as small a hole as you can in the thickest part of the side, about 5cm from the tail. Take about 30cm of thick, hairy parcel string, tie it into a loop, pass it through the hole and back over itself and the fish. The most depressing thing that can happen when smoking is the fish dropping off a hook as it tears through the skin. The hairy string grips to more of the skin surface and tends to pull the hole tighter closed around itself. From now on, lift the fish by the string loop only, but do so very gently, at least until the flesh has firmed a little.

CURE

Plan your cure well in advance. A wet cure is gentle and takes longer, so the results are more controllable when you're experimenting. I like dry cures because they feel like they're tough on surface bacteria and firm the fish up quicker.

A common cure is 60:40 salt to sugar by weight, but I've evolved more towards 50:50 over time. Back in the day, fish salting was all about long preservation, so more salt meant a longer-lasting product. Today we have fridges for the preserving side of things, so taste is everything and we can afford to go towards sweeter cures. You don't have to restrict yourself to plain, refined sugar. Molasses, syrup, honey, demerara or even palm sugar will all add different flavours. The salt should just be a plain, granular sea salt. Avoid table salt because it has 'anti-caking agents' that just aren't necessary here, and also avoid the posh, crystalline stuff or you'll end up spending more on the salt than the fish. Mix the sugar and salt in the proportions you've decided on and add any aromatics you fancy. I rarely go beyond a grind of black pepper, but that's very much up to you. If you're doing a dry cure, mix enough to coat both sides of the fillet. I'd say at least 500g in total.

Now lay the fish on a layer of the cure in a non-reactive container and rub the balance over the top. If you have one, you can use a stainless steel salmon-poaching pan as your curing vessel – the basket in the bottom lets the fish drain freely after the cure is rubbed on – or you can put fish and cure together into a couple of layers of extra-large freezer bags (see sections on bacon and gravadlax, pages 27 and 60). However it's stored, allow the fish to cure for an hour in the fridge.

Next time you smoke you'll be able to adjust the curing time depending on how long you want the fish to hang, how salty you like it, how dried by the cure, etc. You can also tweak the curing mix, but begin with an hour in a dry cure and you'll have an excellent starting point.

CURE VARIATIONS

Good salmon is deeply gorgeous kept simple, but curing is so easy that you might want to introduce some variations to keep your audience on their toes. You can rub the side in an alcohol before salting – whisky is an obvious adjunct to Scottish salmon but you could also try akvavit for a Scandinavian redolence. To really mess with people's heads, try kümmel, which has a subtle caraway flavour. Tequila is suggested in some American recipes, but I can't help thinking that it's a short step from that to Bailey's.

You can also try rubbing with grated horseradish or chilli to add heat, and grated beetroot adds a deep purple hue.

Finally, oily herbs and spices will survive in the cure itself, so juniper, thyme, rosemary, coriander seed and cumin are all possibilities. Parch them in a dry pan to get the flavours flowing before stirring them into the mixture. There are a few Scandinavian recipes that even suggest the addition of pine needles, but I have an awful feeling that would taste like an air-freshener to our effete, non-Viking palates. The only thing I'd counsel strongly against is garlic. As the cure isn't cooked, there's no opportunity for the flavour to mellow, so garlic just kicks everything else, including the fish, into submission.

PELLICLE

Once the fish has cured for an hour, pull it out of the fridge and either rinse and pat dry or just scrape off the remaining dry cure with kitchen paper.

The fish must now be allowed to dry overnight in such a way that it develops a sticky coating called the 'pellicle'. This is vital to the smoking process, as the flavour solids in the smoke will stick to a greater or lesser extent, depending entirely on how well the pellicle has developed. The ideal way to do this is to hang the side, unwrapped, overnight in the fridge, where the cold air forced over it will dry it beautifully. Failing this, lay the fish skin side down on a drying rack.

Once the pellicle has developed, handle it as little as you possibly can. This is where the string loop comes into its own.

SMOKE

Set up your cold-smoking rig and hang the sides in a clear stream of smoke. I go for a 24-hour smoke using a couple of ProQ smoke generators in a clean dustbin. Check every couple of hours to ensure the sawdust is still alight, but don't fret too much if you need to relight it. The fish is continuing to gain flavour just hanging in the residual smoke and it's continuing to dry gently, thus aiding the preservation process. It's rare that I go the full 24 hours without an occasional break in the smoke, but, overall, results are consistent. Move the fish around your chamber during the smoking just to make sure every piece gets the same chances.

REST

I love the smell of smoked salmon and would cheerfully hang the sides in a cool cupboard while the flavours distribute and equalize, but wiser counsels usually prevail at home, so I seal each side into a vacuum pack and keep it in the fridge for between a week and a fortnight.

SLICING

Smoked salmon is traditionally either 'D-cut' or 'long cut'. Both require a long, sharp, flexible knife. In D-cutting you cut on a diagonal away from the tail and turn the blade as you hit the inside of the skin. This gives same-size slices across the fillet in the shape of a capital D. Long slicing takes a little more skill and involves sliding the knife horizontally the length of the side from tail to head end. The long ragged strips look good on the plate and you'll look truly impressive if your knife-work is up to it.

The shelf-life of smoked salmon can be extended by refrigeration, vacuum-packing and freezing. I usually cut a single side into three pieces, one for immediate eating, one vac-packed for eating next week and the third vac-packed and frozen, where it will last up to a couple of months. If there's time, I sometimes pre-slice the pieces and interleave them with greaseproof paper before sealing them up.

SMOKED HADDOCK

FINNAN HADDIE

Finnan haddie is a lightly smoked haddock traditionally prepared in Scotland. The process is almost identical to cold-smoked salmon, with a light, salt-only curing and perhaps a couple of hours in the cold smoke.

The fish is obviously still raw when it's finished and is usually cooked either by baking, or grilling with a moistening dod of butter on top.

SMOKED HADDOCK CHOWDER

100g smoked bacon ★ 50g butter ★ 1 large onion ★ 1 leek ★ 15g plain flour ★ 500g smoked haddock (or other white fish) ★ 400g milk ★ 1 potato ★ 300g single cream ★ a small bunch of fresh parsley or chives, chopped

1. Cut the bacon into small batons and fry gently in the butter until the fat runs but without browning. Remove the cooked bacon with a slotted spoon.

2. Chop the onion and slice the leek, then add them to the pan and cook in the butter and bacon fat until softened. Add the flour to the fat and cook until a pleasant biscuity smell arises.

3. Put the fish into a pan, pour over the milk and poach for about 3 minutes. It will begin to flake but won't be fully cooked through. Remove the fish from the pan, saving the milk. Flake the fish, removing the skin.

4. Take the cooked flour off the heat and slowly pour in the poaching milk through a strainer, whisking as you go. This should give you a thin, creamy white sauce.

5. Cut the potato into 1cm dice and add to the pan with the onions, leeks, bacon and cream. Return to the heat and simmer gently until the potatoes are almost cooked.

6. Just before the potatoes are done, stir in the flaked fish to heat through and strew over the chopped parsley or chives with abandon. Serve with fresh bread.

This is also great (if you are cooking it in August or September) with the kernels scraped from a fresh corn cob added at step 5.

GIVE US OUR DAILY BREAD

CHAPTER FIVE

Home bread-making is about commitment and routine almost as much as it's about technique and recipes, but it's absolutely possible to produce an excellent loaf every day – or every other day – with minimum investment of time, as long as you have certain kit and are well organized. It's worth trying, if only for a couple of weeks, partly so you can see how wonderful homemade bread can be, partly to learn more about dough behaviour and understand what goes into the bread you buy.

Early in the evening, when the kids are doing homework or you're just getting into your first glass of wine, put 385g of strong white flour and 185g of water into the bowl of your mixer.[19]

---

19 If you wish, you can experiment with increasing the 'hydration' of your dough by perhaps 10g of water each time (see page 157).

Crumble in 20g of fresh yeast,[20] 5g of salt and set the mixer running at a low speed, using a dough hook.

After about 10 minutes the dough will become smooth and elastic and leave the sides of the bowl cleanly. Take the dough out and work it for a minute or so on the tabletop. It should not need flour to stop it sticking if it's been worked enough. If it sticks, just keep kneading until it doesn't. Finally, separate 70g of your dough and put it into a closed plastic container in your fridge.

Shape the remaining dough roughly into a ball, put it back into the mixer bowl, cover it with a clean tea towel and go and watch the telly. Check back during the commercials or when refilling the wine glasses until the dough has roughly doubled in size.

Once it's doubled, pour it out on to the tabletop (it may require a little flour this time), knead it for a minute, then shape it or put it straight into a loaf tin. Turn the oven on full, cover the loaf with the cloth and go back to the telly.

When the dough has risen to double height again – this usually takes you to the end of the HBO serial drama you're watching – remove the cover and slide it into the hot oven. You can, if you wish, use a clean garden spray bottle to mist the inside of the hot oven. After 5 minutes, reduce the oven temperature to 180°C and bake for 30 minutes.

Just before bed, remove the loaf, turn it out and leave it to cool on a rack.

That's it. Fresh bread for breakfast.

Next time you do it, start with flour (350g) and water (150g), 20g of yeast and 5g of salt, and add the dough you kept in the fridge overnight before the first 10-minute mix.

---

20 Dried yeast can always be substituted for the fresh stuff. Use half the weight. I find them completely interchangeable but in this case the fresh has a certain air of romance about it.

From then on do the same simple recipe and routine each time, adding the 'old dough' and keeping 70g of the latest batch. Over a few weeks, some of the natural ferments of sourdough will begin to develop in your daily loaf, improving the flavour and character.

Any bread you don't use within 2 days should be sliced and frozen, and, any evening you fancy, you can divert a dough batch into pizzas, or even Chinese-style steamed buns.

BREAD DOUGH 'HYDRATION'

Professional bakers use recipes based on the ratio of ingredients to each other – a system that makes loads of sense when you're scaling recipes up and down for different-sized loaves and batches. The flour amount is 100% and the other weights are expressed as a percentage of that. In the recipe above I've specified 385g of flour and 185g of water . . .

185 ÷ 385 × 100 = 48% hydration

Soft wet doughs, that is doughs with high levels of hydration, offer little resistance to the expanding gases of the yeast and so form light, airy loaves. Professional bakers with years of skill handling and shaping can work with doughs well above 85% hydration, which make award-winning bread but for us would feel like trying to stuff an oiled duvet into a moving bin-liner. If you're happy to use a loaf tin for your bread, you can start at a higher hydration level than suggested above, but if you want to learn to hand-shape your loaves, start down around the 50% level and work upwards in small steps as your skills increase.[21]

21 Ciabatta is a classic example of a high hydration loaf. The texture is massively airy with huge holes but the shape of the loaf looks like it was poured on to a slab and solidified while it was trying to escape.

SOURDOUGH

Sourdough might well be the oldest and most natural form of raising agent in baking but there's nothing simple about it. It usually manifests itself as a kind of bubbling porridge that has to be loved and nurtured like a small and sickly pet in a warm corner of the kitchen. At its heart, sourdough is a nourishing mixture of flour and water which spores of naturally occurring yeast are encouraged to colonize. At the same time, lactobacilli are feeding on sugars in the flour and producing lactic acid . . . that's where the sour taste comes from. In fact the yeasts and lactobacilli have a symbiotic relationship which, one way or another, produces a lot of gas bubbles that can be used to raise bread.

Commercial yeast strains are bred to create big, controllable bursts of gas without too many strong flavours. Naturally occurring yeasts taste more interesting but can be a lot less predictable in behaviour.

There are thousands of different recipes for sourdough starters on the internet and most are useful. They usually vary from this simple one by the use of ingredients with a natural yeast or lactobacillus content – raisins, for example, cabbage leaves or yoghurt – or the provision of natural sugars to help feed them, some recipes suggesting adding malt or fruit juices.

The best yeasts, though, come from the surface of the wheat grain itself and are still present in unbleached, organic flours. Older sourdough starter recipes often specified kicking off the culture with granary or rye flour – even if you transferred to white later in the process – to ensure the yeasts were present. These days we have access to good, unbleached white stuff, so your flour itself should contain all the livestock you need to get going, and if it doesn't work first time, toss it away and try again.

SOURDOUGH STARTER

bread flour ★ water ★ naturally occurring bacteria from the air in your kitchen

1. Mix a couple of hundred grams of flour with enough water to make a thick cream (around 200g).

2. Pour the mixture into a clean preserving jar and cover the top loosely with a piece of kitchen paper.

3. Keep the mixture in a warm place and check every now and again for bubbles. If they haven't appeared after a week, throw the mixture away and start again.

4. If bubbles do appear, 'feed' the mixture by whisking in another 200g of flour, mixed to a cream with water.

5. Two days later the bubbling should be more vigorous. Pour half the mixture away and top up with a fresh 'feed'. To keep the process under control you should begin storing your starter in the fridge. It will continue to bubble but the cold will make the process slower. Continue to pour half away and feed once a week.

6. If the mixture separates at any time, just whisk it back into a cream.

7. Once the mixture is bubbling strongly, it's time to take out insurance. Instead of pouring half away at the next feed, put it into a sealable container and freeze it. If your main starter fails at any point, defrost the 'clone', give it an immediate feed and keep it in a warm place as it comes back to life.

8. When you're ready to bake with your sourdough, extract half to use and replace it with a feed.

YEAST

Yeast is a fungus which consumes carbohydrates, produces carbon dioxide and alcohol and reproduces extremely quickly. Commercial yeast is created by feeding yeast in a controlled environment until a solid mass is created. This can be freeze-dried to make the fast-acting yeast you buy in sachets at the supermarket or simply cut into large blocks which stay 'alive' under refrigeration, the form in which it's delivered to commercial bakeries. Most bakers will supply you with this 'fresh' yeast if you ask politely – in fact, until quite recently, they were required to by law.

Many species of yeast occur naturally and their spores float around in the air. Yeasts are the white bloom on grapes, and some of the growths on food that we commonly refer to as 'mould' are yeasts, so, if you can trap a few and feed them, you can begin to grow a yeast culture that can be used as a raising agent.

Sourdough 'mothers' are just such a culture. Each is subtly different because of the combination of natural spores that makes up its little ecosystem. San Francisco sourdough is reputed to be descended from the 'mothers' that were brought across the West by settlers and it certainly does have a distinctive taste. Commercial bakeries, after many years of working with yeasts, are often riddled with their own individual culture which, they claim, makes their own sourdough special.

In truth a sourdough culture goes through many phases in its life. Its flavour can vary, as can its strength. It can be held like something in a sci-fi movie in cryogenic suspension in a freezer (my own sourdough mother is nicknamed 'Lt Ripley') and revivified whenever needed.

SOURDOUGH BREAD

200g vigorous sourdough starter (see page 161) (half of your starter will weigh 400g, so discard 200g) ★ 300g water ★ 700g strong bread flour ★ 10g salt

1. Mix the starter with the water and half the flour. Whisk, cover with a cloth and leave in a warm place until the mixture begins to bubble. This is a 'sponge', a more liquid environment, without any added salt, where the starter can really get off to a healthy start.

2. Stir in the balance of the flour and the salt and knead until elastic (this can take up to 15 minutes by hand, 10 if you're using a mixer with a dough hook).

3. Cover the dough with a floured cloth and allow it to rise in a warm place until doubled in size.

4. Knead the dough for a minute or so. This is called 'knocking back', and helps to redistribute the gas bubbles in the dough. Put a thick baking sheet or 'pizza stone' into the oven and whack it up to full.

5. Shape the dough into the loaf you want and put it on to a well-floured board or tray, or a tea towel, or put it into a loaf tin. Cover with a floured cloth and allow to rise to twice its size again.

6. Slash the top of the loaf with a sharp knife and then slide it or quickly lift it on to the hot stone. Close the oven door immediately.

7. After 5 minutes, lower the temperature to 180°C but don't open the door. At 35 minutes, check the loaf. It will be done when it sounds hollow when you knock it on the bottom.

BREAD PHYSICS

The combination of flour, water, yeast and heat to make bread seems little short of miraculous, but, in making your own, you're taking control of some pretty wonderful science.

For bread to get that lovely spongy, risen quality instead of cooking down into a crisp pancake, a lot of exciting things have to happen. Gluten (from the Latin for 'glue') is a protein present in wheat. When water is added to flour and the resulting paste is kneaded, the gluten 'develops': at a molecular level the protein strands are agglomerating to form a tough mesh in which starch – the main ingredient in flour – and the raising agent are suspended. 'Strong' bread flour has a lot of gluten in it, which makes it elastic and capable of holding a lot of gas bubbles in a chewy matrix. 'Soft' cake flour has less gluten – still enough to trap gas for light sponges, but not so much that the surrounding cake becomes rubbery. Once the dough has been properly worked or kneaded, its texture changes to a silky, elastic material.

The raising agent is yeast – either the commercial fast-acting type or the naturally occuring ones in sourdough cultures. Yeast is a live micro-organism that feeds on carbohydrates (like starch) and produces carbon dioxide and alcohol. The carbon dioxide is trapped in the elastic gluten mesh, creating bubbles and forming the spongy matrix that will become bread.

Each time the bread dough 'rises' it's being inflated by the carbon dioxide ('yeast farts', if you insist), and each time it is 'knocked down' in subsequent kneadings and shapings, the bubbles are being more evenly distributed through the matrix.

Finally, when the shaped and risen dough hits the searing heat of the oven, each individual bubble of carbon dioxide expands, giving a last burst of expansion to the loaf (this is called 'oven spring') before the matrix is set by the heat into bread.

Most shaping methods are systems of manually folding and pushing the dough in such a way that a tougher outer layer of gluten can build up. This further traps the rising dough – almost like a balloon envelope. It's this outer layer that forms the crust of the loaf and it also explains how cutting a slash in the envelope at the last minute and allowing the insides to rise through creates the fantastically airy shapes of traditional handmade loaves.

A loaf tin is a great way to get usable, sliceable loaves at home, but the skills of hand-shaping are worth seeking out. Unfortunately they are almost impossible to communicate in writing, so it's worth either taking a bread-making course with a talented baker or seeking out a video on line to get you started.

PIZZA

A commercial pizza oven runs at around 400°C, retaining tremendous heat in both the stone base and the brick canopy which sits low over the baking area. A 'proper' thin-based pizza in a wood-fired oven will be cooked through, with topping bubbling, in as little as 60 seconds. Obviously these are not easy conditions to replicate at home, but it's not impossible. Many ovens have a built-in grill function, so it's possible to heat a suitable surface higher than the regular oven temperature to cook on.

You can buy a purpose-built pizza stone from a kitchen supplier or keep your eyes peeled for a granite or marble cheese-cutting board. These can often be picked up cheaply and, once you've cleaned off the rubber feet glued to the underside, will easily build up good heat in an oven.[22] If you're planning to cook a lot of bread or pizza, you can have a piece of granite cut to fit your oven shelf by a monumental mason – I know it sounds a bit odd, but there's not a lot of difference between a gravestone and an oven base except you don't have to get your Nan's name carved on it. Alternatively you can use an upturned cast-iron skillet.

Take a piece of bread dough from one of the recipes above – about the size of a tennis ball. Shape it neatly into a ball, roll it in flour and store it in the fridge overnight. The secret of a good pizza base is that the dough should be sleepy and pretty exhausted by the time it's used. Airy enough not to be solid and biscuity but definitely not bubbly and risen.

Put your cooking surface on the top shelf, right up under the grill, and heat it hard.

Roll your dough out thin using a rolling pin – all that hand-shaping and tossing nonsense is great if you're a Neapolitan and doing it for a living, but for the rest of us life is too short. Place on a floured oven sheet without sides (if you have one to hand, use the base of a springform baking tin or, failing that, a square cut out of the side of a corrugated cardboard box).

Smear on about 20g of canned tomatoes that you've reduced for half an hour over a low heat, mashed to a rough purée and seasoned well. Sprinkle on your toppings (see page 166).

Working quickly, slide out your cooking surface, shoot the pizza on to it and slip it quickly back under the heat. Watch it obsessively until the edges have risen and crisped.

---

22 If you plan to use granite as your baking stone, prepare it by cooking it gently first. Heat it to 150°C and hold it for an hour before whacking it up to full. This will drive off any moisture and should prevent cracking.

IDEAS FOR PIZZA TOPPINGS

To begin with, restrict yourself to simple combinations. The advantage of homemade pizza is that the quality of your topping ingredients gets a chance to show. Try . . .

★ TOMATO AND MOZZARELLA – UNBEATABLE CLASSIC – WITH A FRESH GREEN HERB AND OLIVE OIL

★ RIPE FIGS AND GOAT'S CHEESE – THE CHEESE GETS RUNNY AS THE FIGS GO GOOEY AND CARAMELIZE. ADD A SPLASH OF BALSAMIC VINEGAR

★ SHELLFISH – MUSSELS, CLAMS AND COCKLES WILL STEAM OPEN IN THE HEAT AND THE JUICES WILL SOAK INTO THE BASE. FORGET CHEESE HERE, BUT ROASTED PEPPERS OR CAPERS ARE FANTASTIC

★ VEG OUT – A SMEAR OF ONION JAM CAN REPLACE THE TOMATO SAUCE AND STAND UP TO MORE ROBUST VEG LIKE BEETROOT OR BLANCHED CHARD. TOP WITH SHAVED PARMESAN

PIZZA *Mafia*

The Associazione Vera Pizza Napoletana is the organization that polices authentic pizza. According to their rules the base, made with Tipo 'O' or 'OO' flour, is formed by hand without a rolling pin and cooked for between 60 and 90 seconds at 485°C in a wood-fired, stone-based oven. There are only two topping combinations permitted: Margherita (tomato, mozzarella, basil and olive oil) and Marinara (tomato, mozzarella, garlic, oregano and olive oil).

In other parts of the Mediterranean, different cultures have their own traditions of topped flatbreads. Across the Middle East, flatbread is topped with lamb mince spiced with cumin, cinnamon and garlic, or sometimes just dusted with oregano or za'atar (a spice mix which varies depending on its region of origin but usually contains oregano, thyme, sesame seed, sumac and salt). There is probably a delicious culinary precedent for pretty much anything on a flatbread base somewhere in the world, though it has taken a culture as barbarous as our own to add tinned sweetcorn or pineapple – of which the less said the better.

RYE BREAD (FOR PASTRAMI SANDWICHES)

A proper deli sandwich doesn't stop with the meat. All those Ashkenazi and central European influences should be there in the bread too. But any serious deli lover will tell you that bread is where things begin to fall apart. Proper rye bread is terrifying stuff. It's heavy and dark. Rye doesn't have as much gluten as white wheat flour, so can't make the elastic sponge that allows the loaf to rise into an airy puff. Add to this the belief that good rye should also be sourdough and you're pretty much guaranteed a solid, heavy lump of punishment loaf.

It's perhaps unsurprising, then, that the few remaining delis serving salt beef have modernized their bread to something less 'authentic'. The 'rye' bread you'll be served these days resembles packet toasting bread, barely enlivened with caraway seeds, but it doesn't require the constitution of a seventeenth-century Ukrainian farmhand to digest.

In his book *Save the Deli*,[23] David Sax recalls a dense, moist rye with a crackling crust and, fortunately, this is surprisingly simple to produce.

---

23 David Sax, *Save the Deli: In Search of Perfect Pastrami, Crusty Rye, and the Heart of Jewish Delicatessen*, Mariner Books, 2010.

QUICK RYE BREAD

250g rye flour ★ 250g strong white bread flour, plus extra for dusting ★ 10g fresh yeast (or half a sachet of instant) ★ 10g salt ★ 350g warm water ★ 10g caraway seed, lightly cracked with a rolling pin

1. Combine the lot in a bowl and stir initially with a fork or scraper, then dump into the bowl of a mixer and give it a good 7–10 minutes at medium speed with the dough hook. You could do this by hand, but it will take much longer.

2. Shape into a large ball, coat with a little more flour and place in a bowl covered with a clean tea towel. Leave the dough to rise. In a warm place, it will achieve one and a half times its original size in an hour or two. Slow the rising process down – in a cold porch, or even in the fridge – and it will take all night, developing better, sourdough flavours as it does.

3. Half an hour before you're ready to cook, put a baking sheet into the oven and turn it up to full. Five minutes before baking, fill a small ovenproof dish with hot water from the kettle and stick it in the bottom of the hot oven. Finally, turn your dough out of the bowl, straight on to the hot baking sheet, and stuff it back into the hot, steamy oven as fast as you can. Try to leave the door open for the shortest possible time so the temperature doesn't drop.

4. After 10 minutes, drop the oven temperature to 180°C and open the door. This lets you check on your loaf and allows the oven temp to drop a little faster. After 20 seconds or so, close the door and leave for another 40 or so minutes.

5. At the end of this time the loaf will sound hollow when tapped on the bottom. It should cool thoroughly before you slice it.

CRUMPETS

450g strong white bread flour ★ 1 sachet (usually 7g) of quick-action dried yeast ★ 10g salt ★ 400g warm milk ★ 300g warm water ★ butter for greasing ★ 5g baking powder

1. Put the flour into a mixing bowl, sprinkle in the yeast and the salt and thoroughly combine. Make a well in the middle and pour in the warm milk.

2. Start to work the batter with a wooden spoon, letting it down little by little with the warm water until it's smooth and pourable.

3. Cover and allow to rise in a warm place until doubled in size.

4. Grease some metal cooking rings with butter and put them into a well-greased, heavy-bottomed skillet. Get things quietly sizzling at medium heat.

5. Quickly and lightly beat the baking powder into the batter, then pour a ladleful into each ring, to a depth of around 1cm. You'll need to judge and jockey the temperature of the pan for each batch you cook, but you're aiming for them to rise and set, over about 8–10 minutes, without burning on the bottom. It's a good idea to start with the temperature a little lower than you might think and maybe do a single crumpet as a test.

6. Once the top has just set, flip the rings over, loosen the sides of the crumpets with a knife and push them out of the ring so the top of the crumpet can lightly tan. Serve hot from the pan, with fresh butter.

BATH BUNS

250g whole milk ★ **10g quick-action dried yeast** ★ **650g strong white flour, plus some for kneading** ★ **30g caster sugar** ★ **5g salt** ★ **275g unsalted butter, softened** ★ **50g sultanas** ★ **1 egg, beaten**

To finish
40g caster sugar ★ **20g water** ★ **4 white sugar cubes**

1. Warm the milk to 30°C in a pan and whisk in the yeast. Leave for 10 minutes, until frothy.

2. Combine the flour, sugar and salt in a bowl and work in the butter with your fingertips. Stir in the milk, then bring together into a dough. If you're kneading by hand, allow to rest for 20 minutes; if you have a mixer, fit the dough hook and start kneading until it becomes elastic. This usually takes 10 minutes in the mixer or 15 by hand.

3. Cover the dough and allow to rise in a warm place for 2 hours or until doubled in size.

4. Turn the dough out on to a floured surface and poke it out into a flat shape. Sprinkle on the sultanas and quickly work them in. Divide into 12 pieces.

5. With floured hands, shape each bun. Pull the corners of each piece over and down, pinching them together underneath. Keep stretching and tucking so it looks like the upper surface of the bun is stretched tight over the insides. This membrane will hold the bun's shape as it rises and cooks and give the characteristic smooth crust.

6. Lay the buns on a sheet of quick-release silicone paper on a baking tray, with plenty of room between them for expansion. Allow to rise in a warm place until doubled in size again.

7. Preheat the oven to 180°C. Glaze the buns with the beaten egg, then cook in the oven for 20–25 minutes, or until the underside of the buns sounds hollow when knocked.

8. Dissolve the sugar in the hot water to make a syrup. As soon as the buns come out of the oven, paint the syrup over them. Before the glaze dries, crush the sugar cubes with a rolling pin and sprinkle over the top.

This is my favourite breakfast at Fitzbillies bakery, where I work. Hot out of the oven, split and packed with damson jam and clotted cream.

NOT JUST BAKED

Basic bread dough doesn't always have to be baked. Shape it into a ring, poach it in water for a few minutes before baking, and you have the beginnings of a bagel. You can, of course, deep-fry it. In fact any system that brings enough fast heat to expand the trapped gases and set the dough will work. Pure steam is used to make one of the coolest Chinese street foods, the baozi or steamed bun.

These are not remotely authentic but they're a different way to treat yeast dough and give a surprisingly light and fluffy result. Try the simple Chinese-inspired filling below, but it's much more fun to go off the rails and try other fillings. Curry is fantastic, as are chilli or Bolognese sauce, perhaps combined with a few cubes of appropriate cheese.

These combinations are so wrong, so counter-intuitive, that they shouldn't really be given any sort of name, but they are truly addictive.

(If you don't want to stuff your buns, roll the dough out into a long oval, fold it in half and steam it. It can later be split and used as sandwich rolls. Try them with steamed pork belly, hoisin sauce, spring onions and cucumber . . . or, hell, just about anything really.)

CHAR SIU PORK

1kg pork belly or boned pork shoulder ★ a pinch of five-spice ★ 100g honey (or maltose, see page 340) ★ 1 chunk of fermented bean curd (red and chunky, from a jar) ★ 50g dark rice wine (xiaou tsing) ★ 50g hoisin sauce ★ 2 cloves of garlic ★ 250g dark soy sauce

1. Trim the belly or shoulder of bones and skin, retaining as much fat as possible (you can ask your butcher to do this for you). Slice along the grain into thick fingers.

2. Put the meat into a bowl and sprinkle lightly with the five-spice powder. Don't overdo it first time, a little goes a long way.

3. Put the honey or maltose into a small dish and smoosh in a cube of the fermented bean curd with the back of a spoon until smooth. Add the rice wine and hoisin sauce, then grate in the garlic and stir well. Finally, dilute the lot to a thin liquid with the dark soy sauce.

4. Pour the marinade over the meat and store in the fridge overnight. The high levels of salt in the soy will act as a brine, 'salting' the meat.

5. Drain the meat, reserving the marinade. Set the meat out on a rack over a roasting tin and put 1cm or so of water in the bottom. Cook at around 150°C, basting with the marinade every 10 minutes. The meat is done when the internal temperature reading is above 75°C.

6. Better still, place the meat on a rack in a hot smoker for the same length of time, hauling it out every 10 minutes to dip it in the marinade.

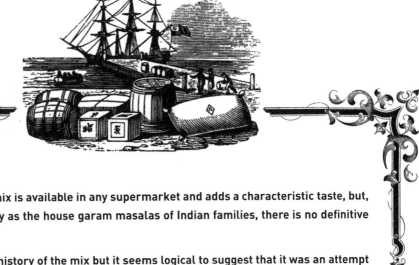

FIVE-SPICE

Chinese 'five-spice' mix is available in any supermarket and adds a characteristic taste, but, in much the same way as the house garam masalas of Indian families, there is no definitive recipe.

Nobody's sure of the history of the mix but it seems logical to suggest that it was an attempt to create a single 'master' condiment that contained the five elements of Chinese cooking: salt, sweet, sour, pungent, bitter.

Traditional mixes include cloves, fennel, cinnamon, star anise and Szechuan pepper. Cassia bark can be used instead of cinnamon, liquorice in place of anise or fennel. Some recipes replace the Szechuan pepper – ground seeds of the prickly ash plant with a weirdly addictive anaesthetic quality on the mouth – with regular black pepper.

Experiment with your own versions. Toasting the ingredients in a hot dry pan before grinding them will help free the flavours, and remember that it's usual for the cinnamon and aniseed to be most dominant.

CHAR SIU STEAMED BUNS

1 quantity of bread dough (see pages 157–8 and note below) ★ **vegetable oil** ★ **5 spring onions** ★ **300g char siu pork (see page 174)** ★ **1 clove of garlic** ★ **10g dark rice wine (xiaou tsing)** ★ **10g oyster sauce** ★ **10g cornflour**

1. Separate your dough into 8 (roughly 100g) portions and form each into a ball.

2. Using a small rolling pin or a length of dowel, roll each ball into a disc about 10cm across. Roll carefully away from the centre to the edge, so the centre of the circle is thicker. You should end up with something looking a little like a thin dough flying saucer.

3. Heat some oil in a frying pan. Add the chopped spring onions and cook for 2–3 minutes until softened, then add the char siu pork, also chopped, and grate in the garlic.

4. Add the rice wine, the oyster sauce and, finally, the cornflour, dissolved to a thin cream in a little water. When the sauce has thickened and become glossy, take it off the heat.

5. Take each disc of dough in the palm of one hand, put a healthy tablespoonful of the filling in the centre and begin pleating and lifting the edges to close the dough around the filling. Finish with a pinch and a twist. If you want a really professional finish, either borrow a Chinese grandmother or go online for hundreds of helpful videos.

6. Let the finished buns rest for an hour or so, so that they can puff back up to delightful fluffiness, then steam them either in a bamboo steamer or in a sieve over boiling water – 15 minutes will do the trick. Use a square of greaseproof paper under each bun to prevent it sticking to the steamer.

NOTE: Ordinary bread dough will make yellow buns, but if you want them white you can buy highly bleached dumpling flour from a Chinese supermarket.

~ PASTRY ~

CHAPTER SIX

Too often today we regard pies as unpleasant products of the cornershop chiller or petrol station forecourt. They have a long shelf-life, are convenient to eat with the hand and can be made from the very cheapest of ingredients . . . no wonder we're suspicious.

But pies have a wonderfully dignified history, hinted at in our traditional nursery rhymes. The 'pieman' whom Simple Simon encountered on his way to the fair would have sold pies for many of the same reasons as motorway service stations do today: as a cheap convenience food for travellers or those without access to their own kitchens. Roman, medieval and Victorian sources refer to pies as the favourite street food of urban Britain, where most of the poor would have had no facilities for home cooking.

In the 'upper crust' of medieval society we encounter 'four and twenty blackbirds' served in a baked piecrust or 'coffyn'. Rich stews or terrine-like fillings would be cooked and brought to the table in giant baked containers that were never intended to be eaten – which explains why live animals could be substituted as a party trick.

Though there's no real evidence to bear it out, it's fun to imagine that it was the servants, usually fed on the leftovers and 'broken meats' of the master's table, who were the first to discover that the bottom crust, soaked with gravy and meat juices, was actually luscious, and may have originated the edible crust.

Hot water crust pastry would have been the best for manufacture of 'coffyns'. It's a lard-based dough which is moulded hot, sets into shape as it cools and can therefore be cooked hard without needing any kind of dish or mould to hold its structure. In modern hot water crust, the quantities are varied to make something that's perhaps less structurally sound but much more pleasant to eat.

Hot water crust is excellent for any pie that's served hot with a gravy-lubricated filling or, better still, for any that is to be served cooled, set and sliced. The best contemporary examples would be game pasties (a mixed game and gravy pie), the noble hand-raised pork pie or the gala pie – which though it lacks live birds, still contains a ghost of that medieval surprise.

Once we'd worked out that eating the case was actually enjoyable, pies and pastry-making began to evolve quickly. Chefs, some of whom began to specialize in the area, devised pastry that was more about taste and less about strength. By increasing the proportion of fat to flour (what bakers call making it 'short'), they made a pastry that crumbled when bitten into. Some began to enrich the mixture with eggs. As sugar became a more common ingredient, it was added to sweeten the pastry. A short, sweet pastry is good enough to need no embellishment and can be cooked dry as a biscuit.[24] Short pastries don't have the robustness of hot water crust so they are often baked 'blind' – baked in a mould while filled with an inert material to hold it in place – which makes them reasonably strong and leakproof before they are filled.

SHORT AND SWEET PIE PASTRY

This recipe is based on the pastry we use commercially in our bakery. It's evolved over ninety years, making it foolproof at any scale.[25] We measure eggs by weight, so there's a conversion inserted for this small amount, which is suitable for four 23cm tart dishes. The finished dough freezes brilliantly, so you can separate it into 250g balls, wrap it in clingfilm and put it into the freezer.

425g plain flour ★ 2g salt ★ 255g butter ★ 217g sugar ★ 107g beaten egg (4 eggs)

1. Combine the flour and salt in a bowl.

2. In another bowl cream together the butter and sugar. You can do this in a mixer with a paddle beater, or by hand, using a spoon or rubber spatula. Once the mixture has lightened in colour, incorporate the eggs.

3. Add the flour and continue to mix until the dough just comes together, then wrap the dough in clingfilm and put into the fridge for 4 hours before using.

---

24 French *bis cuit* or Italian *bis cotti* both mean 'cooked twice'. If sweet dough is cooked once to set it and then again to drive off all moisture, the resulting 'biscuit' will have a long and useful life if stored under dry conditions.

25 As you'll see from the slightly odd weights involved, this size batch is scaled down from a commercial quantity. This system works very well with accurate gram measurements – simply multiply up to create huge tubs of the same stuff – but it neatly illustrates how scaling up '4 eggs' or 'a pinch of salt' by, say, 100 times would quickly get dangerously unpredictable.

Short &

Sweet

FRUIT BAKEWELL TART

For the pastry
1 quantity of short and sweet pie pastry (see page 181)

For the filling
225g very soft unsalted butter ★ 225g caster sugar ★ 3 large eggs ★ 225g ground almonds ★ 1kg bottled fruit (see page 225)

1. Roll out the pastry and line a greased 26cm tart tin. A loose bottom helps when the time comes to pop it out. Cover with clingfilm and refrigerate for at least an hour.

2. Preheat your oven to 200°C. It isn't necessary to blind bake the tart case if you can manage sufficient bottom heat in your oven, so put a substantial oven sheet on the rack and allow that to heat up too.

3. Cream the butter and sugar for the filling, using a wooden spoon, then gently fold in the beaten eggs and ground almonds. Spoon the liquid into the chilled pastry case, then slide it into the oven on top of the hot baking sheet.

4. Bake for 20 minutes, then cover with foil to prevent burning and continue to cook for a further 20 minutes, or until set in the middle. You can test the filling by running a piece of uncooked spaghetti into it – if it comes out clean it's set.

5. Remove the tart from the oven and allow it to cool.

6. Drain your bottled fruit and arrange in a layer on top of the tart. You can, if you wish, save the syrup and reduce it a little to create a glaze which you can paint over the fruit.

7. Serve with clotted cream, because there simply isn't enough joy in the world.

HOT WATER CRUST PASTRY

475g strong white bread flour ★ 5g salt ★ 125g water ★ 175g commercial lard or carefully hoarded beef fat

1. Mix the flour in a bowl with the salt. Bring the water to the boil in a pan and melt the lard or dripping in it, then pour the hot liquid into the bowl of flour and begin combining it with a palette knife.

2. As soon as the dough is cool enough to handle, work it together with your fingers, then form it into a ball. Leave to cool and rest for a few minutes before using. The dough needs to be warm enough to be workable, but if you don't rest it a little it remains elastic and will contract when baked.

This amount will make about 750g of pastry.

GALA PIE

I must have first encountered gala pie at a family wedding, funeral or other licensed brawl. It was a symbol of celebration, an impossibly sophisticated refinement on the quotidian pub pork pie. While uncles fought and boasted and aunts consoled themselves with Babycham, gin and recrimination, I sat under a table on beer-soaked carpet and wondered at the infinite egg. How was it possible that every slice of the yard-long, loaf-shaped pie had a pristine slice of egg in it? Was it even a hen that laid it? Perhaps it was laid by a gala . . . whatever that was. (I think I probably worried too much as a child.)

In my less troubled maturity, I discovered that the infinite egg is a simple trick. A quantity of eggs are separated and the yolks loosely beaten together before being poured into a narrow gauge of sausage skin. After a few minutes in hot water the yolk 'sausage' can be peeled and then carefully inserted into a larger skin along with the combined whites, for a further poaching. Of course the creation of the authentic unappetizing grey ring around the yolk is, and must ever remain, a trade secret.

These days I love a good pie and, though the process has many steps, they are all simple and almost always guarantee a good result. The gala pie is one of those projects that can happily take up an afternoon, but the effect on the audience of wheeling it out is worth all the effort. Rather than indulging in the admittedly hilarious shenanigans of poaching eggs in sausage skins, this recipe contains a simple trick for presentation using whole eggs. It's also worth noting that some consider a gala pie should also contain chicken. You can, if you wish, introduce a layer of poached or leftover roast chicken above or below the eggs. I personally consider this to be a ridiculous affectation; possibly even French.

1kg boned pork shoulder, skin on ★ **200g commercial unsmoked bacon** ★ **2.5g each of mace, nutmeg, allspice and black peppercorns** ★ **2.5g fresh sage leaves** ★ **10g salt** ★ **4 eggs, plus 1 for eggwash** ★ **1 quantity of hot water crust pastry (see page 185)**

For the jelly
1 split pig's trotter ★ **1 stick of celery** ★ **1 carrot** ★ **2 bay leaves** ★ **2–3 fresh sage leaves**

1. Trim the skin and tough connective tissue from the boned pork shoulder and save it. These will be vital elements of the jelly later on. Cut the meat into rough 1cm dice.

2. Cut the bacon into similar-sized pieces. In commercially produced pies, nitrites are added to keep the filling an appetizing colour. There are enough residual preservatives in shop-bought bacon to keep the pie filling pink throughout. If this thought worries you, you can leave out the bacon for an authentically rustic, grey pie interior.

3. To make the jelly, chuck your porky trimmings into a pot with the split pig's trotter, celery, carrot, some bay leaves and sage. Cover with cold water and allow to barely simmer for 2–3 hours, until the trotter gives up the ghost and collapses. Strain the liquid through muslin and keep it in the fridge. Check that it sets to a good consistency – if it doesn't, you can reduce it a little further. This will produce much more jelly than you need but it freezes well, and I like to serve it chopped as a side dish with the pie.

4. Grind the whole spices, then mix them with the chopped sage leaves and a good 10g of salt and season your meat. Remember that the pie is a preserved product, so this is as much about curing as flavouring.

5. Mix the meat and seasonings thoroughly by hand and then blitz half the mix in a food processor before recombining. I like chunks of pork in my pies, but you can vary proportions here to suit your own taste.

6. Place 4 eggs in a pan of cold water, bring to the boil, simmer for exactly 4 minutes, then plunge them into iced water.

7. Preheat the oven to 180°C. Cut off a quarter of your dough to use for the lid. Roll out the remaining dough, fold, turn and reroll until it begins to feel smooth and elastic. Roll to a large circle to line your pie tin. Mould the pastry to fit the tin and allow an overhang of at least 2cm. You can grease it if you think there's not enough fat in this recipe already, but it's not remotely necessary. My tin is round, 16cm across, 7cm deep, with a loose bottom. You shouldn't need a springform, as the pie shrinks away from the sides as it cooks and pops out clean.

8. Put a thin layer of meat into the bottom of the pie case, followed by your peeled eggs. Now here's the cunning bit – make a pen mark on the side of the dish on the centre line of one of your eggs.

9. Carefully pack more filling around and over your eggs, trying to avoid any air gaps.

10. Form a lid with the remaining pastry and glue it on with eggwash, then trim the excess and crimp the edges. Make a small hole in the centre of the pie and, using the back of your knife, mark cutting guides along the centre line of each egg. Finally, eggwash the top, place the pie on a baking tray and put into the preheated oven. After 90 minutes, carefully remove the pie from the tin, eggwash again and return to the oven for 5–10 more minutes.

11. Once the pie is thoroughly cool, wrap the base and sides carefully in a 'bandage' of clingfilm. This will prevent the jelly leaking through any cracks in the pastry before it is fully set. Warm some of the jelly in a pan and pour it slowly through a funnel to fill the air gap between filling and case. Take your time, and keep tapping the pie gently on the worktop to expel any air bubbles. Put back into the fridge so the jelly can set.

12. Slice neatly through the guide lines in the crust and serve.

GAME 'CUTTING' PIE

For the pastry
double quantity of hot water crust pastry (see page 185) ✶ **1 large egg, beaten**

For the marinade
200g Madeira ✶ **2 blades of mace** ✶ **10 black peppercorns** ✶ **4 bay leaves** ✶ **peel from 1 orange** ✶ **2.5g fresh thyme** ✶ **2.5g dried savory** ✶ **10 juniper berries** ✶ **½ a clove of garlic**

For the filling
2 partridges or pheasants ✶ **500g diced venison** ✶ **500g diced mixed game, e.g. rabbit, hare, duck** ✶ **500g pork belly, skin removed** ✶ **100g smoked streaky bacon**

For the jelly
bones and trimmings from game ✶ **1 carrot** ✶ **1 onion** ✶ **1 stick of celery** ✶ **1 pig's trotter or ½ a sheet of gelatine**

1. Remove the breasts from the birds. You can, if you wish, remove the leg meat too and add it to the filling, but I find it's much better employed in strengthening the jelly stock along with the rest of the carcasses.

2. Start a stock by simmering the bird remains in a couple of litres of water with a carrot, an onion and a stick of celery. Add a split pig's trotter if you can get one. If not you'll have to set the jelly at the end, using gelatine. Add any other trimmings to the stock as you prepare the rest of the game. Simmer the stock for about 3 hours, uncovered. Strain, throwing away the flavourings and bones. Reduce the stock to around 200ml over a high heat, then cool and refrigerate.

3. All the non-poultry game should be diced and marinated overnight with the Madeira, herbs, peel and chopped garlic. I suggest letting venison predominate but that's just being fussy. Rabbit, hare, squirrel and, for all I know, kangaroo will all add to the complexity.

4. Mince or chop the pork belly along with the bacon. I like the little twist that smoked streaky gives, but that's your choice. Don't dare to discard any fat at this point. It's vital to the final result. You'll want to add pepper and salt (about 5g each) as you chop.

5. Use two-thirds of your hot water pastry to line a large springform cake tin. A wide, shallow pie suffers less from the shrinkage of the meat during cooking. Preheat the oven to 180°C.

6. Lay half the marinated game in the bottom of the case (I remove the orange peel, but otherwise everything goes in). Season, then add the bird breasts as a middle layer. Season again, then add the remaining game and top with the pork. Game is extremely lean, so the fat from the pork will soak down through the meat, moistening and flavouring it.

7. Take the remaining third of the pastry and roll it out to make a lid. Glue it in place with beaten egg, crimp and trim. Decorate the pie with any trimmings – it's traditional to really go to town with this – and make a small hole in the centre of the lid. Glaze generously with more beaten egg, then bake for 20 minutes. Turn the heat down to 160°C and bake for another hour. The pastry will now be set.

8. Take the pie out of the oven and unmould it from the tin, leaving it on the base. Paint the pie with another layer of eggwash, then return it to the oven and continue to bake until the internal temperature is 75°C.

9. Remove the pie from the oven again and begin cooling it on a wire rack. As soon as the outside of the pie is cool enough to touch, bandage the outer wall with clingfilm and refrigerate the whole thing overnight. The bandaging holds the casing in place and also prevents any leaking during the last stage.

10. The stock should be strained, cooled overnight and de-fatted, which will give you a chance to see how well it sets. Use gelatine sheets according to the instructions on the packet if it isn't setting sufficiently.

11. Warm the jellied stock until it's liquid again and use a funnel to pour it into the hole in the top of the cold pie. Go slowly, giving it a chance to work its way into every remaining crevice. Once set, the jelly is not just delicious but forms an airtight seal around the meat, which, originally, was regarded as a method of preservation.

12. Serve the game pie in cold slices with chutney or piccalilli. It will remain spectacularly good in the fridge for up to a week, where you'll find yourself sneaking to snaffle an extra slice like a character in a P. G. Wodehouse story.

CRAB PASTY

I love crabs, the Armoured Fighting Vehicle of the UK's coastline and one of our most criminally underrated foods. They're plentiful, almost unbelievably cheap, and when served fresh the meat is superior to lobster. The only barrier to this edible goldmine is cooking the damn things and getting the meat out.

In spite of years of trying, we Brits have been pretty much unable to agree on a national dish. Sunday lunch has been suggested but we're never going to get anyone to agree about the Yorkshire puddings. Instead, I'd like to make the case for the crab pasty.

The recipe, such as it is, is so blindingly simple, so utterly right, that it hardly deserves the name. It should just be something we somehow 'know' – like how to queue and that 'tum-ti-tum' bit at the beginning of 'Jerusalem'. Subversively, in a chapter on pastry, I am going to suggest that you use bought puff pastry: pre-made puff is often a by-product of butter over-production, it's machine-rolled and is infinitely more delicate than that you can make yourself without machinery. Check that the ingredient list doesn't run much longer than 'Flour, butter, salt' and you won't be disappointed.

So, take some packet puff pastry. Cut a circle. Put some freshly picked crabmeat on one side, season, fold over the top, seal and eggwash and bake at 180°C until done (around 18 minutes). It is a splendid idea to add sweated shredded leeks and maybe a hint of saffron.

BEEF AND PICKLED WALNUT PUDDING

1 oxtail (approx. 1.5–2kg) ★ stock vegetables (carrot, onion, leek, celery) ★ 350g self-raising flour ★ 150g shredded beef suet ★ 7.5g baking powder ★ 250g beef skirt ★ 50g plain flour ★ salt and black pepper ★ 1 onion ★ 100g red wine ★ 3 pickled walnuts ★ 15g redcurrant jelly ★ 15g vinegar from pickled walnuts ★ 15g tomato purée (optional) ★ 15g mushroom ketchup (optional)

1. The day before you want to serve your pudding, brown the oxtail chunks in a hot dry frying pan and place them in a single layer in a casserole along with whatever stock veg you have to hand. Cover with cold water and bring to the boil. Skim carefully and then reduce to the barest simmer. Keep a lid on the pot and either simmer on a low heat or in the oven at 130°C. Check after a couple of hours, but cook until the meat pulls away from the bones.

2. Remove and discard the stock veg, pick all the meat off the bones and reserve, then strain the remaining liquid and chill overnight so you can lift off (and keep) the fat in the morning.

3. Combine the self-raising flour, suet and baking powder in a bowl and add just enough cold water to bring it to a manageable dough. Use two-thirds of it to line a pudding basin.

4. Cut the beef skirt into neat chunks, toss in seasoned plain flour and brown them in the recovered fat from the oxtail. (Use veg oil if you're not that rugged.)

5. Chop the onion and sweat it in a thick-based pan with a little oil until it softens. Add the browned beef chunks and the red wine and allow the wine to simmer down to about 50% of its volume. Add about 600g of the oxtail liquid, bring to a gentle simmer, then crumble in the pickled walnuts and put a lid on.

6. After about 45 minutes of simmering, the meat will be getting good. Add the oxtail meat and start tweaking. Taste the gravy, then start with salt. You'll also need black pepper. Stir in a little of the redcurrant jelly and taste again. Finally add splashes of the pickling vinegar from the walnuts. Experimentally tasting like this works brilliantly with any gravy or sauce. A little tomato purée sometimes enlivens things, and mushroom ketchup can add a lovely bassy earthiness.

7. Once everything is to your satisfaction, preheat the oven to 160°C. Pour the filling into the pie, roll out the remaining pastry to make a lid and glue it on with water and a paintbrush. Crimp together to seal. Cover the top of the pie with a layer of foil and hold everything in place with a layer of clingfilm. Put the whole basin into a baking tin in the middle of the oven and pour in boiling water to a depth of at least 3–4cm. Cook in the oven for 45 minutes.

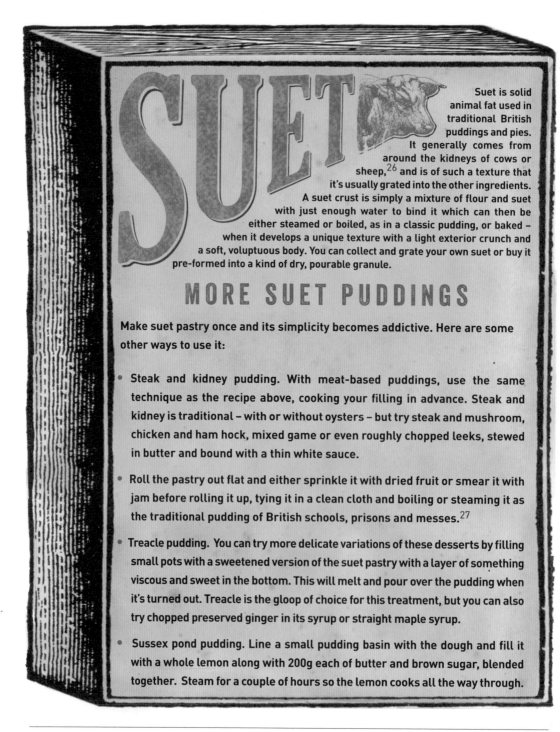

SUET

Suet is solid animal fat used in traditional British puddings and pies. It generally comes from around the kidneys of cows or sheep,[26] and is of such a texture that it's usually grated into the other ingredients. A suet crust is simply a mixture of flour and suet with just enough water to bind it which can then be either steamed or boiled, as in a classic pudding, or baked – when it develops a unique texture with a light exterior crunch and a soft, voluptuous body. You can collect and grate your own suet or buy it pre-formed into a kind of dry, pourable granule.

MORE SUET PUDDINGS

Make suet pastry once and its simplicity becomes addictive. Here are some other ways to use it:

- Steak and kidney pudding. With meat-based puddings, use the same technique as the recipe above, cooking your filling in advance. Steak and kidney is traditional – with or without oysters – but try steak and mushroom, chicken and ham hock, mixed game or even roughly chopped leeks, stewed in butter and bound with a thin white sauce.

- Roll the pastry out flat and either sprinkle it with dried fruit or smear it with jam before rolling it up, tying it in a clean cloth and boiling or steaming it as the traditional pudding of British schools, prisons and messes.[27]

- Treacle pudding. You can try more delicate variations of these desserts by filling small pots with a sweetened version of the suet pastry with a layer of something viscous and sweet in the bottom. This will melt and pour over the pudding when it's turned out. Treacle is the gloop of choice for this treatment, but you can also try chopped preserved ginger in its syrup or straight maple syrup.

- Sussex pond pudding. Line a small pudding basin with the dough and fill it with a whole lemon along with 200g each of butter and brown sugar, blended together. Steam for a couple of hours so the lemon cooks all the way through.

---

26 Solid fat rendered from pork is called lard. See page 317.

27 The resulting slab of fruited carbohydrate, enlivened with a variety of custards and sauces, is traditionally named something deeply unflattering by the happy diners – Spotted Dick, Dead Dog and Dead Man's Arm being some of the more appetizing. We certainly loved it at my school, where we called it Leper's Leg.

PRESERVING

CHAPTER SEVEN

In most European countries, it's possible to walk into a chemist or a hardware store and ask, in a proud, clear voice, for a bottle of plain white alcohol, of drinking quality. For reasons that are depressingly obvious, this simple pleasure is denied us in the UK – we'd probably just drink it. Fruit, nuts, herbs and aromatics, macerated in unflavoured alcohol, are not only preserved but also create an almost unlimited range of drinks – sometimes referred to as schnapps. When additionally sweetened with sugar syrup or honey they become liqueurs. With careful handling, and judiciously chosen flavourings, they can even be transformed into the sublime gin.

FRUIT IN ALCOHOL

So since you can't get hold of plain white alcohol, start with vodka. It is made from either wheat or potatoes. The vegetable starch is turned into sugar, the sugar is fermented into alcohol, the alcohol is distilled and finally re-diluted with pure water. Some brands would have you believe otherwise but a proper vodka is really an almost neutral spirit. Some, particularly the Scandinavian brands, market themselves on their purity and absence of flavours.

Lacking a supply of neutral spirit from the chemist, this is the stuff to choose for your own experiments. Much as I love independent wine merchants and off-licences, by the way, I suggest you go straight to the supermarket for your vodka. It's made by the sort of giant companies that can arrange huge discounts with supermarkets and it's a rare week when they're not shifting the stuff off the shelves at ludicrously low prices or on two-for-one deals. Perhaps there are some advantages to our ambiguous national relationship with alcohol.

Some vodkas are available in half or third sized bottles but if yours isn't, recycle some from other sources; one macerated fruit alcohol is a lovely thing – but five are better.

Fruit for maceration should be wiped clean with a damp cloth but it's not necessary to heat or otherwise sterilize either fruit or bottle. Nothing survives soaking in alcohol. Fruit with a tough skin should be pierced with a needle in a few places to get the juices flowing.

The following may be of interest as starting points but this is one of those occasions where the imagination is the best recipe. Try . . .

Lemon peel, lemon thyme, lemon grass. Seville oranges, Agen prunes, plums, apricots. Fresh cobnuts, coconut, cinnamon. Basil leaves, chillies, cherry tomatoes. Fresh ginger, preserved stem ginger, rose petals or, I am reliably informed, Gummi Bears.

FI'S VIN D'ORANGE

I'd like to make it clear that my friend Fi is not an alcoholic. Alcoholics go to meetings: Fi goes to parties. Granted, she sometimes doesn't come back for a few days, but one thing's for sure: she knows more about drink than any woman alive and she guards with her life the original recipe for vin d'orange, which she inherited from her friend Marie-Odile la Comtesse de Pissy.

Through years of experiment, Fi has evolved the recipe, added and subtracted until the original version, which had an effect not unlike a lobotomy performed with a ball-pein hammer, has become something almost refined.

Wash the skins of 2 small Seville oranges and ½ a lemon and slice roughly. Place in a sterilized jar (see page 68) with . . .

200g sugar ★ **½ a vanilla pod, split lengthwise** ★ **¼ of a cinnamon stick, broken** ★ **1 litre good rosé wine** ★ **200g eau-de-vie**

. . . and stir well with a clean stainless steel spoon.

Cover with the lid and refrigerate for 6 weeks, shaking the jar gently from time to time to dissolve the sugar.

Add 50g of rum and pour through a coffee filter into another sterilized jar or bottle. Cork and refrigerate.

GIN

Gin takes its name from the Dutch jenever or the French genièvre, meaning juniper. Though juniper is and should be the predominant flavour in any gin, a vast number of other 'botanicals' are used to create and refine the complex flavours of various brands. Expensive and classy gins are of the 'distilled' type, which means that base alcohol and the macerated botanicals are passed together through the distilling process. Simpler, cheaper gins are often of the 'compound' type, in which the botanicals are simply added to the alcohol – either in natural form or as extracts.

Distillers will weave all sorts of wonderful stories of how the second distillation combines and mellows the flavours in symbiotic harmony – as they charge you £50 a bottle – but, in truth, an extremely refined, delicate gin can easily be produced by small-scale maceration.

You can macerate in the bottle but that makes it all but impossible to repeat a brilliant recipe. You're dealing with tiny quantities of aromatics and judging how well they've given up their flavours over time entirely by taste. It's much more sensible to do five or more bottles' worth in one batch.

A plastic water bottle of the type found on water coolers will make a usable vessel, or you can buy a plastic jerry-can from a camping store. I managed to pick up a large glass barrel on eBay that's also equipped with a tap. Christened the Gin Beast, it combines the functions of maceration, storage, display and serving. It might also be possible to do away with glasses if I simply lie under the tap and open it.

You can pour the aromatics into the alcohol without further fuss, but if you restrain them in a 'tea ball' or a piece of muslin on a string you can extract them at any time if you need to adjust the flavours or when you feel the gin has reached its optimum.

A good starting set of botanicals for a basic gin is . . .

20g juniper berries, lightly crushed with a rolling pin ✻ 10g dried mandarin peel (available at Chinese supermarkets, or dry your own peel in the airing cupboard) ✻ 5g coriander seed ✻ 5g caraway seed ✻ 1 star anise

These should be combined and stored in an airtight jar. From this master mix take 5g and heat in a dry pan to loosen up the oils and aromatics before adding to the alcohol while still hot.

Very little flavouring is needed for quite large quantities of alcohol, but it's very difficult to control the combinations in small quantities. If I'm honest I should also say that I find the existence of a jar on a kitchen shelf marked 'Gin Mix' quietly encouraging.

This recipe gives a quite simple gin but you can go in all sorts of crazy directions if it takes your fancy. Vanilla, clove and cinnamon are extraordinarily strong flavours and tend to overpower everything else. Orwell describes the awful, state-distilled gin in *1984* as having a strong taste of clove oil – reason enough to leave it out of the mix entirely – but citrus flavours are an excellent addition, using dried peel, lemon or lime leaves, lemon grass or even food-grade citrus oils. The oily herbs – rosemary, bay and thyme – can feature, and any of the more exotic spices can be used in balance; I've even experimented with extracting a small quantity of the alcohol and bubbling smoke through it before gradually adding it back. A faint backnote of log fire is a lovely thing on the palate and the nose.

The main thing to remember is that juniper must remain the predominant flavour if it's to remain a gin, but otherwise you are working in a way more akin to a parfumier than a cook in developing the special individual combination of aromas. You can add a new flavour to the mix at any time but you can't take one away, so if you feel, for example, that everything's spot-on but for a tiny hit of chipotle, then by all means draw off a small quantity and add the new flavour to that. If it works you can always pour it back in and add more of the new ingredient to the mixture. If it has to go down the sink, then the main batch hasn't been lost.

Maceration should take at least a month, but constant, small samplings are an essential and enjoyable part of the process. Many of the oily flavours will successfully transfer in just a few hours, but depth and character develop over a longer period. Once the botanicals have been removed, the shelf-life of the gin in sealed bottles is effectively indefinite.

SLOE GIN

500g sloes ★ 300g sugar ★ 1 bottle of gin

1. Pick over the sloes to make sure you've removed sticks and leaves. Put them into a thick plastic bag and freeze overnight.

2. In the morning, give the frozen sloes a light clobbering with a rolling pin while still in the bag and then feed them into a clean, empty bottle. Funnel in the sugar and top up with the gin.

3. Shake the bottle daily for 3 weeks.

4. Give the bottle a couple of days without shaking to settle, then carefully decant through a fine sieve and a piece of clean J-cloth. Seal and store. Sloes are in season around September to October. Your gin will be drinkable by Christmas but infinitely better after a year.[28]

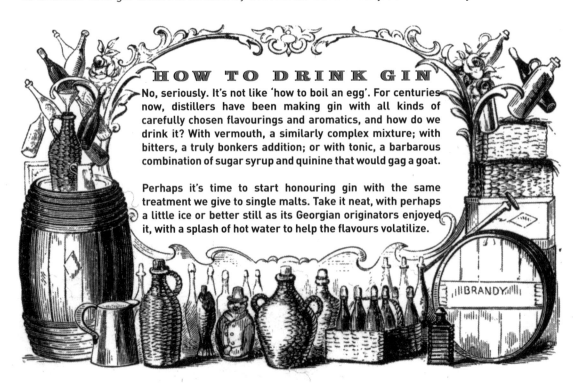

HOW TO DRINK GIN

No, seriously. It's not like 'how to boil an egg'. For centuries now, distillers have been making gin with all kinds of carefully chosen flavourings and aromatics, and how do we drink it? With vermouth, a similarly complex mixture; with bitters, a truly bonkers addition; or with tonic, a barbarous combination of sugar syrup and quinine that would gag a goat.

Perhaps it's time to start honouring gin with the same treatment we give to single malts. Take it neat, with perhaps a little ice or better still as its Georgian originators enjoyed it, with a splash of hot water to help the flavours volatilize.

---

28 Helpful hint: At the same time you make the sloe gin, take a small glass out of a bottle of sherry and replace it with three or four fresh, red hot chillies. Replace the cork and store next to the sloe gin. Chilli sherry is delicious after just a month, so any time you feel the temptation to lash into the gin early, deflect yourself with a nip of sherry instead. To be really traditional, you can top up the chilli bottle with more sherry each time you take a slug.

EXCLUDING AIR

Bacteria need air to thrive, so some of the simplest methods of preservation just prevent air from reaching the food. Sausage skins, to some extent, provide a physical barrier to air and, because they shrink as they dry, they also drive out small air pockets in the meat. Some foods cooked with sufficient fat – confits, for example – are automatically 'sealed' when the fat congeals on cooling. Others, like potted meats, need a layer of clarified butter or lard poured over the surface to create an airtight 'cap'.

RABBIT CONFIT

1 rabbit ★ 10g salt ★ 15 black peppercorns ★ 10 sprigs of fresh thyme ★ 4 sprigs of fresh rosemary ★ 3 bay leaves ★ 10 cloves of garlic ★ 16 juniper berries ★1 shallot ★ 1 litre olive oil

1. Skin the rabbit and joint it into 8 pieces – or have your butcher do it for you. Put them into a dish.

2. Combine the salt, ground peppercorns, half the fresh herbs and half the chopped garlic and rub into the rabbit pieces. Cover and allow to marinate overnight in the fridge.

3. Preheat the oven to 120°C. Pack the rabbit pieces into a casserole or other heavy, lidded pot, sprinkling the remaining seasonings between the pieces. Tuck in the sliced shallot. Pour over enough olive oil to completely submerge everything.

4. Cut a circle of greaseproof paper big enough to sit on the surface of the oil and make a small hole in the centre to act as a steam vent. Lay on the paper cover, then put the lid on and place the casserole in the hot oven for 3 hours. Check occasionally. The oil should not simmer, maybe just give the occasional bubble, and a probe thermometer should read between 100°C and 120°C. Shift the rabbit pieces every now and then, to make sure they're not sticking.

5. When the meat is soft but not falling off the bone, allow it to cool in the oil and refrigerate for up to 4 days. To serve, remove from the oil, warm in a hot oven to an internal temperature of 75°C, then either sear the outside in a dry pan or quickly crisp on a hot charcoal grill.

PARTRIDGE ESCABECHE

4 partridges ★ 75g olive oil ★ 4 onions ★ 1 carrot ★ 8 cloves of garlic ★ 5g sherry vinegar ★ 125g white wine ★ 4 bay leaves ★ 2 or 3 sprigs of fresh thyme ★ 1 sprig of fresh parsley ★10 peppercorns ★ 5g smoked paprika ★ salt

1. Clean the partridges and tie them with string so they keep their shape.

2. Heat the olive oil in a cazuela or a large, heavy casserole and brown the birds, then lift them out and put them to one side.

3. Peel and slice the onions, carrot and garlic. Add, along with the remaining ingredients, to the pot and boil for 3 minutes.

4. Pack the partridges into large preserving jars.[29] Remove the solid ingredients from the pot with a slotted spoon and distribute between the jars, then pour the hot liquid over the birds, ensuring it's divided equally.

5. Top up the jars with hot water to ensure that the birds are well covered and seal them up.

6. Lower the jars into a large pan of boiling water and poach for 55 minutes.

7. Lift the jars, allow to cool, then refrigerate. Escabeche tastes good after 2 days' storage and will remain excellent for up to 7 days. Either serve whole, or shred the meat from the carcasses, return it to the liquid and reheat. Serve with cooked beans or lentils.

---

29 I pack 2 birds at a time into 2 litre Le Parfait Super preserving jars. You can usually pack a single average-sized bird into a 1 litre jar. I find the Le Parfaits are particularly good for processes where the food is actually cooked in the jar. I'm sure other brands work well, but where high pressures and food preservation are concerned, go with something you trust.

DUCK CONFIT

30g salt ★ 15g black peppercorns ★ 4 sprigs of fresh thyme ★ 4 cloves of garlic ★ 4 large duck legs ★ 750g duck fat

1. Mix the salt, crushed peppercorns, thyme leaves and crushed garlic in a bowl and rub the mixture hard into all surfaces and crevices of the duck legs.

2. Allow the duck legs to cure overnight in the fridge, then rinse off the marinade and pat the legs dry with kitchen paper.

3. Pack the duck legs skin side down into a pot, casserole or oven tray so that they cover the bottom neatly in a single layer. Pour over the melted fat to cover the meat, and poach gently at 85–90°C for 3 hours.

4. To store the confit, pack the cooled legs into a jar, pot or plastic box and pour over enough of the fat to cover. Tap smartly on the worktop to dislodge any air bubbles before allowing to cool and set. Store the confit in the fridge. Each time you remove a leg to use, gently re-melt the fat so it settles back neatly, sealing the remaining confit.

5. To serve a duck leg, drop it skin side down into a hot, dry pan. This will crisp and brown the skin beautifully. Then flip it over to quickly sear the other side. Remember you're not cooking the duck here, just warming it through while making the exterior doubly delicious. Serve with potatoes, roasted or fried in some of the fat from the same jar, and a green salad or French beans.

6. As you work your way down through the confit you'll find you have more fat left over than you strictly need, so hoick out a lump every now and again to fry potatoes or even (be still, my bleating heart surgeon) your breakfast eggs.

7. This recipe will also work well for goose, which like duck has a delicate flavour that's present in the abundant fat. It doesn't work so well for chicken, which somehow just comes out bland when confited. The tough legs of any of the small game birds can be confited and are often served as such alongside the breast fillets, which have been more speedily cooked. As they lack fat of their own they are usually done in duck fat.

TERRINES/PÂTÉS

There's no great dearth of terrines, no dreadful famine of chicken liver parfait and, as far as I'm aware, the meat-paste market still thrives in its own quiet way, but where, oh where are the great slablike pâtés of my youth?

Pâté came from two sources when I was a kid. There was the stuff from the supermarket or the deli that came in oval ceramic crocks (my mother, as I remember, would flirt openly with the spud-faced geriatric in the butchery section, who dispensed the empties as gifts to his 'special ladies'). The tops were ferociously aspicked and coded with various arcane trimmings. The wrinkled orange slice meant the 'Ardennes', a liverish concoction that looked like a lateral section through a life-threatening tumour and may, or may not, have contained duck. Best, though, by far, was 'pâté de campagne', which looked like dogfood but was packed with enough French military-grade garlic to knock out a passing camel.

Some women in the 1970s were different. They wore huge broad floppy-brimmed hats, had hair like in the ads, ran through fields in soft focus and did all their own cooking. I think Mum was one of those . . . or at least she thought she was, and so, one dark day, she got a shiny cookbook down from the shelf, bought a pail of guts from the spud-faced butcher and boldly made her own.

I was truly impressed. It was a hell of an achievement and what was more, it made the shop-bought stuff taste like year-old meatloaf. I'd never been to France but now I knew exactly what it would taste like and I was sold on pâté.

Today, pâté seems as hard to find as a bottle of Blue Nun or a tin of smoked oysters. Maybe the naff *Abigail's Party* connotations have pushed it from fashionable menus. But that's a shame, because a decent pâté de campagne is a thing of beauty and not remotely difficult to knock up. Recipes are legion and variations huge, but that's half the fun. The main points to remember as you go off-piste are that all the flavour is in the marinade and the texture depends on proper cooling while tightly wrapped, so the longer you take over things the more brilliant the finished product will be.

There's something lovely about an even-tempered terrine, and a chicken liver parfait will always be a welcome addition to the starters section, but let's act before it's too late, to rescue the pâté our parents found so exotic.

PÂTÉ DE CAMPAGNE

500g pork shoulder ★ 250g pig's liver ★ 250g pork backfat ★ 2 rashers of unsmoked back bacon ★ caul fat (see page 223) or 10 rashers of streaky bacon ★ 1 egg ★ salt

For the marinade
5g fresh parsley ★ 2 sprigs of fresh thyme ★ 3 allspice berries ★ 75g sherry ★ 75g white wine ★ black pepper

1. Cut all the meaty ingredients, except for the caul fat or streaky bacon, into rough 2cm cubes.

2. Chop the herbs finely, crush the berries, then munge all the marinade ingredients together with the meat in a plastic bag with lots of black pepper. Leave in the fridge for at least 24 hours.

3. Discard the marinade, then mince coarsely or blitz lightly in a food processor. Don't purée unless you like it boringly smooth (this is pâté de campagne, not pâté de suburb).

4. Prepare your tin. A terrine tin with a lid is great, but you can use a regular loaf tin with sloping sides. If you are a perfectionist, you can cut a lid from a piece of wood or thick card and wrap it in foil. Line your tin with a layer of foil, a layer of clingfilm and a single layer of caul fat. Try to keep the fat evenly spread out – it's mainly a decorative wrapping. If you can't get caul fat you can line the tin with bacon rashers (bacon is never inappropriate).

5. Add an egg and 15g of salt to the mixture and work through with your hands. Pack the mixture into the prepared tin, folding the caul fat closed over the top.

6. Preheat the oven to 180°C. Wrap clingfilm round to form a tight seal, then close up the foil before putting on your lid or your foil-covered board (the lid isn't vital but makes for a more elegant finished product). Place the tin in a big roasting pan and pour in boiling water to just below the top of the tin. Slide it carefully into the oven and allow to cook gently for 2½ hours.

7. Remove the terrine from the oven and weight the lid. Do not be tempted to unwrap at this stage. Once it's cool enough, transfer to the fridge overnight, keeping the weights in place.

8. Unwrap, like a large and meaty pass-the-parcel. While cooling, the pâté will have reabsorbed most of its juices and fats, which will then have set. Wipe the surface clean of excess jelly and fat to expose that lovely layer of caul. If you're feeling rustic, you can smear the jelly on your bread before serving.

POTTING

POTTED LOBSTER

Lobster and crab meat can be potted the same way as shrimps. If you're cooking a fresh crab you can take a mixture of the white and brown meat and treat it exactly the same as the cooked shrimps in the recipe on page 222. If you've bought a cooked lobster, then the same recipe is a terrific way to add flavour back into the shredded meat. If, on the other hand, you can find raw frozen lobster tail, or, better still, you're not averse to 'homarcide', try the recipe below, which harks back to Escoffier and uses a broadly similar technique to create possibly the most decadent starter imaginable. In technical terms what's going on here is very similar to the terribly fashionable 'sous-vide' technique, though obviously in a far more DIY way.

1 raw lobster tail (weights vary wildly) ★ **around the same weight of clarified butter, plus a little extra to seal** ★ **a pinch of black pepper** ★ **a pinch of ground mace** ★ **½ a bay leaf** ★ **lemon juice**

1. Slice the lobster tail into 0.5cm rounds.

2. Warm the clarified butter to 85°C and add the seasonings.

3. Pack the lobster slices into a preserving jar, pour over the melted butter through a sieve and seal. Choose your jar size carefully so it's well packed with meat before adding the butter, otherwise you'll end up with lobster-flavoured butter rather than butter-flavoured lobster.

4. Lower the jar into barely simmering water so that it comes halfway up the sides of the jar. The lobster will be cooked in 10–12 minutes.

5. Lift out the jar, open it and break the meat up a little with a fork before closing, tapping to remove air bubbles, cooling and chilling.

6. Once everything has reset, pour on a further layer of clarified butter.

7. Serve in the same way as potted shrimps but with considerably more smugness.

CHICKEN LIVER PARFAIT WITH MADEIRA JELLY

500g fresh chicken livers ★ 500g unsalted butter ★ 3 shallots, chopped ★ 1 clove of garlic, sliced ★ 2 sprigs of fresh thyme ★ 100g Madeira ★ 50g brandy ★ 5 large free-range eggs ★ 10g salt ★ 2 pinches of freshly ground black pepper

1. Trim the chicken livers of any stringy bits and anything that looks a little discoloured. Warm the butter gently so it's just liquid enough to pour, and preheat your oven to 130°C.

2. Put the shallots, garlic and thyme into a small pan and add the Madeira and brandy. Bring to a simmer and allow to reduce to about half. Strain the liquid into your food processor.

3. Add the livers to the food processor and begin blending. Add the eggs one at a time over about 3 minutes or so, until entirely smooth.

4. With the motor running, begin pouring in the liquid butter. This will emulsify with the liver in the same way as a mayonnaise – though it can also split in the same way if added too quickly or at too high a temperature. Stop pouring before you hit the milky liquid under the butter.

5. Traditionally a chef would taste the mixture at this point and adjust the seasoning but, as raw offal and raw eggs are both high-risk food products, this would be strictly forbidden in a modern professional kitchen. I've suggested a starting point of 10g, though under-salting isn't catastrophic in something as rich as the finished pâté. Black pepper is useful at this point too, but set the grind very fine if you don't want flecks in your pink parfait.

6. Pour the parfait into individual serving jars or pots and set in a bain-marie. I usually fold a tea towel into the bottom of a large baking dish to stop the bottoms of the pots overheating, slide it into the preheated oven, then add boiling water to come at least halfway up the jars.

7. After 20 minutes begin checking the parfaits with a probe thermometer. At 65–70°C they will be set, beautifully pink and with a smooth spreadable consistency. Remove from the bain-marie, allow to cool to room temperature and refrigerate for at least 4 hours.

8. You can top the cooled, set parfaits with clarified butter, which would be a traditional finish, or you can make a simple jelly of Madeira (see port jelly, page 361) and pour it on the top, where it will set, seal and form its own delicious accompaniment.

POTTED SHRIMPS

400g brown shrimps ★ **400g clarified butter** ★ **a large pinch of ground mace** ★ **a large pinch of black pepper** ★ **15g fresh lemon juice** ★ **5g anchovy paste**

1. If you can find fresh, live shrimps, boil them for 10 minutes in seawater and peel painstakingly. In fact, most shrimps are boiled, peeled and frozen the moment they're landed, so there's no shame in buying them pre-prepared.

2. Keep back 100g of the butter for sealing and melt the rest gently in a pan. Add the shrimps and the rest of the ingredients.

3. To really get the shrimps tasting their best, it's worth keeping them in the melted, flavoured butter for as long as possible, but they won't take any further cooking. It's best to keep them near enough to the heat that the butter stays liquid, but definitely not to apply any direct heat once the shrimps are in the pan.

4. Use a slotted spoon to lift the shrimps out of the butter and pack them loosely into ramekins or preserving jars. Pour over the flavoured butter.

5. Fold a tea towel into a pad of four or more thicknesses, lay it on the worktop, and tap the jars firmly on it to dislodge any air bubbles. Then refrigerate until set.

6. Melt the remaining butter and pour a layer over the set shrimps, ensuring that none are poking above the surface. Chill again until set.

7. Allow to return to room temperature before serving with hot toast. Potted goods are fine in the fridge for up to 2 weeks, though they should be eaten quickly once the seal is broken and should not be 'reset' after they've been served (it's a good idea to set them in single-portion containers). They also freeze well.

FAGGOTS

120g caul fat ☆ 500g pork liver ☆ 300g skinless and boneless pork belly ☆ 1 clove of garlic ☆ 5g fresh thyme ☆ 5g fresh sage ☆ 5g ground mace ☆ 100g fresh white breadcrumbs ☆ 100g oil or dripping, to cook

1. Soak the caul fat in cold water. This helps to make it easier to handle.

2. Thoroughly combine the rest of the ingredients in a bowl. Take a tiny pinch and fry it quickly in a hot pan so you can test your seasoning, then adjust accordingly.

3. Take small handfuls of the meat, about the size of a billiard ball, pack loosely and wrap in a piece of the caul fat. Pack the finished faggots into a shallow dish and chill them until they're firm.

4. Fry in oil or dripping for 6–8 minutes, in batches if necessary, and serve with rich gravy and mashed potatoes. Peas are the traditional accompaniment, but the key words here are definitely 'marrowfat' or 'mushy' rather than any kind of affected, frozen petit pois.

Caul fat is a beautiful lacy membrane which stretches between an animal's internal organs. It's tough enough to hold loose ingredients together but largely melts away in cooking. In doing so it lubricates and moistens the meat.

Pork caul is most commonly used in charcuterie. It can be obtained from your butcher with enough notice, or directly from the online suppliers on pages 370-71.

In any sausage recipe the filling can be wrapped in caul rather than piped into a casing. This gives a more rustic finish, but is just as tasty in a terrine that's cooked in a dish. The effect of the caul is largely decorative but in traditional West Country faggots, it's vital. Nothing but caul will hold together those glorious nuggets of chopped offal.

IN SUGAR

A concentrated sugar solution is as hostile to bacteria as a salty brine. It seals out the air that the bacteria need to survive and in some cases physically destroys them by osmosis. Many fruit can be preserved in a simple syrup (water and sugar in equal quantities by weight), which is the way much soft fruit is bottled or canned. By cooking the fruit in the syrup, water is driven off and the sugar concentration is raised. If this is done repeatedly, the result is 'candied' fruit, which has a quite astonishing shelf-life.

If soft fruit are stewed with high quantities of sugar, the result can be a jam or preserve in which pectin present in the fruit causes the mixture of juice and syrup to set around the preserved fruit.

DAMSON CHEESE

1.5kg ripe damsons ★ 1kg sugar

1. Wash the fruit carefully, removing leaves, stems and any bruised or damaged material. Pour into a non-reactive pan and add 200g of water. Simmer until skins and stones begin to float to the surface.

2. Pass the mixture through a sieve and weigh the purée.

3. Add half the weight of sugar to purée, then heat the mixture, gently, until the sugar has dissolved, stirring to ensure nothing catches or burns.

4. Simmer gently until the mixture is thick enough to leave a noticeable trail when a spoon is pulled through.

5. Pour into flat, tray-like containers – margarine tubs that have been through the dishwasher or takeaway-style foil trays are great. While the mixture is still hot, cut a piece of greaseproof paper to fit the surface and push it down on top of the cheese, working out any air bubbles.

6. Put on any lids you have, wrap in clingfilm and refrigerate. The cheese will mature over weeks and last up to 3 months.

FRUIT IN SYRUP

Storing fruit in syrup is an ancient kitchen standby. Even before we had sugar in the UK we were preserving fruits like figs in honey. The recipe below is the absolute basic method adapted from a traditional Lebanese recipe and works brilliantly with the kind of figs we tend to get in the UK – the syrup compensates for the sweetness they have not developed from the Mediterranean sunshine.

By macerating the fruit overnight in sugar, some juice is extracted from the figs to create a flavoured syrup. Further cooking of the fruit in the syrup kills any remaining spoilage bacteria. This method would also work with, for example, peeled pears, quinces, lemons, cherries or robust plums.

PRESERVED FIGS

1kg figs ★ 500g sugar ★ 15g lemon juice

1. Leave the figs whole. Put them into a bowl, toss them in the sugar, then add around 100g of water and let everything sit in the fridge overnight.

2. In the morning pour the contents of the bowl into a heavy saucepan and bring to a low simmer.

3. When froth appears on the surface, skim it off, then add the lemon juice.

4. Simmer gently for 1 hour or so, stirring carefully so as not to burst the figs. Stop when the liquid is thick and syrupy.

5. Pour into a sterilized jar (see page 68) while still hot and store in the fridge. Should last up to a month, improving with age.

OUTDOOR COOKING

CHAPTER EIGHT

If Brits ever think about cooking outdoors, it's likely to be a barbecue. If they're well-off it will be a gas-fired monster, dripping with accessories and probably requiring a special 'comedy' apron to operate. If they're broke it will be a cheap tin affair, loaded with briquettes and firelighters, or one of those tinfoil disposable jobs.

This is a shame, because cooking outdoors with fire should be an exciting way to add new flavours and textures to food. Charcoal, even the good stuff, is wood that has already been burned once so that any aromatic element has gone.

HOW WOOD BURNS

When wood burns in the presence of a good source of oxygen it will give off heat, light and smoke. If it's deprived of oxygen, heated wood gives off all its moisture, all its tasty, smoky impurities, and becomes charcoal. Charcoal needs more heat than wood to ignite but, in turn, gives off more as it burns.

HEAT

- 'Heat' is the transfer of energy from a hot body to a cooler one. In general terms, as long as heat energy is applied – be it through fire or another heating element – the temperature of the cooler body will rise until it reaches the same temperature.

- Leaving aside, for a moment, the evil microwave, heat is transferred in two ways that interest the cook: a) conduction, where the heat source is in physical contact with the food; b) convection, where the heat is transferred through the movement of a fluid – that's water, oil and, importantly, air.

- Hot fluids rise, cool fluids fall.

- Some materials transmit heat quickly and efficiently – think of the bottom of a frying pan. Others – like the stone floor of a bread oven – store heat. The pan will cool quickly once it's taken off the heat source; the bread oven can take days to cool after the fire is put out.

- Cooking is about understanding how heat affects food, mainly how direct heat affects the surface and how heat is transferred within the food.

Charcoal is a good source of clean heat for cooking but does nothing to impart flavour or character. Wood, on the other hand, needs to be much more carefully managed.

The initial flames from burning wood will char food and give it an unpleasant taste but, as it burns down, the more acrid combustion products will have been driven off and we're left with hot, smouldering coals.

The trick with any wood-burning cooking method is to manage this initial burn in a way that doesn't harm the food and then take advantage of the hot stage. It's always going to be a matter of balancing the smoky flavours against the heat.

There are several ways to manage burning. When hot-smoking, for example, restricting the amount of air reaching the fire will prevent flaring up but allow the combustion to continue, creating lots of smoke but less heat and no flame.

In a bread oven the burning takes place first, allowing the heat to build up in the stones, but all the combustible material is raked out before the dough goes in.

In a firepit, the simple principle is to burn the wood away from the food and then physically move the hot coals under it to cook.

An offset barbecue is designed so that the heat and the smoke are created away from the food but either can be controllably directed towards it.

A gas barbecue . . . you might as well hook up an extension hose and drag the kitchen gas cooker out on to the deck.

FIREPIT

The very simplest way of cooking with fire, and the one that's been with us pretty much since we lived in caves, is the firepit or hearth.

Clear a patch of bare earth and, if you're feeling particularly fancy, build a low wall around it with bricks. You can also dig the earth out a little, if you wish, so you have a shallow, flat-bottomed hole. Store your firewood nearby, but outside the pit.

Create your firepit in an oval or rectangular shape because you're going to have two separate fires going in it at once.

At one end of the pit, build a small pyramid of thin pieces of wood and light it. As the fire takes hold, add larger pieces of wood and allow them to burn until there is no more flame but the logs are still glowing red through grey ash. Using a shovel or tongs, lift the glowing coals to the second fire position and then put some fresh logs into the first pile. You can now cook over the second fire.[30]

It's that simple. But hey . . . we could do this before we'd evolved language, so it can't be that tough. Now for the civilized refinements. Flat rocks under the cooking fire will tend to absorb and store heat, which means that it will remain more regular during cooking. More rocks, creating a back and sides to the fire, will also store heat and tend to reflect it back towards the food. At the very least, put a large slow-burning timber – literally a 'backlog' – at the rear of your

BRONZE AGE PIT COOKING

All across the British Isles, archaeologists have turned up examples of early Bronze Age cooking arrangements called fulachtaí fiadh. Each site is similar, comprising a hearth, a mound of stones and a trough-shaped hole, often lined with wood. Each fulacht fiadh was built on a small mound near a source of water, rocks and timber, and it's believed that they were used as ritual kitchens. The rocks would be heated on the hearth before being dropped into the water-filled trough until it boiled, then food – judging by the size of the hole, anything up to the size of a deer – was dropped in and poached.

It's also been suggested that the pits could have been used for ritual bathing – perhaps using the same water in which dinner had been cooked – and there have even been successful attempts to brew beer in them.

The idea of Bronze Age Britons wrecked on beer and eating poached venison in a bath full of hot fatty stock might seem a bit far-fetched, but I can't be alone in finding it strangely appealing too.

---

30 Real backwoodsmen favour a 'keyhole' fire: a circular blaze for heat, light and jollity, with the embers raked forward into an 'apron' on which a pot can be heated or meat cooked.

fire to help throw the heat forwards. It's a simple tweak but it will improve the efficiency of your pit several-fold. See, that took ten minutes . . . it probably took our ancestors a thousand years.

Many cultures still cook their food using pointed sticks but we should be able to do better. A thick iron frying pan or pot can be laid directly in the coals, a metal grating can go over the top or we can rig any sort of spit to hold larger pieces.

The firepit can be so rudimentary it can be improvised wherever you are, or it can be built as a permanent feature. It's probably the single most versatile arrangement for cooking with fire, which is why the majority of the world's population still use it in one form or another to this day.

BEANHOLE

The beanhole is one of the simplest of earth ovens. It's commonly associated with pioneer woodsmen in America, lumberjacks and loggers who would set up the beanhole to cook overnight, open for breakfast and then return to it for dinner before doing it all over again. Yes. They ate a lot of beans.

You can make a beanhole as permanent or as temporary as you like, depending on whether you roughly fill the bottom with rocks or build a firebrick retaining wall inside. If you make the extra effort it will also pass as a tandoor or the kind of pot-oven used in some Chinese cooking.

A traditional American bean pot would have been ceramic but you can also use a cast-iron casserole or cauldron – as long as it has a good, tight-fitting lid and you can arrange some sort of wire handle for lifting it in and out of the hole.

The size of your beanhole depends very much on the size of your bean pot. Place it on the ground and mark out a circle that will just contain it. If you're planning a brick lining, lay out a couple of courses around the pot on top of the ground and mark another ring around the outside, then start digging.

The hole should be straight-sided and at least three times as deep as the height of your bean pot.

Pour in gravel to a quarter of the depth and then lay the brick lining if you're using one. Now put large pebbles into the bottom until the hole is half full.

Drop in a layer of crumpled newspaper and some small kindling followed by charcoal or larger pieces of wood, light the paper and allow to burn vigorously. Keep feeding the fire for an hour or so, then let the flames die down. The large pebbles in the bottom should be visible through the glowing ash.

A flat stone or piece of tile makes a good diffuser under the pot, which should be lowered in and covered with a sack. The remaining quarter of the hole should then be filled with clean sand or earth. It helps to keep things neat if you can allow the corners of the sack to stay on the surface, where they can be used to lift out the top layer when the time comes.

Leave the beanhole undisturbed overnight or for at least 8 hours. Whether you use the time to chop down enormous trees is entirely up to you.

To serve, lift or dig off the top layer, lift out the pot and dig in.

SCIENCE of COOKING

UNDERGROUND

Underground cooking appears all over the world, as hungi in New Zealand, luau in Hawaii, in various forms of pig roast and clambake. They've evolved because though a fire is easy to start, its initial heat is hard to control. By using the earth itself as an insulator and stones as heat stores, it's possible to create a hot fire and then remove it before cooking. The firebricks in a beanhole store the heat from the fire and, insulated from above by a layer of earth, transfer it gently to the food in the pot.

Long, slow cooking renders even the toughest cuts of meat gloriously tasty, yet, because the cooking temperature is low, it doesn't overcook the more tender parts. It's therefore a method ideally adapted to cooking a whole animal carcass – like a pig roast – or mixtures of food, like the shellfish, lobsters, corn and potatoes in a New England clambake (see page 260).

Beanhole

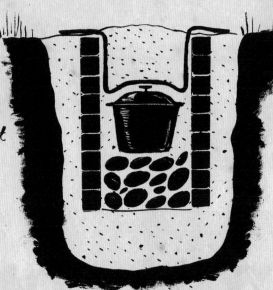

Damp Sack
OR
Tarpaulin

Brick lining,
optional
3x height of Pot

large rocks
OR
Pebbles

Gravel for drainage

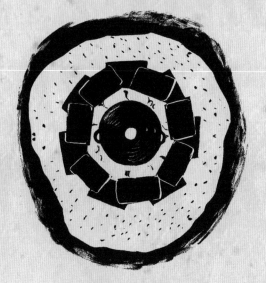

BEANHOLE BAKED BEANS

500g dried haricot beans ✴ 1 white onion ✴ 1 x 400g tin of tomatoes ✴ 5g English mustard powder ✴ black pepper ✴ 20g molasses ✴ 250g fat pork belly, salted (smoked optional)

1. Soak the beans overnight in unsalted water.

2. Drain the beans, cover with fresh, cold water, bring to the boil and remove any grey scum. Drain the beans again and pour them into your bean pot.

3. Chop the onion coarsely and add to the beans. Pour in the tinned tomatoes, breaking them up with your hands.

4. Add the mustard powder, a twist or two of black pepper and the molasses and top up with hot water until the beans are covered. Stir everything around until it's well mixed and then bury your piece of pork right into the centre of the beans.

5. Cover the pot with a layer of tinfoil, put on the lid, then scrunch up anything that sticks out of the sides to help create a better seal.

6. At this point you can lower your sealed pot into the beanhole or put it into a 120°C oven for 6 or more hours.

If you don't feel sufficiently lumberjackish to dig a beanhole you can try a modern twist on the wartime 'haybox' technique. During rationing, the Ministry of Food recommended saving fuel by heating casseroles and then storing them hot in a box insulated with a thick layer of straw, in which they would continue to cook for hours. You can do this even more efficiently by heating your bean pot until it's simmering gently, then wrapping it in a blanket or towel and placing it in a beer cooler.

STICKS AND SPITS

Soon after the firepit in the evolution of cooking came various ways of holding food near the heat to cook it. Simplest is a sharpened green stick which enables you to roast small lumps of meat directly in the flame and, with luck, won't catch fire itself. It's worth trying cooking on sticks for one simple reason. Once three or four pieces of expensive meat have dropped into the ashes at precisely the moment they were starting to look and smell stupendous, you'll realize why even the most primitive humans quickly evolved better ways to do it.

Metal is a great material for a spit because it won't burn and also conducts heat to the centre of the meat, speeding up and evening out cooking. Unfortunately meat slips around a simple rod, making it frustratingly difficult.

It's unfortunate that we don't carry swords or spears any more. Cultures that do can spit meat directly on to the broad blade and cheerfully flip it backwards and forwards over the heat. Odysseus and his buddies favoured this way of kebabing, according to Homer. The simplest spit, therefore, to knock up yourself is a piece of mild steel stock 2–4cm wide and thick enough not to bend under the weight of the meat. Use a grinder to put a rough point on the end, which will make it much easier to thrust through the meat.

Larger, commercially made spits often have fork-like arrangements which slide along the bar and clamp in place to hold medium-sized pieces of meat.

For full-on hog or sheep roasts, a scaffold pole makes a great spit but it's best to drill a series of holes along its length so that sharpened pieces of metal rod can be shoved through the carcass and the spit crossways.

GRIDIRONS AND PARRILLAS

A gridiron is much like the metal grill that holds the meat over a garden barbecue ... it's just bigger and a whole lot butcher. Gridirons are usually made to order by a blacksmith and are made of more substantial metal rod rather than wire. This means that the grill itself stores heat and will make those fantastic lines of carbonization on the meat. (I love the idea of gridirons so much, I've got one tattooed on my arm.)

SPITS, FRAMES AND GRIDIRONS

In South American cooking the gridiron is called a 'parrilla' and is sometimes arranged so it can be lifted up and down over the coals with chains and a crank handle. Some gridirons are constructed as two hinged halves which can be closed around a piece of meat or fish to make it easier to turn over during cooking. A common trick among seriously redneck barbecuers is to open out a pig or lamb and sandwich it between two sheets of reinforcing mesh or crowd-control fencing. Once the mesh is wired together the whole beast can be flipped over the coals at will.

COOKING FRAMES

Once the meat is fixed to its spit, you'll need something to support it. Simple piles of rocks or forked sticks will do when camping, but something altogether more grown-up is necessary for anything more serious than a rabbit.

Metal poles, either on firm bases or driven into the ground, will support the weight and are even more convenient if there's an easy way to adjust the height. A series of stepped hooks or rests is a good start.

In South American asado cooking, whole pigs, sheep or goats are opened out along the front[31] and attached to metal cross-frames which are propped vertically around a central fire. In this case, flames can pass straight up without catching the meat, while the radiant heat does its work and a certain amount of light smoking takes place. As the fire burns lower, the frames are angled down lower over the coals.

Asado refers not only to the method of cooking but also to the social event, a family gathering lasting the whole day and into the evening, where everyone participates in the long cooking, snacking on smaller things like sausages or grilled kidneys to stave off hunger pangs and gently maintaining the atmosphere with chilled beer until the big meat is ready. If there is a spiritual home of fire cooking it's surely neither Bondi Beach nor the American suburban backyard but somewhere out on the grasslands of Argentina.

---

31 Your butcher will be happy to supply a whole lamb, pig or goat given sufficient notice. The only special preparation required of him will be to partially split the spine along the inside of the ribcage. This means that the carcass can be opened out like a book. It's not necessary to split the spine further towards the tail, as there's plenty of flex in the hip joints. If you don't think your veterinary physiology is up to it, you can also ask your butcher to point out the places around the hamstrings that are strong enough to support the whole carcass, which you'll need to know in order to wire it to the frame.

COOKING A COW It's probably too elaborate a set-piece to carry off in most back gardens, but at some large asados and country fairs, a whole cow is cooked on a frame. In order to manage the transfer from a vertical position to an angle over the firepit, a small crane or winch has to be used. I find it encouraging, as a DIY cook, to remember that there are people out there, right now, barbecuing cows with cranes.

HOG OR LAMB ROAST

You'll need a shovel, a dozen cheap concrete paving slabs, two stepladders, a length of scaffolding pole, a few lengths of reinforcing bar, some wire and several bags of barbecue charcoal. Oh . . . and a pig.

Choose a scaffolding pole about twice the length of your pig. At the midpoint, drill a hole through it big enough to thread a piece of reinforcing bar through. Drill two more holes about 50cm either side. About 10cm in from each end, drill two more holes, at right angles to each other, through the spit. Thread the pole up the middle of your pig, through the mouth, if it still has its head on, and out beneath the tail. Locate the animal in the middle of the pole. Take three pieces of reinforcing bar, about 50cm each in length, and poke them horizontally through the carcass, through the holes in the pole and back out through the other side (you might find it useful to roughly sharpen one end with a file or grinder). At this stage, while the inside of the carcass is still accessible, season it liberally.

You'll need to restrain the carcass into as near a tubular shape as possible to make the cooking even, so you can either tuck up the legs and wire them into position or wrap the whole carcass in chicken wire and stitch it closed with a lighter gauge of steel wire.

Keep two extra pieces of reinforcing bar handy. By inserting them into the holes at the ends of the spit you can rotate the whole thing or lock it into place.

Dig a V-shaped trench four paving slabs long and line it with two runs of slabs at a diagonal to each other. Now lay in the last four slabs horizontally. This creates a firebed with ventilation beneath and two reflecting panels that concentrate the heat on the meat. Clear a patch of ground near to the spit where you can start a second fire to keep up your supply of coals during cooking. Erect the two stepladders at either end of the firepit, well back from the heat with their steps facing inwards. The steps will enable you to adjust the height of the spit.

Pour a couple of bags of charcoal into the pit and light it. You can use a chimney to start the fire at three or four points along the length, or a blowlamp. Always work in the same direction along the pit so that the heat will remain consistent when you refuel. Once the coals have a covering of white ash and are glowing fiercely, bring the spit into position and prop it on the steps of the ladders, using the reinforcing bars to lock it in position.

Rotate the spit regularly to achieve even browning and carefully extinguish any flare-ups caused by dripping fat. A cup of water usually does the job and hardly reduces the heat at all.

Half an hour into cooking, start to pour a bag of charcoal on to the cleared patch of ground and light it. Once it's glowing, shovel it into the firepit to keep the heat steady and start another bag burning for the next refuel.

Once the outside of the animal is browned and the fat is beginning to melt and flow, you can lower the cooking temperature by raising the spit a little or by reducing the amount of charcoal in each refuel. If you place your hand next to the carcass above the coals and can only keep it there for 3 seconds, you're at the right temperature.

Now it's just a matter of refuelling, turning, drinking beer and being patient. Use a probe thermometer to check internal temperatures and after about an hour or so you should be able to make a reasonable estimate of your finishing time.

Once the internal temperature of the meat at the thickest point (usually in the muscle at the top of the leg) reaches 75°C, lift the spit off, have a couple of hungry assistants move the ladders to somewhere quiet away from the fire, then replace the spit on the ladders so the meat can rest. Half an hour or 45 minutes is not an unreasonable time to rest a whole pig or lamb. It will retain its heat, but keep rotating the spit during resting as it helps to redistribute fat and juices.

ROASTING 'ON A STRING'

Not many cookbooks quote George Eliot – perhaps not enough – but this reference pops up in *Silas Marner* and acts as a kind of catnip to the enquiring food geek:

'There was something in front of the fire, too, that would have been inviting to a hungry man, if it had been in a different stage of cooking. It was a small bit of pork suspended from the kettle-hanger by a string passed through a large door-key, in a way known to primitive housekeepers unpossessed of jacks.'

Roasting 'on a string' or 'on a key' was a common way of cooking joints of meat in working-class homes, which usually lacked ovens.[32] On the plus side, the domestic fire is still the very best place to roast meat. Roasting requires radiant heat and an open environment where moisture can escape.[33] Large kitchen fires in old houses sometimes had spits for roasting, but ordinary homeowners hung their meat vertically in front of the fire. If they were well off they'd have a clockwork 'jack' which slowly rotated the meat in front of the flames; if they were poorer, a piece of string or wire would do and the joint could be rotated by hand, possibly by a small child.

Obviously a piece of string tied around the meat would slip as the meat cooked or possibly even burn, so, as in the Eliot quote, a big door key could be thrust through a piece of meat, like a rough skewer, the handle preventing the meat from slipping off and then being tied on to a string fixed to the mantelpiece or kettle hook.

The advantage of vertical cooking is that, much like the great elephant leg in your local kebab shop, the cooking juices and fats travel down through and over the meat, effectively basting it. A pan or dish placed underneath Marner's joint would catch the 'drippings', which could then be ladled back over the top.[34]

---

32 Grand houses, farmhouses and small communal bakeries had always had ovens for bread, but the kitchen range, with its metal box oven, was a Victorian invention and, even then, they were luxuries. Ordinary working-class homes survived with the fireplace as the only source of cooking heat right up until the 1930s.

33 What takes place in an oven, even today, is strictly 'baking', not roasting.

34 In really hi-tech Victorian kitchens a 'hastener' could speed up the roasting. This was a large curved metal screen which could be placed around the front of the rotating joint, reflecting the heat back on all sides. Hasteners were sometimes designed with a dripping catcher and in some cases a small door, which could be opened for basting.

BUILDING BARBECUE 'PITS'

American barbecue pits come in two basic patterns. Either a lovely old brick-built object, permanently installed, or a trailer-mounted job that can be towed to tailgate parties, family reunions and, most importantly, barbecue competitions.

Because most people build their own, there's no set pattern but the basic physics stay the same.

The main smoking chamber needs heat controllable between 75 and 300°C and should be designed, as far as possible, to lock in moisture and smoke – the vital ingredients of good barbecue.

Containing the fire in trays makes it easier to control its position relative to the food. As with all barbecues, the heat of the burn is controlled by airflow and the smoke is directed over the food.

With this sort of simple rig the pitmaster can easily cook a dozen or so shoulders or racks of ribs, moving each around to control flavour and temperature. Some of the more obsessive pros trick their pits out with fans to control airflow, temperature probes and even computers. Most build their own trailer barbecues, as it requires little more than skill with a grinder and welding kit and ends up costing a lot less than the few models commercially available.

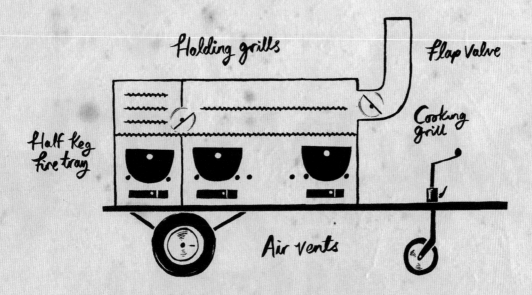

Mobile Competition Barbecue Rig

Holding grills

Flap Valve

Cooking grill

Half Keg fire tray

Air vents

Most use a scrap propane cylinder as the base – though it's important to note that these require specialized procedures to cut. Even an empty cylinder contains enough gas mixture to go off like a bomb when ignited by grinder sparks, so under no circumstances start chopping into an old cylinder yourself. If you're not comfortable with cutting and welding then it's time to speak to a local light engineering company.

All the important basics are present in the mobile model: the offset firebox, the ability to control heat and smoke flow, vents and holding space. It's simple to imagine a similar arrangement built in brick, block or stone with perhaps a metal flap or doors. This is the usual arrangement in barbecue restaurants, particularly those temples of piggery where the entire hog is spatchcocked and slow-cooked over the coals.

An alternative pattern, favoured by home builders, arranges the chambers vertically. This takes up less garden space – it's the size of a large double fridge – and can, if you are so inclined, be combined with a wood-burning bread/pizza oven. Brick and block work is probably easier to contemplate for the British DIY-er, the smoke chamber door can be timber and the fire chamber can be left open-fronted, but for the best smoking, the longest working life and frankly a smarter result, it's definitely worth approaching a local engineering company for custom-made steel doors.

With the firebox offset and low, it's possible to build vertical smokers that can run cool enough for cold-smoking, though it can require delicate control of the fire.

GYM LOCKER OFFSET BARBECUE SMOKER

A quick and affordable way to make something approaching the towable competition rig is to use a second-hand gym locker as a ready-made pair of chambers. You'll need to rig up some wooden trestles or brick piers to support it, or, if you don't mind working bent over, at a pinch you could hold it in place with piles of earth.

If you can find a locker with a top section as well as the long 'coathanging' bit, drill as many holes as you can manage in the shelf between them (if your locker is single-section you'll just have to 'offset' by building your fire at one end and cooking your meat at the other).

By propping the locker on one back edge you create a V-shaped channel for the fuel which acts as its own fire tray, and you should be able to cut some heavy-grade steel mesh to fit across the widest point as a cooking grill. The chimney isn't necessary but it's fun.

Be sure to have a big 'burn' in the cabinet before attempting any cooking. If paint or other coatings are going to bubble off with the heat, it's better to get them out of the way before any food gets involved.

CARDBOARD BOX VERTICAL SMOKER

A well-tended barbecue pit should never rise above 95°C, so counter-intuitively it's possible to build one out of something we'd normally consider flammable. Two strong cardboard boxes, slid together, create a tower and enclosure that will keep all the elements of a barbecue pit in place and be recyclable after use.

Push timber dowels through the box to support a cooking grill near the top and a foil tray of water nearer the bottom. The water keeps the cooking environment moist and helps dissipate some of the heat.

Heat and smoke come from a cheap electric hotplate and a metal tray or skillet filled with soaked woodchips. It's possible to smoke and slow-cook a pork shoulder for hours in this rig, with the only real time limitation being the operator's ability to stay awake and tend to the smoke generator.

The dial thermometer at the top of the stack gives the cooking temperature, which should stay just shy of 100°C. If it's too hot, turn down the hotplate; if it's not hot enough try cutting the boxes down to bring the meat closer to the heat, or even lining the box with tinfoil to stop heat escaping through the sides.

The box smoker won't generate enough heat to crisp up the surface of the meat, so be ready to flash it in a hot oven or on top of a regular garden grill before serving if you want a real crust.

Vertical Smokehouse

Optional Metal door (Can be left open)

Door in wood or Metal

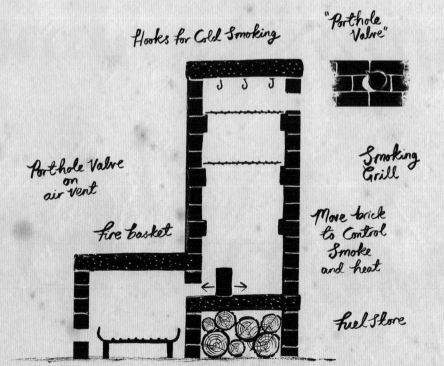

Hooks for Cold Smoking

"Porthole Valve"

Porthole Valve on air vent

fire basket

Smoking Grill

Move brick to Control Smoke and heat

fuel Store

COLD SMOKEHOUSE

There's something phenomenally restful about a cold smokehouse. In the UK the outdoor temperature is only really suitable for long cold-smoking during the winter months, so the smokehouse sits at the end of the garden on a crisp misty day, silently emitting wisps of gorgeous-smelling smoke as the leaves or snow settle around it. You can't hurry smoking, and the feeling that a couple of sides of stonking salmon are dangling in there getting slowly more and more lovely is enough to make a man misty-eyed. A cold smokehouse can be elegant, craftsmanlike, traditional; unlike a barbecue pit it should have no taint of redneck bodgery but hint more at the cool aesthetics of Scandinavia. If you get it right it can look like a sauna for a small Norse god; wrong, it will look like a steaming outside lavatory.

The cold smokehouse is built on the same principle as the barbecue pit, but the connection between firebox and smoking chamber is extended to ensure that the smoke is properly cold by the time it reaches the food.

Dig a shallow pit and place a paving slab in the base, then build up a brick wall on three sides. Leave out half a brick near the top of the wall on the side nearest to your smokehouse, and cap off with another slab. Put a length of metal downpipe or air-conditioning duct through the hole in the side of your firebox and then bury it in soil.

At the other end of the pipe, build a brick plinth slightly higher than your firebox and erect your smokehouse on top. Many garden centres sell small kit-form wooden sheds, sometimes called 'tool stores', which can quickly be assembled into a good-looking, weatherproof smokehouse. Cheaper alternatives, though somewhat undermining the aesthetic, are a couple of tea chests on top of each other, an old cupboard or wardrobe, a galvanized dustbin or even a plastic water-butt.

Almost anything that can be made weather- and animal-proof and is reasonably smoke-tight will do the job. I've actually seen someone at a food festival smoke salmon in a cheap tent.

Cold Smokehouse

Fire chamber built of bricks & slab, buried in earth

Drain pipe or A/C duct

Any weather/bug /animal proof enclosure

Brick plinth raises height above fire box

DEEP-FRIED TURKEY

Most normal people, when told of a cooking technique that puts hundreds of people in hospital every year and results in the burning down of many houses, would probably choose not to read on. By now, I firmly believe you are made of stronger stuff.

When performed properly and safely, deep-frying a whole turkey or chicken produces amazing results. A crisp skin, moist meat with both leg and breast evenly cooked and no trace of greasiness beyond the lubricating loveliness of poultry fat.

What causes the damage is the large tank of oil, brought to a rolling boil over a naked flame, and thoughtless handling of a socking great lump of meat. Across the American South, though, thousands of families successfully deep-fry a turkey for Christmas or Thanksgiving without ending up in the emergency room or watching their house burn.

The only heat source controllable enough to be safe is a large gas ring. These are available from camping or hardware stores for between £30 and £50 and hook up to a propane cylinder. They are stable on the ground, easy to light and, more importantly, easy to switch off.

You'll also need a large pot. Catering suppliers and many Indian or Chinese specialist supermarkets sell cheap aluminium pots big enough to boil anything from a rabbit to a small ox, so this should be your first port of call. They will probably stock the large drum of worryingly nameless vegetable oil that you'll also need.

Deep-frying works best with a 4–5kg bird; any larger and the outside will be overdone before the inside is finished. Make a hanger by twisting a small metal pot lid on to a straightened wire coathanger and then forming a strong loop in the other end. Feed the wire through the bird, neck end first, so it's doing a sort of yogic shoulder stand on the pot lid and has 30cm or so of wire with a loop in it sticking out of the vent end.

Lower the bird into your pot and then carefully fill with water until the bird is just submerged. Lift the bird out, letting all the water from the cavity drain back into the pot, then, using a piece of wood as a dipstick, mark the level of water left. This will be the correct quantity of oil for the job. Most accidents are caused when too much oil is loaded into the pot and it overflows into the flames when the bird is lowered in. If the water level in the pot is more than two-thirds the height of the pot, stop at once – you're going to need a bigger pot or a smaller bird.

Pour the water from the pot and dry it carefully with kitchen paper. Also dry the bird thoroughly inside and out. Excess water can mix with the hot oil and immediately cause it to bubble up and over – another potential fire hazard.

Pour oil into the pot to the water level marked on your dipstick. It may not look much, but you now know for certain that it's enough to cover your turkey and no more. Turn on the gas and heat the oil until it reads 175°C on your thermometer.

Once the oil is at the correct temperature, TURN OFF THE GAS and allow the flames to die completely before slowly and carefully lowering in your bird. It should take at least a minute to fully submerge. There will be a ferocious bubbling, particularly in the final seconds as the oil flows over into the body cavity, but as long as the oil level is less than two-thirds the height of the pot it should not boil over. If, by some catastrophic error, it begins to, there is no flame to ignite it and it's not too late to lift the bird out and rethink.

Once the bird is submerged, relight the gas, bring the oil temperature back to 175°C, and fry for 3 minutes per 500g plus an extra 15 minutes.

When cooking time is up, TURN OFF THE GAS, lift out the bird, making sure that all the oil drains from the cavity, and place it on a serving plate. The turkey will need a short rest, in which time you can secure the oil. It will remain hot enough to injure for several hours, so take whatever precautions are necessary to ensure that children or animals can't get near it.

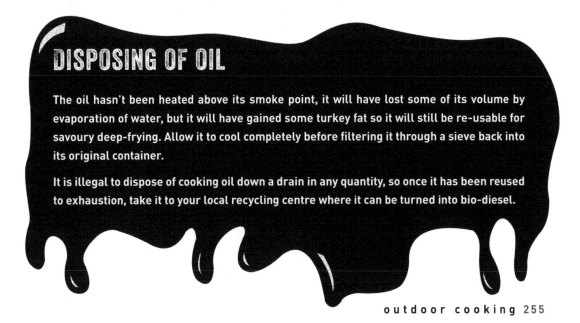

DISPOSING OF OIL

The oil hasn't been heated above its smoke point, it will have lost some of its volume by evaporation of water, but it will have gained some turkey fat so it will still be re-usable for savoury deep-frying. Allow it to cool completely before filtering it through a sieve back into its original container.

It is illegal to dispose of cooking oil down a drain in any quantity, so once it has been reused to exhaustion, take it to your local recycling centre where it can be turned into bio-diesel.

ÉCLADE DES MOULES

An éclade des moules is a traditional French method of cooking mussels outdoors. It originates in the Charente-Maritime departement, where pine trees cover the coastline and mussels are plentiful. The fact that the French had this marvellous idea first should gall us immensely, because there are many parts of the UK where the mussels are superb and there's just as much pine about. This is a superbly flash trick for a family barbecue on holiday.

Drive a single 10cm nail into the centre of a large wooden board. This can be up to a metre square or, if you lay your mussels out in a slightly different configuration, a metre-long piece of plank or driftwood. The board will get scorched but otherwise be completely reusable, as long as the mussels keep coming.

Prop your board flat, on rocks, on a sandy part of the beach, well away from any trees or other flammable bits of nature, and prop 4 mussels up against the nail with their hinge edge and pointed ends upwards.

The next stage is best left to nimble-fingered children while adults watch and consume beer. Prop more mussels around the central four, all in the same 'hinge-up' direction and forming concentric circles. You should be able to stand several kilos this way, allowing time for inevitable amusing 'domino effect' disasters.

Carefully lay handfuls of dry pine needles[35] over the raft of mussels, building up layers until they're around 15cm thick, then light the needles at several points around the edge.

The resinous needles will take a short while to catch and then go up spectacularly, burning with intense heat and causing the seawater trapped in the mussel shells to boil, steaming the flesh and opening the shells.

When the fire has died down, flap at it with a folded newspaper (quality broadsheet obviously) or possibly a light boogie-board, to blow away the remaining ash, then dive in and eat with your fingers. This is rustic, fisherman-style cooking, so no extra sauces or flavourings are required, though you might fancy bringing along a loaf of fresh bread.

---

35 If you're out of the pine needle season or in a resolutely deciduous part of the country this can apparently be done with hay or straw.

CLAMBAKE

A clambake is another of those excuses for a joyous, rambunctious group eating session based around a cooking method almost as old as mankind. On the East Coast of the USA clambakes are often held for whole communities, using pits dug with backhoes and hundreds of kilos of seafood. This method is a little calmer and can be performed far from the beach by the simple use of a metal wheelbarrow and some materials from the local garden centre.

Whip the front wheel off the barrow if you ever have ambitions to use it again. The tyre will melt and burst in the heat otherwise.

Pour a bag of sharp sand into the bottom of the wheelbarrow and create a dip in the centre. Build a good hot fire in the dip, using a bag of barbecue charcoal, and insert into the glowing coals half a dozen rocks around the size of a tennis ball. Granite or similar boulders are good, while shale and flint have the tendency to crack and split alarmingly.

Keep the fire burning merrily for an hour or two, until a drop of water vaporizes immediately on hitting the rocks.

Soak a sack in water and lay it over the hot stones – you'll need to work fast so it doesn't dry and scorch – and immediately top with half a bag of seaweed (ask your fishmonger nicely when ordering your shellfish. Seaweed is sold at fish markets, where it's used in fishmongers' displays).

Pour your shellfish in a single layer into the seaweed along with ears of sweetcorn (still in the husk) and baking potatoes wrapped in foil. Cover the lot with the rest of the seaweed, another layer of damp sacking and a second bag of sand.

By spreading the sand and patting it down carefully you should achieve a pretty good seal around the food – pack on extra handfuls where steam escapes.

You can check the temperature inside the clambake with a probe thermometer and you'll see it rises very quickly and holds stable.

Cooking time depends on the amount of food you have inside the chamber, but half an hour will do a reasonable-sized lobster and a couple of kilos of clams and mussels.

Warren's

OF
KITTERY, MAINE

WHERE THE LOBSTER REIGNS SUPREME

Every Meal a Pleasant Memory

OPEN THE YEAR ROUND

BUTCHERY

CHAPTER NINE

It's one of the great truisms of the professional kitchen that the better your preparatory work – your 'prep' – the easier will be the service, but for me, in the home kitchen, there's a much more important reason not to skip it.

The supermarkets have convinced us that we're all too busy to cook and so they can offer us the service of doing the prep for us – obviously in exchange for money. We buy our meat jointed, our veg washed, peeled and even chopped and sometimes we buy whole meals, ready to be reheated. This is sold to us in the name of convenience – an advantage, I acknowledge – but robs us of our relationship with our food, our understanding of it and ultimately our control over what goes into our bodies and those of our families.

Doing our own prep puts us back in the driving seat.

Unless you're really in a hurry it's a good idea to do your own butchery whenever you can. Buy a whole chicken and reduce it to parts yourself. It will give you better control over the portions you're using, plus you'll get the carcass and trim for stock. If you need steaks for a barbecue or cubed meat for a stew or tagine, buy the whole piece, on the bone, and trim it out yourself. Removing silverskin, tendons and the other stringy bits that spoil your dinner, you'll learn more of the physiology of the animal. Along with the bones, all that waste goes to make useful stock and even the fat is saved for later rendering.

A traditionally trained butcher looks at the animal as a whole and, driven by the economics of the small shop, will sell high-quality meat but minimize waste. Good butchers offer a selection of carefully prepared cheaper cuts – including some of the odd ones that our parents' generation understood were full of flavour but have now all but disappeared. The really diligent ones turn trimmed material into their own sausages. Supermarkets increasingly sell only prime cuts, which means that more is wasted or repurposed into processed products. If your idea of meat is a clingfilmed steak, perhaps it doesn't matter, but if you care whether a carcass is used economically then the loss of traditional skills is a problem.

HARD WORK BRINGS ITS OWN REWARD

When choosing meat there are a couple of rules which help assess how a cut is going to taste and what cooking method it will take to most. Generally speaking, the harder worked a muscle is, the better it tastes. If you think, for example, of muscles like those in the rib-eye, which keep the spine straight, they've never stopped working at keeping a ton of animal from crumpling into a heap since the first day the calf stood up. Rib-eye will be full of flavour and tender in texture without too much cooking. A rib-eye steak will require searing heat and a good long rest to be spot-on.

It's the fat in meat that contains so much of the flavour. External fat should be preserved wherever possible, so that flavour isn't lost, and when choosing meat look, with your butcher's help, for 'marbling', which means deposits of fat inside and between the big muscles. Like humans, animals lay down fat differently depending on the individual, so it's important to examine every piece before forking out big cash.

The marbling in a well-worked muscle will melt quickly at quite low temperatures, lubricating and flavouring the meat beautifully – this explains why Wagyu fillet, bred for marbling, is so highly prized.

Beef that has been 'finished' before slaughter by feeding on a grain-rich diet will often have better, more reliable marbling. Aficionados, though, sometimes prefer meat that's been finished on grass, which, they argue, has a better flavour without the need for the fatty boost that the marbling gives.

A beast isn't only made of big, expensive and well-worked muscles, though. Look at a shoulder joint in a pig, lamb or cow and there are dozens of small muscles, laid over each other and intertwining, each ending in tough tendons, wrapped in 'silverskin' and interrupted here and there by knobbles of cartilage and bone. On most quadrupeds, the rear legs are the muscular power source; the front legs are more about balance and staying upright. It's not impossible to get small joints out of the nuggets of pure muscle in a shoulder but it takes a great deal of physiological understanding and fine knife-work. This is the mysterious art of 'seam' cutting that butchery nerds whisper of wherever they gather – careful, almost surgical dissection of individual muscles from a complex group, delicate trimming and arcane tying methods. This gives flavourful pieces from smaller worked muscles that can be fast-cooked.

Most of us, though, learn to compensate for complex joints by a different type of cooking. The collagens and gelatine that make up all that connective tissue, tendon and cartilage are also unctuous. They have flavour but they also add a fantastic gelatinous richness when, melted by long-slow-low heat, they combine with the muscle fibres.

A boned and rolled shoulder can be slow-roasted, pot-roasted, braised or cooked by any other method that encloses, moistens and allows low heat to work on it for the longest possible period. If time is short it can also be cut into small pieces and cooked in liquid – a classic stew.

LAMB

Lamb is one of the great successes of British farming. Because sheep thrive outdoors, on grass, in our strange climate there's usually little commercial gain in dosing them with drugs or devising intensive, indoor rearing methods. There's a fair chance, therefore, that the meat that reaches us is free-range and near-organic by default. This may be part of the reason that sheep farming is not a licence to print money. Whenever there's any kind of agricultural crisis we hear horror stories of farmers getting so little for their sheep that it's not worth feeding them or taking them to slaughter; yet somehow a leg of lamb still ends up costing an unconscionable amount by the time it gets to the supermarket.

Many cultures would consider us mad to pay a professional to butcher something as simple as a lamb. It is the easiest animal to break down competently into simple joints, and most butchers will be happy to sell you one (by adding a reasonable mark-up on a whole lamb the butcher is taking a small profit yet saving himself time, effort and storage space). If your local butcher won't cooperate, there are dozens on the internet who will.

A lamb carcass is not necessarily a scary object. On the exterior you should see the stamps applied at the abattoir, which indicate that the animal has been properly slaughtered, inspected and declared free of disease. There's no remaining blood. At around 12 kilos it's not difficult to lift or move, and, being from a young animal, most of the bones are comparatively easy to cut. There's also a surprisingly lovely smell, not the kind of meaty funk you might expect but a delicate combination of lanolin and fresh grass. Lamb doesn't respond to long hanging times like beef or game, so there's no macho mould development, no blackened areas to be cut away, in fact it looks reassuringly like a piece of very good meat – it's just several times bigger than you may be used to dealing with.

I was lucky. When I first told my butcher what I planned to do he invited me in to watch him cut up a lamb, but many now run courses that will take you through the process more thoroughly.

The main difference between butchering at home and the way a professional would do it is that the butcher, with access to a bandsaw, begins by dividing the carcass down the spine. You may be able to persuade your butcher to do this for you at a price but it's not strictly necessary. The simplest way to handle things in your own kitchen is to divide the animal into three parts: the fore end (shoulders and neck), the rump (both the back legs) and the saddle area, which encompasses the bottom of the ribcage and the abdomen. Once this is done, the sections look a lot less challenging and are easier to work with. The simplest breakdown will give two leg joints, two shoulders, a pair of rib racks and some loin chops. The cheap, forgotten cuts of neck and breast are a bonus, as are the kidneys. To extract the full value and for extra smugness points, be sure to make stock from the bones and the pile of trimmings. Lamb stock freezes brilliantly and makes a superb base for any lamb stew.

The first time you do it there will be a few mistakes – perhaps one or two major joints might have to be quickly repurposed as diced stewing meat, and there might be a few ragged edges or bone chips, but, by the time you've done a couple and have got the hang of the physiology, you'll be happily turning out more exotic cuts.

Don't get me wrong here. A Master Butcher has the training and skills to do a beautiful job of this, to turn out a greater variety of cuts, to minimize waste and to store and manage his fridges so you can have just the prime piece you want, in peak condition, at the moment you need it – but when supermarkets are selling meat processed by semi-skilled factory operatives and sold by staff in fancy-dress butcher's costumes, home butchery feels like a moral duty. If you have freezer space of your own and you're interested in trying all the cuts, then with a little practice you can make a good enough job of this to meet your needs and, oddly enough, I haven't been able to find a Master Butcher anywhere who hasn't been positively encouraging of the idea.

The carcass is probably too big for the fridge, so it can be hung overnight somewhere cool and under cover. A shed is ideal.

I use a regular boning knife and steel, a smaller boning knife, a meat saw, hooks and swivel and a cleaver. The saw is nice to have but you can easily do the job with a clean tenon saw from a tool shop. The hooks aren't essential but they cost a couple of quid at a butchers' supply store and make handling a bit easier.

Lamb

B

D

Neck

Shoulder

Best
end

Breas

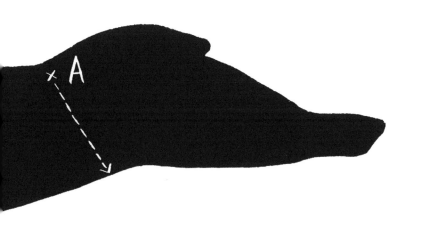

A

guide

loin chump leg

Find the top of the pelvic girdle by pushing with two fingers and mark with your knife.

A) Take a line perpendicular to the spine and as close as possible to the top of the pelvis, and slice neatly down through the side to the spine. You should have clear space to saw where the spine meets the top of the pelvis. Saw or cut with the cleaver.

B) With one hand inside and one outside the ribcage, count off five ribs from the neck end and mark with your knife. Following the line between ribs five and six, cut down, away from the spine, turning towards the tail end at the bottom. Having cut both sides, saw through the spine.

C) Do the same thing at the back end of the ribs to separate the loin – cut from spine to belly behind the last rib and saw through the spine.

D) Going back up to the ribs, measure halfway along the front rib with your finger. Saw through the ribs on both sides.

The traditional way to handle the loin now would be to split it in half by sawing directly through the middle of the vertebrae, which is fine if you have a commercial bandsaw. If you're feeling particularly rugged you can do this with the hand saw but it will take a while. The most elegant trim for a rack involves 'chining' or cutting away the half of the spine anyway, so this simpler method gives a better result without the donkey work.

Using the boning knife, cut down one side of the pointy-up bits of the vertebrae. Let the knife do the work, sliding downwards then turning out. Stop when you can see or feel the point where the ribs attach. Repeat on the other side.

Stand the double rack firmly on end and cut the ends of the ribs away from the spine with a few blows of the cleaver. The bones are soft, so it's easier than it sounds. Using the cleaver leaves less bone dust than using the saw, so the finished joint is cleaner.

Now we need to detach the meat from the ends of the ribs furthest from the spine. This technique, traditionally called 'frenching', leaves a clean bone 'handle' on each cutlet. Working from the inside, use the tip of the knife to slide up either side of the last third of each rib. This will begin to free the meat from the ribs. Now slip the knife down behind the ribs, detaching the meat as a flap from the ends. Turning back the meat outside the ribs, trim and scrape between them. Now use the knife to scrape any remaining meat or membrane from the rib tips and to scrape through the membrane inside the ribs.

Finally, trim away the flap and tidy up the bone ends. Congratulations – you've made a rack. The front rib plate you sawed off earlier can be trimmed from the bones and rolled, or you can leave it all intact and slow-cook it, spare-rib style.

Back to the loin. Trim off the ends around the point where the joint thins so the skin/meat ratio gets a bit pointless. Choose the thickness of your chops and cut outwards from the spine. To avoid too much traumatic bone work, try to choose a point where there's a convenient intravertebral joint. I usually fail dismally, but as the bones are soft enough to use the cleaver, the only downside is a messy trim and maybe a bone chip or two. Once you've cut, use the cleaver to go through the spine.

Going back to the fore end, cut all round where the neck joins the body . . . and use the cleaver to remove the neck. The neck can look a bit messy, and butchers often slice it into cheap chops, but I'm forced to save it whole for my mum – she has happy memories of stewed neck as a kid but can't get it from her butcher.

Saw the fore portion in half, directly through the spine, and cut away the sternum through the soft ends of the long ribs. Working from inside, get the knife behind the ribs – again, let the knife do the work, following the bones – trim back up towards the spine and remove ribs and vertebrae in one piece.

Find the triangular shoulder blade and trim down either side and behind it. Use your fingers to work down around the bone until you find the ball and socket joint, then cut through the tough tendons with the tip of your knife to free it. Look out for a raised 'rib' running down the back of the shoulder blade and try to avoid cutting out through the skin as you free it.

There you go . . . one boned shoulder. Not the easiest joint to handle but you've done it. Roll it, stuff it, tie it. You'll have worked out by now exactly how full of connective tissue this joint is, so you'll be itching to slow-roast or braise it. Good plan. If it's really messy, though, you can always cube it for stew.

On to the rump. Pointing the legs up in the air, cut down either side of the tail. Use a little pressure to pop the hip joints and your knife will find its own way. There. Don't they look lovely? If you're feeling rustic you can just go straight ahead and roast them as they are. But we're getting all cocky about our butchery skills now, so let's clean them up a little. Trim any excess fat inside the thighs. Feel around the inside top of the joint and work your knife under and around the socket part of the pelvis. It's obvious and comes out cleanly. Again, use the knife tip to cut the tendons around the joint.

LAMB SHANK REDEMPTION

Lamb shanks are a gastropub classic, but are often disappointingly dry. The trick to redeeming flavourful joints like the shank is to braise 'slow and low' and to give the meat something wonderful to exchange flavours with. I've suggested Marsala, a sweet, heavy Italian wine. You could substitute port, sherry or Madeira, or use red wine, but sweeten later with redcurrant or other fruit jelly.

olive oil ☆ 4 lamb shanks ☆ 4 shallots ☆ 1 carrot ☆ 100g Marsala ☆ 250g chicken stock ☆ 5g juniper berries or thyme leaves ☆ 1 clove of garlic ☆ 1kg large roasting potatoes ☆ salt and freshly ground black pepper ☆ 200g unsalted butter

1. Preheat the oven to 140°C.

2. Heat a little oil in a thick-bottomed casserole on top of the stove and brown the lamb shanks. Remove them to a safe distance, then, in the same pot, gently soften the shredded shallots and finely chopped carrot.

3. Pour over the Marsala and allow it to bubble and reduce. This cooks off the alcohol – it should end up looking like a sticky syrup.

4. Reintroduce the lamb shanks to the pot and roll them around in the gloop before pouring over the stock so that the shanks are almost covered. Bring everything back to a bare simmer. Add the juniper or thyme, and grate in a little garlic. As you slow-cook the lamb, you should, ideally, lose almost none of the liquid, so put a piece of foil over the top of the pot and then drop the lid on. This will make for an even better seal. Put the pot into the oven.

5. Wash your potatoes, wrap them in foil and put them into the oven with the casserole.

6. After at least 3 hours, check the shanks – they should be so tender that they barely hold together. Lift them out of the liquid and put them to one side while you bring the juices back to the boil and reduce them to a treacly consistency. You should, at this stage, adjust the seasoning of the sauce (see Proper Gravy, page 320).

7. Unwrap the potatoes, cut them in half and spoon the insides into a mixing bowl. Add the butter in small pieces, beating well. Season the mash. Serve the shanks on a pile of mash, with the gravy poured around. You can, if you wish, sieve the gravy, but this is an unnecessary refinement. I rather like the shallot shreds.

NECK OF LAMB WITH MISO GLAZE

1 lamb neck ⭑ olive oil ⭑ stock vegetables (carrot, onion, leek, celery) ⭑ 100g white miso paste ⭑ 10g dark soy sauce ⭑ 10 small carrots ⭑ 10g clear honey ⭑ 10g butter ⭑ a pinch of salt

1. Preheat the oven to 120°C.

2. Brown the outer surface of the lamb in a hot dry pan.

3. Heat a little oil in a casserole dish and sweat the finely chopped stock veg, then place the browned lamb on top and add boiling water to a depth of about 1cm.

4. Seal the top of the casserole with foil and put on the lid. This will keep all the juices and moisture inside. Put the casserole into the oven for 3 hours.

5. Lift the lamb neck out of the pot and place it on a rack in a baking tray. Increase the oven temperature to 180°C.

6. Mix the miso with the soy sauce and paint on to the lamb, then put it back into the hot oven for 20 minutes, repainting halfway through.

7. Peel or scrape the carrots and place in a saucepan with the honey, the butter and a pinch of salt. Barely cover with boiling water, raise to a ferocious boil and keep going, with the saucepan uncovered, until all the water has evaporated and the butter and honey have formed a glaze on the just-cooked carrots.

8. A lamb neck is hugely romantic. It will serve 2 people and is best presented on a single plate so you can both pull off the sumptuous shreds of juicy meat. The miso glaze, much like the more traditional anchovy, adds both saltiness and umami, which contrasts handsomely with the sweet glaze on the carrots.

KNOTTING BUTCHER'S STRING

There are many different knots taught by professional butchers which involve dextrous and flashy tricks, wrapping the string around various fingers, pulling loops through holes and flicking wrists. Butchers have had their entire careers to perfect these and will be happy to demonstrate them to you. The one thing of which you can be absolutely positive, though, is that when you come to try them yourself you'll have forgotten how to do it, your joint will fall apart or you'll end up having lashed yourself to the bread bin.

To preserve all our sanities, here's how to tie up a piece of meat using the one knot we all know. You know the one. The one we learned before we could tie our shoelaces, the simplest of the lot where you make a loop and push the end through.

Pull a length of string off the roll and tie one of those simple knots about 10cm from the end.

Now. This is the only complicated bit. Using whatever technique you prefer – be it pulling through a loop, holding the end in your teeth or picking up the roll of string and tossing it from hand to hand – contrive to tie another simple knot, around the string below the first knot. This will give you a 'lasso' type loop in the end of your string, which should be passed around the meat.

Pull on the end of the string attached to the roll. The lasso will tighten around the meat, AND the second knot will slide around the string until it is suddenly stopped short by the first knot.

Now cut the string off the roll, leaving 10cm loose still attached to the meat, and finally, lock everything up by tying a simple knot with the two 10cm ends.

There. The most complicated professional knot made out of three of the very simplest.

BEEF

3-RIB ROAST BEEF

Beef is pricey stuff that we don't get to eat often. A big, show-off roast is an expensive investment and you'd be justified in leaving the work to the pros and getting your butcher to do it. A standing rib roast, though, is probably one of the best big cuts for a celebratory family meal and by butchering it yourself you'll learn a lot, you'll rescue lots of interesting trimmings for other uses and you'll have a much bigger glow of pride as it's paraded to the table.

The rib roast comes from high up on the back of the beast. Starting at the back of the neck, imagine working back till past the shoulder and then cut downwards. Now continue backwards until you hit the last rib and cut down again. Along the top of this central chunk runs the spine, which is held firm, supporting the entire weight of the animal's body by two long, roughly cylindrical muscle groups. These sit outside the body cavity and on either side of the feather bones or spinal processes (these are the bovine equivalent of those knobbles down your spine). The carcass is sawn in half at the abattoir.

The rib roast, then, is a slice taken through one half of this section. It looks like the cut of meat beloved of Fred Flintstone, a rack of curved bones with a red, teardrop-shaped chunk of meat alongside. The meaty part – a cross-section of that huge, well-worked muscle cylinder – is called the rib-eye, for reasons which should now be obvious.

Looking at the end of your piece of meat you should be able to identify the rib, the rib-eye, the external fat and half of the vertebra and feather bones.

Unless you have your own meat saw, ask the butcher to cut through the ribs but to leave the spine and feather bones attached.

Stand your joint up with the feather bones flat on the chopping board and, starting at the sawn tip of the ribs, begin slicing the external fat away from the meat in a single sheet. Continue detaching the fat until you are about halfway down the joint, well into the rib-eye.

Now slice down, along the surface of the ribs and across the top of the rib-eye so you can lift out most of the fat and any other non-rib-eye pieces. How much of this material you have and its composition will vary depending on where in the rack the ribs were taken from.

Trim the meat from between the ribs as far down as the rib-eye and scrape the bones clean with your knife. Wrap the fat back over the top of the rib-eye and secure it with a loop of butcher's string between each rib and around the ends if there's enough meat beyond the bones to get any kind of purchase.

To really simplify carving you can slip your knife along the feather bones and remove them along with the spine, though it's a good idea to tie them back on once you've done this. It provides a firmer base when roasting and none of the flavour in the bones is wasted.

Now separate the remaining meat trim from the fat as neatly as you can. The thin muscle layers are tender and full of flavour. They stand up to quick, hot searing so they're great for fajitas, stir-fries, etc. The interstitial muscle trimmed from between the ribs is some of the finest hamburger meat available. Its complex structure of interwoven fibres and connective material stands up well to grinding but maintains a great taste. Alternatively, all the meat trim can go straight to the stockpot along with the leftover bones at the end of the meal.

COOKING A LARGE ROAST

Traditional cooking instructions for a large roast would be to place it in as hot an oven as possible for around 20 minutes to half an hour, then drop to 160°C and allow 10 minutes for every 500g/lb of meat for 'rare', 15 minutes for 'medium' and 20 minutes for 'well done'. This should be finished off with at least a 30-minute 'rest'.

This has worked reasonably well for generations, even though ovens vary in their temperatures and times vary depending on the starting temperature and texture of the meat. It's still a good way of working out the answer to the inevitable question 'What time will dinner be ready?'

Since most of these instructions were first evolved, probe thermometers have dropped in price and become ubiquitous in the catering industry. Your Christmas turkey or standing rib roast may cost you over £50 in ingredients, so is a tenner for a cheap probe thermometer too much to invest in cooking it to perfection? Probe temperatures for guaranteed bang-on-the-button cooking are 50–55°C rare, 55–60°C medium/rare, 60–65°C medium, and anything over is what beef lovers refer to as 'ruined'.

BEEF

3-RIB

ROAST

BEEF

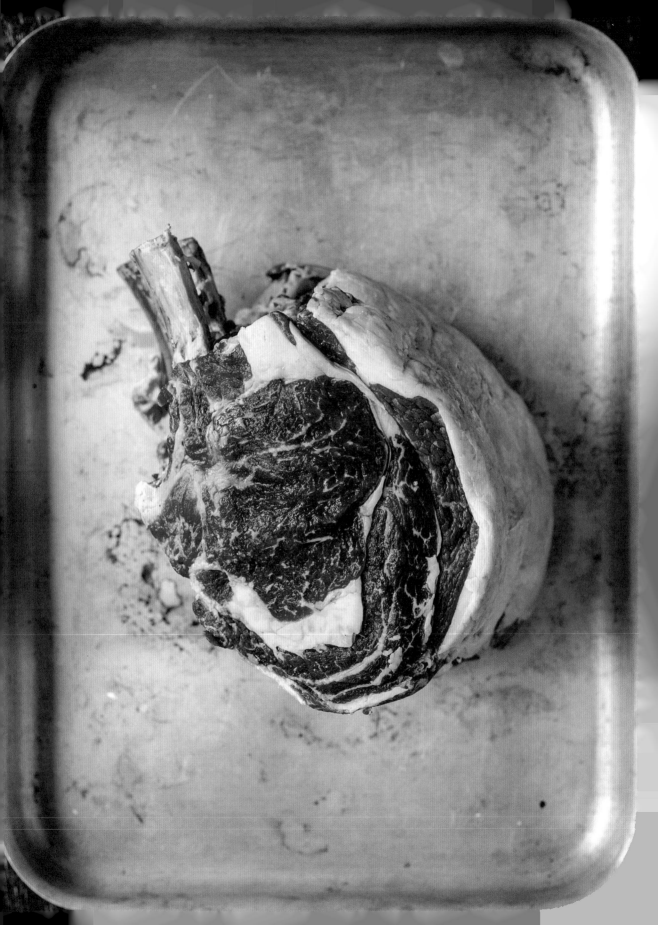

CHICKEN

In Britain we seem to buy chicken in one of two ways: it's either whole for roasting – and truly sublime it is too – or jointed down into convenient portions, the most common of which, the skinless, boneless, bloodless and tasteless breast, is usually packaged so you can cook it without ever realizing that you've touched meat.

Buy a chicken whole and do your own butchery and you'll end up with much more interesting cuts, meat that will stretch further for less cash, and you'll be left with a carcass and trim that's ideal for stock.

In classic French cooking, the whole roast chicken is a rare beast (poaching is preferred) and it was Escoffier who documented the easiest and most efficient pattern of jointing. This is an adaptation of his method.

1. Before diving in with the knives, work both leg and wing joints vigorously in their sockets. Particularly if the chicken has been refrigerated, this loosens up the muscles and makes everything easier to get at.

2. Remove the giblets, if they're inside the bird, and any large lumps of fat – these sometimes occur in corn-finished chickens and make a great cooking fat.

3. Put your fingers inside the neck end and feel up either side of the hole. You should be able to feel the hard ridges of the wishbone. Use the tip of your knife to scrape through to the bones and expose them from top to bottom. The top is attached to the breastbone and should be neatly snapped free; the bottom ends should be cracked and twisted away. Removing the wishbone is the fiddliest and most complicated bit of the process, but it's worth every bit of the effort. It makes it much simpler to carve the bird if it's been cooked whole or, if you're going on to joint it, you'll end up with two extra beautifully trimmed cuts.

4. With the chicken breast up, pull one thigh away to the side quite firmly and begin slicing downwards. Once through the skin, the muscles will separate with little effort and you'll quickly expose the hip joint. Use extra force to dislocate the joint and the tip of your knife to cut through any tendons. Now flip the bird over and continue to cut in a neat circle around the back of the hip. Keep your knife against the main bones of the body as you do this, to keep the maximum usable meat on the thigh.

5. Lift the leg clear and lay it on the table. Wiggle (I believe the correct veterinary term is 'articulate', but I like to wiggle) the knee joint until you can clearly visualize where the bend point is, then slice straight towards it from the back. You should find that the knife hits the joint at cartilage and you can slice straight through with little effort. If you find you're hitting tough bone, bend the joint open as far as it will go and then a little further, which will open a void that will guide the knife.

6. The thigh is your first 'joint'. Trim any excess skin and, if you wish, remove the thigh bone completely from the inside. A boned thigh joint cooks almost as quickly as a breast but the meat is much juicier, more full of flavour and much more tolerant of accidental overcooking.

7. Using the heel of your knife, cut straight through the knobbly knuckle at the bottom of the drumstick. The scaly ankly bit can go straight into the stockpot; the drumstick is your second joint. A drumstick cooks at the same rate as a thigh with the bone left in. It has the same taste and juiciness but has the additional benefit of a handle. Bone-in thighs and drumsticks make tremendous fried chicken and cook beautifully in casseroles, as they both hold their shape and yield good flavour.

8. Having removed the second leg in the same way, place the carcass breast upwards again with the wing end towards you. If, at this stage, you cut diagonally through the ribs from the tip of the keel bone and through the spine you'll be left with a 'crown'. This is the breasts, left on the bone and with the skin on in such a way that they can be roasted quickly. A whole roast chicken needs to be cooked until the juices from the thickest part of the thigh run clear, so the breast is usually woefully overcooked, dry and dull. A crown can be roasted in just over half the time, retains much of its juiciness and can still be carved at the table with considerably more flair than just plopping down a couple of skinless breasts.

9. If you're not going for a crown, slice through the skin and down one side of the breastbone until you hit the ribs, then, turning the knife outwards, work down, over the surface of the ribcage. Look out for a spur of bone that shoots up the inside of the breast muscle towards the rear – you may need to get your knife behind it to free the breast. The tenderloin may separate from the back of the breast too, but just hold the pieces together and keep working down towards the spine and back towards the wing joint. Once you can see the wing joint, fold the wing back the 'wrong' way until you can see a way in with the knife, separate the joint and then slip the knife in a circular movement, round the shoulder, to detach the whole piece.

Chicken

Thighs

Breasts

Tonight

Legs

Wings

10. You should now be looking at a whole breast fillet with the wing attached. Slice straight through the first wing joint, leaving one bone attached to the breast, then through the second joint, detaching the wing tip. The tip goes into the stock, and the wing pieces can too, though they can also be added to a collection in the freezer so that, after a few chickens, you'll have enough for 'buffalo wings' or a marvellously elegant French-style chicken wing salad.

11. The remaining breast with a small wing-stub 'handle' is what the pros refer to as 'airline trim' or 'hotel cut'. With the pointy end trimmed up, it's the smartest way to present a chicken breast on a plate and it takes well to breadcrumbing or other crusty treatments. Slice a 'pocket' into it and you have the basis for a splendidly ironic chicken 'Kiev'. You can leave your breast pieces exactly like this or slice each one across diagonally. This will give you two breast portions on each side, one with the bone 'handle' but all of roughly equal portion size with the thigh and drumstick.

12. Fully jointed, the chicken can be massaged with oil or butter and roasted quickly in an open pan. I like to start the thighs and drumsticks together, then add the breast portions 10 minutes later. As with any roast meat, a good long resting period before serving gives the internal temperatures a chance to stabilize and stops juices wastefully departing.

CARVING CHICKEN OR TURKEY

If you're going to need to carve a chicken or turkey publicly, perhaps for Christmas dinner or some other celebration, it's not cheating to do a little backroom preparation.

Follow the instructions in the section above for removing the wishbone. Also, work the hip joints of the bird, dislocate them, then, using the tip of your knife, cut through to the joint from the inside of the vent and sever any tendons holding the thighs in place. Close the legs back into position and truss together with butcher's string.

Once the bird has been roasted, follow the same procedure as for jointing the raw chicken. With the hip joints already dealt with, the legs will come off with a deft flick of the knife and with the wishbone gone the breasts can be gently separated from the bones and lifted away. These large, equal-sized 'chunk' portions look good on the serving plate and hold their warmth and juices better than the traditional way of attempting to make long 'slices' along breast and thigh.

BONING A CHICKEN

Boning a chicken is often regarded as one of the toughest tests of your knife skills. The traditional method involves removing the skeleton without cutting the exterior at all, so the flesh and skin has to be turned back, like a thick meaty glove, as it's freed from the bones. Very few recipes still call for a bird boned this way and it certainly isn't necessary for the three-bird roast on page 294. Here we bone the bird but end up with it opened flat. Much easier – if you take the process slowly it can be simple and intuitive and, if you manage it without loss of fingers, you may well feel you can tackle it old-style next time.

This technique combines many of those mentioned in the section above on jointing a chicken.

Remove the wishbone and loosen the leg and wing joints. Begin by slicing down one side of the spine and teasing away skin and flesh with the tip of your knife. When the hip joint becomes visible, detach it carefully and keep going . . . use the tip of the knife and repeated short strokes to keep moving around the body, going through the wing joint and stopping as you reach the keel bone.

Now turn the bird around and follow exactly the same procedure on the other side. You should now be left with all the meat removed, attached to the skin and only still attached along the ridge of the keel bone. This is really the only tough part: trying to separate the skeleton where it attaches so closely to the skin along the front. Fortunately, a few small holes are not a problem for this recipe.

Once the carcass has been lifted clear you'll have a messy-looking, flattened chook with only the thigh and wing bones still attached. Run the blade down from the hip joint along the thigh bone to the knee. The bone will, after some hockling, be free enough to twist out, leaving the thigh opened like a book. You can continue to open up the drumstick if you wish, but the knee is so complicated and close to the skin that it's not usually worth it. Cut them off, along with the wing bones which are usually too much trouble to bother with, and add them to the stockpot.

SPANISH CHICKEN

1 free-range chicken ✶ stock vegetables (carrot, onion, leek, celery) ✶ 75g olive oil ✶ 1 onion ✶ 2 cloves of garlic ✶ 10g pimentón (smoked paprika), plus extra to sprinkle ✶ 75g sherry ✶ 1 jar of roasted red peppers ✶ 2 cans of 'judión' or butter beans ✶ salt and freshly ground black pepper ✶ fresh flat-leaf parsley

1. Joint the chicken and set the trimmings and carcass simmering with a few veg for stock. If you use the giblets (of course you will), discard the liver as it gives the stock a less clear flavour.

2. Heat the olive oil in a pan and brown the chicken pieces, one or two at a time. As each one is finished, lay them in a flat ovenproof dish in a single layer.

3. Preheat the oven to 190°C. Chop the onion and garlic and soften them in the pan using the oil and chicken fat left behind. Once the onions are clear, add the pimentón and allow to cook for a minute to release the oil-soluble flavour compounds, then splash in the sherry and allow it to bubble ferociously until it's reduced to a treacly consistency.

4. Add the red peppers, drained and cut into strips, and the drained beans, then lower the heat as far as humanly possible and let things stew for a minute or so, just so the flavours can start to combine. Finally, pour everything over the chicken.

5. Add a couple of ladles of the hot stock, which should come about halfway up the chicken pieces, add a screw of pepper and a sprinkle of salt, cover with a lid or foil and place in the oven for 45–50 minutes. The meat is cooked when a probe thermometer reads 70°C at the thickest part of the thigh.

6. Check on things every now and again while cooking and add more stock if things are drying out. I usually remove the foil for the last 10–15 minutes and add a last sprinkling of pimentón, which gives a lovely crispness to the skin. Strew with roughly chopped flat-leaf parsley before serving (will feed 4).

COQ IN HOCK

1 medium free-range chicken ★ stock vegetables (carrot, onion, leek, celery) ★ 150g mildly smoked bacon ★ 75g butter ★ 10 small onions or shallots ★ 200g button mushrooms ★ 1 carrot ★ 1 large onion ★ 2 sticks of celery ★ 40g plain flour, seasoned ★ 1 x 75cl bottle of hock or riesling ★ 4 sprigs of fresh thyme ★ 2 cloves of garlic ★ 200g whipping cream

1. Joint the chicken and set the carcass, trimmings and giblets (minus the liver) on a light simmer with a few vegetables to create a stock.

2. In a large frying pan, sweat the bacon until it's just beginning to brown, then lift it out and put it into the bottom of a big casserole. Add half of the butter to the bacon fat left in the pan and brown the peeled small onions. Once they look a healthy colour, put them to one side and then roll in the button mushrooms. Let these take a little colour but they mustn't be allowed to become mushy. Put the mushrooms aside. Add more butter if necessary and use it to sweat the carrot, large onion and celery sticks, all very finely chopped. Once they've gone soft, lift them into the casserole.

3. Roll the chicken pieces lightly in seasoned flour and brown them in the fat. Add more butter if necessary and take it slowly. Don't crowd the pan, and get a good golden finish on each piece before lifting it out and into the casserole.

4. Deglaze the pan with a glass or so of the wine and then pour it into the casserole along with the rest of the bottle. Bring to a quite fierce simmer for 10 minutes, then lower the heat to a really gentle simmer and add the small onions, thyme and finely grated garlic.

5. Simmer for around half an hour, then add the button mushrooms and continue for another 10 minutes or so, until the chicken pieces are cooked (70°C internal temperature at thickest part of the thigh or until the juices run clear when skewered). Add hot stock during the cooking if the liquid reduces much below the top of the chicken.

6. Use a slotted spoon to lift out the chicken, onions and mushrooms to your serving dish and whack up the heat under the remaining sauce until it's bubbling merrily. Pour in the cream and reduce the lot to about three-quarters before pouring it back over everything else.

This could be served with boiled potatoes or fettucine (one chicken will easily serve 4), but I prefer great lumps of fresh bread, as the sauce is like an infinitely more refined version of a childhood favourite, cream of chicken soup.

3-BIRD ROAST

There's a long historical tradition of show-off feasting dishes made by inserting progressively smaller animals into each other. Perhaps the most famous is the Rôti Sans Pareil quoted by Norman Douglas in his 1952 collection of aphrodisiac recipes, *Venus in the Kitchen*.

Originating in a nineteenth-century French cookbook, this monster had twenty stages, beginning with a sliver of anchovy stuffed into an olive inserted into some tiny and endangered warbler and ending several days later when a turkey is shoved up a bustard – an ornithological outrage which not only flouted eighteen separate game and public decency laws but also required a large crane.

The Rôti Sans Pareil is a difficult one to replicate these days, for all sorts of very good reasons, legal, technical and aesthetic, but, down another winding byway of culinary history, there's a multi-bird roast that opens up better possibilities ... the almost legendary turducken.

Google 'turducken' and you'll be able to trace the brief history of this strange dish – half recipe, half urban legend. Originating in Louisiana and of lineage both recent and fiercely argued, the turducken combined a TURkey, a DUCk and a chicKEN to produce a dish with arguably the least appetizing name in the history of food.

But though it sounds like a redneck experiment in grotesque overeating, the turducken is distinguished by the addition of three separate 'dressings' – that's stuffings to those of us who've left the bayou – stuffings that save the roast from the awful dryness and tedium of the standard large poultry and complement the different flavours of the birds.

We should probably think about an upper size limit. There are recipes for 24-bird roasts that will feed upwards of 100 people, and certainly 13kg turkeys are a common enough starting point for roasts in the Southern states, but this version will feed 8 with just the usual ridiculous amount of leftovers.

1 Aylesbury or Gressingham duck (about 2.2kg total weight) ★ 1 free-range chicken (1.2–1.4kg total weight) ★ 1 pheasant (500–700g total weight) ★ 350g good smoked streaky bacon, rind removed ★ to roast: 3 large carrots, 2 medium onions, peeled

Stuffing #1
500g of your favourite sausages ★ 200g cooked chestnuts, roughly chopped ★ 150g dried cranberries, soaked overnight ★ 1 leek, chopped, sweated in butter and allowed to cool ★ 1 blade of mace ★ allspice berries ★ 15g fresh thyme leaves ★ freshly grated nutmeg

Stuffing #2
150g fresh, good-quality white bread ★ 1 large onion, chopped, sweated in butter and allowed to cool ★ 15g fresh sage ★ salt ★ white pepper

Kit
Small boning knife, large kitchen knife or chopper, needle and butcher's thread – this is a shiny, food-safe cotton which slides easily; ask your butcher nicely for some. Regular string will probably work but it will make the job tougher. Unwaxed dental floss is a surprisingly effective alternative. Clean tea towel.

PREP (CAN ALL BE DONE AT LEAST A DAY IN ADVANCE)
1. Bone all three birds (see method on page 289), keeping the skin intact. Leave the leg and wing bones intact on the duck, remove all bones from the chicken and remove legs and wings entirely from the pheasant. Salt liberally, cover and refrigerate overnight.

2. Save 1 sausage, then remove the skins from the rest. Put the sausage meat into a bowl and add the chestnuts, cranberries and leeks. With a pestle and mortar, grind the mace and allspice and add the thyme leaves. Add to the stuffing along with a liberal grating of nutmeg. This will be Stuffing #1. Cover and refrigerate.

3. Reduce the bread to crumbs in a food processor, and add the onion, roughly chopped sage, salt and pepper. Resist at all costs the temptation to add an egg. There's no need to bind the stuffing and it just gives it a horrible rubbery texture. This is Stuffing #2. Cover and refrigerate.

ASSEMBLY (PREHEAT THE OVEN TO 200°C)
4. Lay the duck skin side down on the worktop. If you wish you can put a clean tea towel underneath to help with handling later on. Brush off any excess salt and then grind on some white pepper. Smear Stuffing #1 on to the duck, stopping just short of the edge.

5. Lay the chicken on top, skin side down, legs and wings matching the duck. Again brush off the salt and add pepper. Smear on Stuffing #2, being careful to pack it into the pockets formed by the tops of the wings and legs where the bones have been removed.

6. Lay the pheasant on top, skin side down, and top with the reserved sausage.

7. Wrap the pheasant tight around the sausage and pull up the edges of the chicken around the stuffing and the pheasant. You can temporarily skewer the roll closed if it helps. Using the tea towel if necessary, pull the duck and Stuffing #1 up around the chicken. Don't worry if the edges don't meet exactly.

8. Using about 150cm of thread, make a first stitch at the vent end of the central line. Only pull half the thread through and don't fix the end. Take large stitches, about 3cm apart, and at least 2cm back into the skin on each side, and work towards the head end. Leave the stitches loose at first. When you get to the head end, tuck in the flap and stitch tightly across the neck hole.

9. Using both hands, massage the bird vigorously to redistribute the stuffing into the shape you want. Starting at the head end, pull each stitch individually tighter as you work the stuffing into place. Thread the needle back on to the tail end of the thread and pull it tight. Stitch across the vent end and tie off.

10. Use the carrots and onions to make a trivet in a big roasting tin. Place the bird on top, sutures down, season, drape bacon over the breast and top with a tent of foil.

COOKING (FIGURES FOR A 3.5KG BIRD)

11. Place in the preheated oven – chances are you won't have much choice of shelf, but near the middle if you do. After half an hour, drop the temperature to 150°C and drain off the fat and juices with a bulb baster or a small ladle.

12. Cooking times are dependent on so many variables that it's almost impossible to recommend. I favour slower, longer cooking (around 150°C), which has larger margins for error. You could guesstimate cooking time at around 1 hour 15 minutes per kilo, but in the end the only safe measure is a probe thermometer, which should read 70°C.

13. Allow at least half an hour's rest under the foil tent before even considering cutting. It will easily stay servably warm for an hour and will only improve.

14. Slice across the middle to gasps of admiration and serve it forth.

MAKING SAUSAGES

Cooking a proper sausage, and by that I mean one with a high meat content, well packed in a natural casing, is a matter of delicately balancing heat so the meat cooks without the pressure of the expanding filling bursting the skin. Some people – I name no names – seem to enjoy pricking the sausage, believing that the relief of pressure will prevent the banger bursting. This will, of course, stop the skin splitting uncontrollably but only at terrible cost: allowing all the juices to escape into the pan.

Sausage prickers convince themselves that the leaked liquid is largely fat and thus conclude that a pierced sausage is a healthier sausage. Further still, to entirely rob the banger of its vital fluids and turn it into a health food, they like to grill or roast them in a hot oven – because frying means fat and fat is evil. Oh yes, the stabbed and grilled sausage is a healthy, sensible and nourishing foodstuff; it's also a shrivelled, limp travesty and an insult to the proud majesty of the banger.

There is, to my mind, only one way to correctly cook a proper sausage. Take a deep frying pan and pour in enough oil to come halfway up the sides. Slip in the sausages, bring the oily bath up to a temperature at which they barely simmer and hold them there. The intention is not to shallow-fry the sausage but to lovingly poach it. The skin, remember, is impermeable to fat, so none is going to leak in or out. The oil bath anoints the casing, keeping it supple so it is less inclined to split, and the gentle cooking preserves all the juices inside the banger. This is not a speedy, slapdash process – at least half an hour is required for the full ritual – but at the end the sausage is firm, bursting with rich juices, lightly tanned and requiring only a brief wipe with a cloth before being proudly served (see note on page 255 regarding oil disposal).

Failing this, massage each sausage individually with oil first, then slide them into an oiled pan and keep them rolling, on a low heat, for as long and as continuously as possible.

Trust me, even 25 minutes of gently rolling them back and forth, jostling their plumply greased little bodies against each other, is not too long. As the skins change to a light tan, then begin to caramelize as what is known as the Maillard reaction takes place, you'll find yourself shifting into the right meditative state to honour your sausage.

There are few foods that reward a bit of care and attention quite as well as the simple banger. A poorly made supermarket sausage can be an awful thing; recycling the worst waste meats and packed with fillers, fluids and modifiers. Yet a properly made artisanal sausage from an honest butcher calls forth hymns of praise from the lucky consumer. What too few of us seem to realize is how little effort it can take to go one better and actually make our own sausages, controlling quality and flavours and producing something immeasurably more transcendent than the dispiriting slurry-packed condom in the styrofoam tray on the chiller shelf.

Sausages require little more than pork, seasonings, casings and a mincer. So let's deal with the biggest of those first. It's possible to buy hand-operated mincers which not only chop the meat but also, with the blade removed, pack it into the skin for you. These are reasonably successful, but producing a single kilo of sausage will leave you with a hypertrophic forearm like a fiddler crab on steroids. Far better to search the houses of friends and relatives and seek out the individual with the biggest kitchen mixer. The best can be fitted with a mincer, so it's worth clubbing together with friends to buy the attachment for the rare occasions it will be used.

SAUSAGE SKINS

Sausage skins, or 'casings' as they're known in the butchery trade, are traditionally made from cleaned lengths of the digestive tract. There are obviously some fairly stringent methods employed to clean what is effectively a pipe full of poop.

Lengths of gut are turned inside out, scraped to remove the soft lining material and repeatedly washed. What's left is a tough membrane, impermeable to liquids, edible, though without any flavour, that shrinks as it dries.

You can order casings from your butcher or the online suppliers on pages 370–71. They will arrive salted, vacuum-packed and probably in ludicrous lengths. First thing to do is unpack and sort them. Cut them into lengths of about a metre, then repack them into smaller batches and freeze. They'll keep indefinitely frozen.

To use a batch of natural casings, unpack them and soak in several changes of clean water. This will remove the salt and make them softer and more manageable.

There's no polite way of describing the next bit. You need to pick up the wet membrane and slide it on to your sausage horn like a wet sock, wrinkling it up so you can pack as much on as possible. You'll probably be able to load it up with several metre lengths.

Different gauges of sausage casing come from different parts of the digestive tract and from different animals. Medium to large size, from the large intestine of a cow or pig, will work well for fat bangers and salamis, chipolatas will need the small intestine of a pig, and merguez is usually done halal style, using the small intestine of a lamb.

THE SAUSAGE HORN

A sausage horn or nozzle is not vital but it makes shovelling mince into a damp piece of casing a minor chore rather than an extended comedy sketch. If you own a mincer you may find that a set of horns – in various sizes to fit the bore of the different casings – comes as an accessory. If you can find these, remove the blade from your mincer and attach the nozzle, loaded with casings, then the mincer's helical drive will act as a packing machine, forcing the meat into the sausages.

If you don't have a mincer, a set of plastic horns will set you back a few pence and you can pack the meat in with a combination of spoon and vigorous application of the thumb.

Always try to avoid air bubbles when packing the skins. They can cause a banger to burst and are occasionally hideaways for spoilage bacteria.

BASIC PORK SAUSAGES

Sausages generally need 1.5–2% of salt. 4% is probably the highest you'll need to go in a homemade one. The best way is to start with the smallest amount and fry test batches.

natural sausage casings (see pages 370–71 for suppliers) ☆ **5g dried savory** ☆ **2.5g dried sage** ☆ **2.5g allspice berries** ☆ **2.5g white peppercorns** ☆ **15g salt** ☆ **1kg pork back** ☆ **1kg pork belly** ☆ **200g white breadcrumbs, dried in the oven**

1. Soak the hog casings to remove the salt.

2. Select your spicing mix. For a traditional English breakfast-style sausage I suggest savory, sage, allspice and white pepper in the amounts above. You'll also need plenty of salt. Grind the spice mix in a pestle and mortar but keep the salt to one side.

3. Remove any skin and bones from the pork and slice the meat into cubes small enough to fit into the throat of your mincer. Salt generously, then put into a freezer for half an hour or so. This stiffens the meat and makes mincing easier.

4. Pass the meat through the mincer once. I prefer a coarse plate for a chunkier sausage, but use a fine one or pass the meat through twice if you want something more smooth and shop-bought in style.

5. Add breadcrumbs (10% by weight) and half your spice mix and work thoroughly through the meat with your hands. Fry a teaspoonful in a hot pan to check the seasoning and adjust accordingly. The breadcrumbs soak up some of the fat and juices that might otherwise be cooked out of the sausage, so drying them carefully in the oven before adding them to the mix will ensure that they're super-absorbent.

6. Slip the wet casing over the funnel attachment of your mincer. Remove the blades, mount the stuffing funnel and set the machine going on its slowest setting. Keep your fingers around the rolled casing, paying it out as required. Leave a good length empty before starting to fill.

7. Don't allow the meat to pack too tight, but don't let air in either. Beginners should fill about a metre of casing at a time then cut it off, leaving plenty of spare casing at either end.

8. Tie off one end of each length of casing, then gently squeeze enough space to twist the sausage a few times between each link.

TOAD IN THE HOLE

2 eggs ★ 125g plain flour ★ 75g milk ★ 75g water ★ salt ★ 50g lard, dripping or duck fat ★ 6 of your own sausages ★ 50g chopped red onion

1. Whisk together the eggs, flour and milk, then let down with the water until it's the consistency of double cream: pourable and smooth. Salt or otherwise season.

2. Successful toad is entirely dependent on the heat of your fat, so choose an oven dish you can get really hot. Heat the fat in the bottom of the dish and use it to quickly brown the outside of the sausages, then lift them out and put the dish and fat into the oven, cranked up as high as it will go, for 10 minutes or so.

3. Take out the oven dish – the oil will now be smoking – and pour in the batter. Arrange the sausages in the batter and sprinkle the red onion in between.

4. Put the dish back into the oven and bake for 25–30 minutes, until inflated and crispy.

5. Serve with gravy (see page 320) and something green.

SAUSAGE VARIATIONS

Sausage recipes can be varied in all sorts of directions from the basic recipe:

- Vary the herbs. Sage is traditional with pork in the UK, juniper works brilliantly with game, and more Mediterranean oily herbs like thyme or oregano combine well with garlic. Quantities are entirely a matter of taste, but if you start with small pinches, testing samples in the frying pan as you go, you'll build flavours quickly without endangering the whole batch.

- A Cumberland sausage is simply seasoned, predominantly with pepper, and formed into a coil without twisting into individual links. Hold it together in a spiral shape with wooden skewers for cooking.

- Use a splash of red wine, chopped smoked bacon and a healthy amount of crushed garlic – say 10g per kg – in your sausage meat for a reasonably authentic saucisson de Toulouse. This is the sausage to use in a cassoulet.

- If you want to add a fruit element in the form of prune, apricot or apple, use 20g of dried fruit per kg of sausage meat, chop it finely and work it through the mixture.

- Adding 10g of smoked paprika per kilo and cutting the pork fat into coarser cubes gives a good chorizo.

- Adding fennel (5g) and minced garlic (10g) to the mix makes very acceptable Italian salsicce.

- Try replacing the lean back pork with beef, lamb or venison, but always retain the fatty pork, which is still necessary for texture.

- By replacing the pork entirely with equal quantities of lamb shoulder and lamb breast and seasoning liberally with harissa paste, you'll end up with enviable merguez.

The world isn't just your oyster, it's also your sausage.

EST. 1770

HARRIS
WILTSHIRE
SAUSAGES

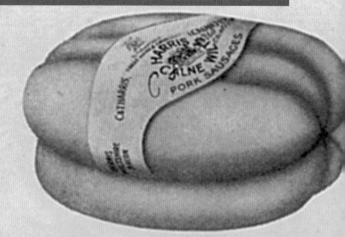

DROËWORS

Droëwors is an excellent South African recipe which combines elements of sausage, salami, bresaola and biltong making in one recipe. By now, most of the techniques will be familiar to you. It's one of my absolute favourites and the starting point for dozens of fantastic flavour experiments. Try it once, then go off-piste with the ingredients.

Droëwors uses lean beef because fattier meats tend to rancidity in the South African heat.

thin sausage casings ★ 1.5kg beef or venison ★ 500g beef fat or lamb breast ★ 15g salt ★ 5g coarse ground black pepper ★ 10g coriander seed ★ 1g ground cloves ★ 100ml white wine vinegar

1. Soak the sausage casings.

2. Chop the meat into 3cm cubes, mix with the dry ingredients and put through the mincer on the coarsest plate.

3. Pack directly into the soaked casings.

4. Use a rolling pin to squash the sausages into a slightly flattened shape, wash the outsides in the vinegar and hang them to dry in a biltong box or desiccator (see page 99).

5. For added character, pull the sausages out of the box after a day and give them a quick session in the cold-smoker (see page 141).

6. Continue to dry in the box for another day or two or until they achieve 30% weight loss.

7. Vac-pack or wrap and freeze to prevent further drying out.

SCOTCH EGGS

The original 'Scotched' egg was a snack devised by royal cornershop Fortnum & Mason to fortify travellers leaving Piccadilly on the stagecoach for points west.

It's fitting that the Scotch egg was born as a travel snack from a posh grocer's, because to this very day you're most likely to encounter one either in a motorway service station or in one of those morale-sapping trays of pre-made 'canapés' from the supermarket. The 'cocktail' Scotch egg, tiny and enticing, offers vague promises of quail's egg and a delicately fragranced forcemeat but in fact is a deposit of egg mayonnaise in a cornified pig-slurry cyst.

It's a crying shame because, as cuisines all over the world have shown, the deep-fried morsel of something lovely, wrapped around or stuffed with something even lovelier, is as near perfection as any recipe can approach.

Other traditional English savouries have had similar names – the Welsh Rabbit, the Scotch Woodcock – with a xenophobic air and a patronizing ring. The name implies that the dish is somehow less than it pretends to be. The proper Scotch egg has no such inferiority. It is grander than the mere egg, more filling, more flavoursome, a nobler, better, higher thing. A just-set egg in sausage meat with a light and crisp crumb coating is a lovesome thing and worth every bit of the effort in its preparation.

If you're making the sausage meat on page 303 in quantity, you can put aside a portion for Scotch egg manufacture, but they're also quite simple to do in small batches and with all sorts of interesting variations, so this recipe assumes you're starting from scratch.

500g pork shoulder, boneless and skinless ★ 5g salt ★ 2.5g allspice berries ★ 2.5g dried savory or thyme ★ 2.5g black peppercorns ★ 2.5g dried sage ★ 9 medium eggs, at room temperature ★ 150g breadcrumbs ★ 1.5 litres vegetable oil, for frying

1. Chop the pork, salt and flavourings in a food processor. Chunky is good for sausages but an absolute nightmare to wrap round a small, softish egg, so go for a quite smooth finish.

2. Preheat the oven to 180°C. Carefully place 6 of the eggs in a pan of boiling water. After 4½ minutes, whip them out with a slotted spoon and plunge them into iced water to cool completely for about 15 minutes.

3. Peel the eggs incredibly carefully. You may want to do this while they're still immersed in the iced water. Dry each egg with kitchen paper.

4. Divide your sausage meat into 6 portions and roll each one out between sheets of greaseproof paper to a diameter of 15cm. Place an egg in the centre of each one, then carefully fold the meat around the egg and press to seal. Refrigerate for half an hour to make handling easier.

5. Beat the other 3 eggs in a bowl, then dip in the Scotch eggs and roll them in the breadcrumbs.

6. Heat 3cm of oil to 180°C in a pan and fry the Scotch eggs in small batches for 3 minutes. Then transfer to the oven and cook for another 15 minutes.

7. Serve while still hot, preferably with homemade piccalilli (see page 68).

Quite justifiably, the Scotch egg is enjoying a revival as gastropubs go to town with variations. Every kind of egg is getting the wrap-and-fry treatment and the results are, with few exceptions, excellent. The recipe above can be simply adapted by varying the egg, the forcemeat and the crumb. A gull's egg in a smoked haddock and mash jacket could be crumbed with oatmeal. Perhaps a quail's egg wrapped in a crab forcemeat rolled in Japanese 'panko' crumbs. Finely minced salt beef (page 53) would hold together around an egg, and matzo meal makes a good crust. All that would need is a pickled gherkin for completeness.

Maybe it's the 'bar-snack' image of the Scotch egg that encourages daring but, once you start imagining, the possibilities are dangerously various. Why not a Scotch pickled egg (page 74)? A Scotch pickled onion (page 66)?

BLACK PUDDING

Black pudding is probably one of the most challenging DIY projects for most people, as obtaining a bucket of blood, keeping it liquid and pouring it into skins in your kitchen is well beyond the comfort zone of a lot of cooks. That said, if you're untroubled by the fact that it's blood then homemade black pudding is one of the most rewarding things to make – for the simple reason that most of the commercial stuff is radically over-spiced and loses all its subtlety.

There are places where you can get into a three-month debate on seasonings and a stand-up fight over serving blood pudding. It's regarded as a national dish in parts of Ireland, Spain, rural France and the north of England . . . all places where the finer points of culinary debate can be ferociously defended. I tend towards a morcilla style but only because my friend Rachel McCormack, a Glaswegian expert on Catalan food, scares me so much that I follow her advice:

'Black pepper – and in Asturias a tiny bit of cinnamon. In Extramadura, cumin. In Burgos onion and pinenuts. In a village in Andalucia almonds and they also do one with quite a lot of chilli (but won't give me the bloody recipe). Mallorcans make butifarros and I've had them with fennel and also with marjoram but that's very very Mallorcan.'

I'm sure you can vary your flavourings to reflect the traditions of Bury, Cork or Paris, and I promise I won't set Rachel on you.

(Morcilla is often made in smaller-gauge skins and twisted to form small, almost spherical puddings which are fried whole after poaching. If you fancy this, reduce the poaching time accordingly. I'd suggest 45 minutes as a starting point.)

1 litre pig's blood ★ 350g shredded suet ★ 300g milk ★ 60g oatmeal ★ 15g salt ★ 3 medium onions ★ large-gauge sausage casings

1. Your butcher may be able to supply pig's blood if you ask nicely and well in advance. Traders dealing with pork at farmers' markets are always a good bet too. They usually have some sort of relationship with the abattoir and may well be sympathetic to your experiments. In order to prevent clotting, the blood should have a little vinegar added and preferably be stirred regularly. If you can't get your hands on fresh blood, you should be able to buy the pasteurized and dried variety from a butcher's supply house (see pages 370–71). There's no shame in this. Food hygiene regulations mean that many artisanal manufacturers are now using the dried product.

2. Mix the blood with the rest of the ingredients apart from the casings and pour or spoon into the skins. Don't overfill, as the filling will expand as it cooks. Try to leave some slack in the skin before tying off, but also ensure there are no air pockets. A centimetre or so of skin, squeezed flat and empty, before the knot should do the trick.

3. Gently poach the puddings in water just short of a full simmer for 90 minutes, at the end of which time they should be firm and cooked through. Allow to cool in the poaching liquid.

4. The puddings should be sliced cold and fried before serving. They can be stored under refrigeration for a day or two but should be vac-packed or film-wrapped and frozen if you want to store them for longer. If you freeze the pudding in slices you will find they defrost quickly . . . often in the time it takes to properly fry a sausage (see page 299).

5. You can serve your black pudding in the classic manner, fried crisp on the outside and surrounded by the supportive elements of a Full English Breakfast. Profoundly unpatriotic as it may seem, I like mine crumbled and fried with equal quantities of cubed chorizo, stirred into lightly scrambled eggs and served rolled in a burrito. To be really elegant, slice thinly and serve fried with slices of a sharp, acidic apple, such as a Cox's Orange Pippin.

HAGGIS

A sheep's 'pluck' is the windpipe, lungs, heart and liver, which you'll need to order direct from a butcher. If you've been good to him all year, he probably won't charge you. Slaughter regulations mean that any food-safe pluck will have had the windpipe removed and the lungs will have been cut across for inspection. This makes little difference as, in traditional recipes, the windpipe was merely hung over the edge of the pot to remove 'impurities' (read sheepsnot) and not included in the stuffing. You will, however, have to keep your eye on the simmering pot as the same 'impurities' can cause a disturbing brown froth to form if boiled too hard. Not in any way to the detriment of the finished product but visually reminiscent of something in a cheap 50s sci-fi shocker.

Scottish haggis was traditionally contained in the sheep's fourth stomach or rumen. These are difficult to obtain from English butchers, as anything with the slightest possibility of 'fecal contamination' requires special cleaning and there's, tragically, not enough demand down here. The best alternative, ox bung, is available from specialist sausage suppliers (see pages 370–71) and comprises the last metre or so of the large intestine of a cow, cleaned and salted.

You'll need some coarse oatmeal (500g), a large onion, and dried rosemary, sage, thyme and savory. If you can get it, 500g of lamb suet will add yet more flavour but you can substitute packaged, refined suet as I did. You'll also need salt, pepper and butcher's string.

Though the recipe is simple, scaling it is almost impossible. Ox bungs don't come in standard sizes, and sheep's plucks range in size from something that might comfortably squeeze into a large breakfast bowl to something you'd have trouble beating into a wheelbarrow with a stick. I filled my bung in two pieces, ending up with a 2kg and a 850g haggis. Unless you're lucky (as I was) or incredibly clever, you should expect to throw away either some stuffing or some bung. On the other hand, as total ingredient cost will come in at something under £3, this shouldn't be too painful.

Wash the pluck and simmer it gently in unsalted water until it's tender – usually about an hour and a half. Let it cool overnight in its own cooking liquid. Keep the liquid for later and chop the heart and lungs finely – I used a mezzaluna, but a food processor will do the job if pulsed gently. Remember that you're looking for a gravelly texture, not pâté. Grate the liver – a weird and strangely satisfying sensation.

Toast the oatmeal for a few minutes in a medium oven while chopping the onions. Season the meat with salt, coarsely ground white pepper, sage, thyme, rosemary and savory. There's no need to go overboard here – particularly with the pepper. This isn't, after all, an English sausage. Add the onions, the oatmeal, the suet and a pint or so of the liquid in which the pluck was poached. The mix should be moist but not enough to hold together as a single mass.

The ox bung will have been thoroughly cleaned and salted, so rinse it inside and out with cold water and pat it dry with a kitchen towel. Spoon the stuffing into the bung until it's half full; I wanted to make two, so I stopped early and cut the bung short. Expel any air left in the casing, tie the opening tightly with several turns of butcher's string, and work the filling back out into the full length of the casing. The stuffing will expand in cooking as the oatmeal absorbs the fat and meat juices. The most important trick is to allow space for this expansion while preventing any air bubbles which might turn the entire thing into an offal-themed *Hindenberg* disaster.

Lower the haggis into gently simmering water. The casing will contract and the stuffing will swell. Use a skewer to pierce and release any trapped air. Remember that cooking time is based on thickness, not mass; the long sausage shape of the bung means that this one took just over an hour and a half to cook. Lift out on to a plate and pat dry.

This is a genuinely monumental piece of food. There's something about the steaming, bulging shape of it, the astonishingly welcoming smell, that could easily inspire ritual and poetry in a nation less emotionally constipated than the English. And the taste . . . oh, the taste. I can't ever remember eating anything quite so rich. The grains absorb the fats and flavours, the powerful aromas of the meat are dispersed throughout, the velvet liver is offset by a nutty texture – it's completely astonishing. With the combination of fat richness and slight livery aftertaste I found myself thinking of foie gras – but more fun.

FATS

Our relationship with dietary fats is an odd one. Mainly we're terrified of anything with the faintest hint of it and have formed the suspicion that the evil substance somehow passes straight into our bloodstreams and forms great ugly clumps in our aortas. The slimmest sliver of fat on our steak and we start imagining something like Raquel Welch had to fight with in *The Fantastic Voyage* . . . only made of lard.

There's one simple thing to remember about dietary fat. Butter is nearly pure fat but every gram you eat doesn't stay in your body. All but a trace amount is passed or metabolized. The effect of different fats and how they are laid down in the body is down to a huge number of variables, some to do with us, some to do with the fats.

We could discuss indefinitely the benefits and risks of various fats in the diet, the effects of different types of cholesterol, the genetic, societal and environmental factors involved in obesity and its relationship to heart disease. If you wish to find out more about this endless and ferocious debate, I commend you to the internet.

The one thing most cooks and food lovers know is that fat tastes great. Good cooking isn't simply a matter of how well you can include fats in a dish but sometimes it seems that way.

Fat creates a mouthfeel that we're designed to crave and carries fat-soluble flavourings around the mouth in a way that delights us. Frying creates flavours and textures that we can hardly resist. We can't and shouldn't stamp fats from our diets, but we should understand them so we can use them well. Chicken fat, for example, is almost liquid at room temperature. This makes it, in the opinion of some health experts, less damaging (my Jewish medical friend, on the other hand, ascribes to it astonishing curative powers). There is fat in chips, the terror of middle-class parents, but very little of it if the chips are fried at a high enough temperature and properly drained; certainly considerably less oil than you'd use in dressing a crisp green salad and a tiny portion of the amount in a smear of artisan Camembert on crisp baguette or a lump of beurre d'Isigny on your fresh steamed Jersey Royals.

Many fats that are by-products of cooking or butchering processes can be saved and reused in wonderful ways.

RENDERING FATS

Pork fat comes in two types. Leaf fat is the solid white stuff that accumulates around various organs inside the body cavity, particularly the kidneys, which can be used without further treatment as suet. Large lumps can sometimes be 'snapped' out of the inside of pork joints and saved to be grated into pastry, particularly hot water crust. The other useful pork fat is the subcutaneous variety that we're used to around the outside of a good pork chop. This can be thick and with more flavour than the leaf type. If you're lucky enough to find fat from the back area 3cm or more thick, count your blessings and look at the section on curing it as 'lardo' (page 38). This backfat is also the best for larding.

Other trimmings from more general pork butchery should be collected in a pot, a little water poured over them to create steam and start the process of rendering, then placed over a low heat. The water will quickly boil and bubble off, by which point the fat will begin to melt and run, a gorgeous clear liquid. After an hour or so, gently and carefully smoosh any remaining lumps with a potato masher – this releases any fat still trapped in cells – and finally filter the liquid through a sieve and into a jar for refrigeration. This is pure lard.

The fat recovered from the top of a chilled pork stock is also lard and has a near neutral flavour. It's ideal for general pan greasing as well as for sealing jars when potting.

Hard lamb or mutton fat from around the organs is used as suet – particularly for traditional puddings – but the recovered or rendered subcutaneous fat has few culinary uses and tends to go rancid quickly.

Beef fat from inside the carcass is also usable as suet and, until 'wiser' counsels intervened, was the favourite fat of fish and chip shops all over the country. The fat which dribbles off a roasting joint, combined with the jellified juices of the meat accumulating in the pan, is 'beef dripping'. This should be smeared on sourdough toast like a sublime butter and occasionally enjoyed as a benison of the roasting gods. Rendered subcutaneous fat retains a strong beef flavour. In spite of the fact that it sounds delicious, it somehow doesn't find as many uses in my kitchen as one might imagine. This is probably good because, as it sets harder than any other common kitchen fat, it's considered more dangerous.

A roast duck can yield up to a quarter of its original weight in gorgeous clear fat. Extra trimmings can be poached in it to create more – plus the scrackly pieces of skin that get trapped in the sieve when you filter it are posh 'scratchings' and beyond sublime. This is the best fat, without question, for roasting potatoes. It can be used several times over for confiting duck legs and, in Italy and France, is also used to preserve small sausages in jars.

RECIPE FOR DRIPPING

The *Antiseptic Manual* was published in 1835 and subtitled: 'or the art and mystery of preserving every description of alimentary substance, animal and vegetable, for any length of time, by various approved and recently discovered processes, for domestic use, foreign consumption, on long voyages'.

'Take 6lbs of good beef dripping, bring it to the boil, let it set and then scrape off any layer of jelly or impurities at the bottom. Repeat [the anonymous writer suggests eight times but this may be overkill if you're not going to be out of sight of land for eight months or more]. Place in a pan with 6 bay leaves, 12 cloves, some peppercorns and half a pound of salt. Warm until liquid enough then pour through a strainer, into a pot.

'In this manner you may prepare any quantity of dripping you please; and the best way to keep this or any other sort is to turn the pot upside down, and then no vermin will get at it. It will keep on shipboard, and make as fine a puff paste crust as any butter whatever, for either pies or puddings.'[36]

STOCK

Many of us have a particular image of the Victorian stockpot – a huge vat, sitting on the stove for months on end, reducing every kitchen scrap from plate scrapings to rancid bacon into a nutritious broth – but it turns out to be a bit of a culinary myth. Several well-meant handbooks for the working classes did suggest just such a pot, but there's little evidence anyone actually used one; meanwhile, Mrs Beeton, Eliza Acton and Alexis Soyer wrote really quite sensible recipes for sophisticated, pure-flavoured stocks we'd recognize in a restaurant kitchen today.

The idea of extracting all available flavour from your ingredients seems so sensible, yet home cooks often don't bother. Perhaps it's the convenience of stock cubes, perhaps it's the worry that it's somehow complicated and involved. The truth is that stock-making isn't so

---

36 *Antiseptic manual,* Joseph Thomas, London, 1835 (author unknown).

much about recipes as a regime. It's a kind of commitment to a way of working in the kitchen that involves little investment in terms of time or organization and can yield astounding results. People who get organized to bake their own bread are evangelistic about it and attract a certain amount of admiration, but stock-makers are a different breed. They have a secret that endows them with a feeling of righteousness for using every last ounce plus the knowledge that their cooking will taste better.

Having stock in the freezer means that homemade soup can be made from any seasonal ingredient in minutes. Stews and casseroles take on a new and complex richness. Sauces are transformed. In fact, though you could justifiably characterize me as a bit of a swivel-eyed stock extremist, I can't think of any other culinary trick or technique that has transformed my own cooking as much as making and using stock.

Chicken is a great starting point, partly because a carcass is a common kitchen by-product – you don't have to go to the butcher's in search of special ingredients, you just reuse something you'd usually toss away – and partly because chicken stock, with its chameleon-like ability to work with almost any other flavour, is just so damned useful.

PORK JELLY CUBES

How well your stocks jellify depends on the amount of gelatinous material in the bones you choose. The traditional cook's standby was to add a trotter, which did nothing to the flavour but guaranteed it would set to a rubbery consistency and add extra richness whatever its final use. Because we don't make stocks in the quantities we used to, this recipe just extracts the gelatinousness and conveniently packages it for addition to smaller stock batches.

2 pig's trotters ★ water

1. Place the trotters in a stockpot and cover with a couple of litres of water. Bring to the boil, spoon off the initial risings of scum and then reduce to a gentle simmer. The trotters will eventually disintegrate – usually after a couple of hours. Strain the stock through a sieve or muslin and chill until set in a shallow tray.

2. Lift off the fat layer – this is tremendous for cooking – then lift the block of jelly, scrape any sediment off the bottom with kitchen paper, and slice into cubes. Freeze these separately on a baking sheet, then toss them into a bag and bury them in the freezer. They'll last, effectively, for ever, taking up little space and just waiting to bail out a limp stock or man-up a stew.

PROPER GRAVY

'England has three sauces and three hundred and sixty religions, whereas France has three religions and three hundred and sixty sauces.'

Talleyrand

What Talleyrand and others were incapable of comprehending, however, is that we don't need sauces in England because we have gravy.

Proper gravy, not brown gunge made from powder, is a complex creation which, when done well, balances all the available flavour sensations in the mouth while elegantly complementing the meat. It brings the plate into harmony like a talented choirmaster and makes the soul soar. Gravy is better than any sauce and the secrets of its creation should be shared among us.

For a brief time, chefs would have had us believe that the best gravy was the simple juices of the meat. Not only is this palpable nonsense but it also misses the point that properly cooked meat shouldn't be losing its juices in enough quantity to fill a gravy boat.

Here, then, are a series of instructions for proper gravy. Do not regard this as a recipe – a gravy with a recipe is a sauce – but as part of your cultural heritage.

1. Finely chop or slice some onions or shallots and sweat them in butter or a fat appropriate to your meat.

2. Once they are clear, add a glass or so of a suitable wine and reduce hard until there's nothing much left but a syrup.

3. At this point I usually add my vinegar. This may sound counter-intuitive, but gravy should have a distant hint of sour to play against the sweet. You can use red or white wine vinegar, perhaps a little aged balsamic, but my secret weapon is the vinegar from pickled walnuts. There's always loads left over and it keeps for ever in a small squeezy bottle in the fridge. Add a shot and cook until the acetic, eye-watering effect subsides.

4. Now you can turn to your pan juices. Your meat will obviously be resting, ready to be carved, by now, so put the baking dish on the hob and start the juices and fat sizzling. If you believe in a thickened gravy you can add flour here, but make sure it cooks well in the fat. Lumps are avoided by the simple expedient of a small wire 'magic' whisk – that's the sort your Nan had, made with a bit of spring threaded on a wire. It looks retro but nothing does the job better.

5. The flour, cooking in the fat, is creating a roux which will thicken the gravy a little, and here you can also add an alcohol with a little more body. Port, sherry, Marsala or the princely Madeira. The alcohol will cook off as it hits the heat but the flavours will be preserved.

6. Scrape all the contents of the oven dish into the first pan with the onions and reduced liquids and turn everything down. All the flash, hot stuff is over now and the contemplative artistic process begins.

7. Add some appropriate stock if you have it – of course you do.

8. Begin tasting. You'll doubtless need salt and perhaps pepper but you'll also need to adjust the sour and sweet – things like redcurrant jelly and a shot more of your favoured vinegar work particularly well here.

9. Think about gravy like a painting or a musical score. To express that deep meaty flavour, have we enough highlights? If you're lacking power in the midtones you can try a shot of that other great British standby, mushroom ketchup.

10. Keep the liquid – which we can finally dignify with the word 'gravy' – just simmering so everything can combine and mellow. Pass it through a sieve into a warmed gravy boat and serve forth to the acclaim of your family.

CHICKEN, QUICK CHICKEN AND BEEF STOCK

BASE RECIPE

·1· BROWN BONES

For beef stock, preheat the oven to 220°C. Put the bones and whole peeled onion into a tray and roast in the oven until they begin to brown.

For chicken stock, bones and wings can be browned if you prefer a darker stock, as with the beef stock.

·2· ADD VEG

Coarsely chop the vegetables, place them in a large pot with the carcass and wings (if it has wings) and top up with cold water until everything is covered.

BASE + ADDITIONAL INGREDIENTS

BASE INGREDIENTS

- 1 ONION
- 1 LARGE CARROT
- 1 LEEK
- 1 STICK OF CELERY
- 1 BAY LEAF
- ½ CLOVE OF GARLIC (OPTIONAL)
- BLACK PEPPER
- SALT

FOR CHICKEN STOCK

Raw chicken and wings, and a very little tarragon or some thyme

FOR QUICK CHICKEN STOCK

Bones, trimmings, leavings and scrapings of 1 roast chicken

FOR BEEF STOCK

Raw beef bones, 5g tomato purée, ½ star anise (a small pinch of sugar can help bring out the flavours)

·3·

SEASON

Add primary seasonings, bearing in mind that they will strengthen in flavour if the stock is reduced. For quick chicken stock, salt may not be necessary if the roast chicken was well seasoned.

·4·

SIMMER

Bring the stock to the edge of a simmer, then immediately back off the heat so just the occasional bubble breaks the surface.

Keep at the point just short of full simmering, skimming off any floating scum that rises in the first half-hour or so. Add more cold water if the ingredients are no longer covered or if the temperature gets out of control and it begins to simmer too aggressively.

·5·

ADJUST SEASONING

Use salt and other seasonings by taste

·6·

STRAIN & CHILL

After 2–3 hours, drain the stock through a sieve and chill it.

DEFATTING

Any fat will rise to the surface and solidify in the fridge so you'll be able to lift it off.

·7·

REDUCE — or — STORE

Quick chicken stock tends to be cloudy no matter how careful you are in cooking. Because it has less gelatine content it won't set either so there's little point in reducing it. It's best used 'as is' in soups or stews. By more aggressive simmering you can reduce your stock to about half to create a thick gloopy 'glaze'. This is the best point to freeze it. Do this in ice cube trays or flat in a freezer bag so you can snap off a little whenever you need it to enrich a sauce, gravy or stew.

FORTIFY

·8·

With chicken and beef, the stock can be used as is, or fortified with a shot of Madeira.

- Vegetable and fish stocks, often known as fumets, are so delicate they don't really benefit from long cooking or reduction. Because they don't reduce much you can add aromatic herbs and even salt without fear that the flavours will concentrate and dominate. I usually make fish or veg stock as I need it, using only slightly more water than the eventual quantity I'm looking for. A bay leaf is a good addition, along with carrots, celery and a small quantity of onion. I find turnip a little assertive in fumets. Really mince the veg to release maximum flavour and use all the trimmings from your fish – skin, scales, heads and tails.

- If you spot smoked hock or smoked belly pork going cheap at your butcher's, snap it up quickly. Smoked pork stock is a tremendous standby, making a near instant soup with almost any pulse. Dried peas are my favourite, though canned white beans create something that might be considered more sophisticated.

- A less elegant but nonetheless useful stock can be made from the leftovers of a roast chicken. Break up the carcass, add any leftover bones or trimmings from the plates, plus fresh stock veg, and be sure to deglaze the roasting pan to salvage any last useful juices. It's extremely unlikely you'll be able to keep a cooked chicken stock clear, so it's less important to keep the water below the simmer. Most of the good stuff will have been extracted in an hour or so – going much further will produce a 'bony' or 'fowly' taste.

- Keep stocks clear by simmering them long and low. You can remove the fat easily by refrigerating the stock overnight and lifting off the solidified top layer the following day. If you're really hard-core, you'll store the fats and find a way to cook with them, but we can still be friends if you throw them away.

- To completely clarify a stock, freeze it solid then allow it to defrost slowly, overnight, in a colander lined with a clean linen cloth or several layers of muslin. Personally, I reckon life's too short for consommés, but just in case you ever have to, that's how it's done.

PRESSURE COOKERS

You can make stock amazingly quickly in a pressure cooker. In the time it takes to roast a chicken, for example, the giblets, trimmings, wingtips and knuckles can be reduced to a rich stock which, added to the pan juices, makes cosmic gravy. I'm told it's possible to keep stock clear in a pressure cooker but I've never quite managed it. That said, if you need it in that much of a hurry, it probably doesn't matter.

REHEATING AND RESEALING

Stock has a shelf-life of a few days when refrigerated but there's no denying it's an excellent home for bacteria. It's so convenient to have liquid stock ready to be spooned into anything that it seems worth the effort of bringing it back up to the boil every 2 or 3 days to ensure it stays healthy. Keeping the fat layer means that every time the stock is reheated it forms an airtight cap.

USING STOCK

- When grilling or pan-frying anything, deglaze the pan with a little wine then add a small quantity of stock and season. Enriched pan juices are the most appropriate sauce for almost anything.

- If parboiling potatoes for roasting or frying, add stock to the water. The flavour added is subtle but astonishingly good.

- Most vegetables, for example potatoes, alliums, peas, tomatoes and all manner of roots and squashes – whatever happens to be cheap or in season – can be poached in stock and water and then blitzed into a fantastic soup.

- In stews, casseroles or any other dish that cooks slowly in a liquid, consider using stock in place of plain water.

PHO

Pho is street food, a Vietnamese noodle soup so simple, so deliciously comforting and so flat-out addictive that Anthony Bourdain once said, 'I would jerk a rusty butterknife across my best friend's throat for this.' I learned to make pho from Uyen Luu, whose family fled Vietnam in the 80s and settled in Hackney. She's a filmmaker who blogs about and teaches Vietnamese cooking. This is an adaptation, but I never cook it without remembering its importance to her family and her.

½ an oxtail, chopped into chunks ★ 3 beef ribs ★ 1 litre clear chicken stock ★ 1 spice bag (10g each of fennel seed, coriander seed, black peppercorns, plus 1 piece of cassia bark or cinnamon stick, all tied in muslin) ★ 100g mooli, peeled and quartered ★ 2 onions, peeled ★ 2 thumb-sized nubs of ginger root, peeled ★ 15g star anise ★ 30g rock sugar ★ 'Three Crabs' fish sauce (nuoc mam)

To serve
1 x 500g pack of dried medium flat rice noodles ★ 100g beef fillet ★ 6 spring onions, thinly sliced ★ a large bunch of fresh coriander ★ a bunch of fresh mint ★ a bunch of Thai basil ★ a bunch of Thai parsley (if you can get it) ★ 2 shallots, thinly sliced ★ 2 hot red chillies, thinly sliced ★ Sriracha chilli sauce ★ fresh limes

1. Fill a large pot with water, bring to the boil and drop in the pieces of oxtail and rib. Allow to simmer for 5 minutes and then drain the meat (discard the water) and wash it in cold water. This will prevent the stock becoming cloudy.

2. Put the meat back into the clean pot, add the chicken stock and top up with 2 litres of cold water. Bring back to just below the boil and allow to simmer extremely gently. The surface of the stock should shimmer rather than bubble. Add the spice bag and the mooli.

3. Heat up a griddle and, without adding oil, scorch and burn the surfaces of the onions and ginger pieces. Once you've achieved charred black patches, drop them into the stock and then scorch the star anise pods and add them too. Add a couple of big lumps of rock sugar.

4. Now comes the interesting bit. Simmer for at least 3 hours, skimming regularly and tasting constantly. You can add more rock sugar for sweetness, spoon out the star anise if they become too predominant for your taste, and begin adding salt. Stop short with the salt though, and instead add the vital fish sauce in great healthy splashes once the stock is beginning to taste near ideal and you've removed it from the heat. The stock will be usable after an hour or so but will be better if allowed to simmer for as long as possible with constant adjustment. The gelatine will begin to cook out of the oxtail, adding a sublime velvet texture to the liquid.

5. To serve: blanch your noodles in hot water until they're soft and place them in the bottom of deep bowls. Cut the fillet steak into transparently thin slices and drape them over the noodles with a handful of chopped spring onions and fresh coriander. Pour over the hot stock, which will cook the fillet, and add a few juicy pieces of the stock meat. At the table, each diner should have chopsticks, a large spoon and free run of the trimmings and sauces. Tear up the mint, Thai basil, the rest of the coriander and the Thai parsley and scatter over the soup. Add the shallots, chillies and chilli sauce to taste and squeeze in the lime juice.

-DIY-
TAKE AWAY

CHAPTER TEN

I love junk food as much as the next person. There's nothing quite as satisfying as a filthy burger, chicken-in-a-bucket or a late-night kebab (occasionally and in moderation, apparently). But why on earth would you bother to DIY junk food when it's just five minutes away in the car or comes delivered to your door?

Have you ever wondered how we ended up with the fast-food options we have? It's certainly not because they taste awful...it's usually because they are simple things to make delicious out of the cheapest of ingredients, because they are full of big fat flavours that please the maximum number of people and offend the least and because they're almost impossible to mess up. Recreating some of these favourites isn't just fun, doesn't just give us something amusingly ironic to serve to our mates, but it helps us understand what's good and bad about 'junk' food.

FRIED CHICKEN

Woody Allen once opined that sex is like pizza – even when it's rubbish it's pretty damn good. I feel the same way about fried chicken. The truth is, it would take effort and skill to screw up succulent chicken meat, dredged in seasoned flour and cooked in boiling fat. Like many other food lovers I have a problem with the moral implications of KFC's chicken meat, but I can't, with my hand on my (rapidly congesting) heart, say it doesn't taste pretty good when fresh from the bucket.

But I'm lucky enough to also have sampled the real thing. I lived for several years in rural North Carolina and married a local girl. The reception was held on a hot summer evening, on the banks of a sleepy river on the family farm, and was a pot-luck affair. In the course of the evening a couple of hundred people turned up, most carrying trays covered in a cloth and containing a personal variation on fried chicken.

Your personal 'secret recipe' for fried chicken is a pretty serious business in the South, and a newbie outsider like me could be forgiven for believing that all those family reunions, church picnics, barbecues and tailgate parties were just a front for a bitterly fought and endless competition to produce better and better fried chicken. I personally reckon the world would be a much better place if we all got together every now and again in a 'healthy' competition over fried chicken. It sublimates family tensions, draws communities together and generally makes it socially acceptable to eat like a starved weasel in the name of politeness.

Commercial fried chicken is a completely different beast. It varies hugely from the homemade product in three important ways. First, the quality of the meat used. Fast-food fried chicken companies have never really made any attempt to suggest that they use anything other than intensively reared birds. It wouldn't be possible to keep prices so low if they didn't. Bucket chicken, though, doesn't really depend on the quality of the meat.

The proprietary cooking methods originated by Colonel Harland Saunders and seemingly ripped off by thousands of imitators around the world require a 'secret' blend of herbs and spices for the coating flour and special deep-fat fryers which operate under pressure.

It's difficult to see quite what pressure adds to the frying arrangement, but I've a horrible feeling it might have something to do with the devastatingly moreish oily texture of the meat once it's been through the process.

There have been several attempts to replicate the Colonel's mixture and most have been reasonably successful. What's most noticeable is that, as you'd expect from an evolved fast food, no single polarizing flavour predominates.

The combined hit of chicken, fat and flavour in commercial fried chicken is disorientatingly powerful. It's the sort of comprehensive sensory seeing-to that's both best and worst about drink, drugs and sex. So very good and so very bad. No wonder teenagers live on this stuff. But trying to apply any kind of critical approach to the flavour is surprisingly hard. You can't decode that famous mixture of '11 secret herbs and spices' for a very good reason, because you can't distinguish any particular flavours amid the assault.

My version may seem complicated and random but, like the original, it combines the piquant spices which provide a high note, the woody, oily herbs that create the mid-range, and the MSG that supplies the stonking bass-line. Like the original, it's overdone and lacking in subtlety. Like the original, it approaches the divine.

Cooking from scratch enables us to do things that the Colonel can't: use great chicken, drain the grease more efficiently, achieve texture through an elegant poaching rather than pressure-frying.

A single bite of homemade fried chicken is enough. It's like biting into a dew-fresh ripe peach after eating a canned one. It's obviously the same thing but an order of magnitude better. As in the secret recipe, none of the flavours predominate enough to be identifiable but, having made up the mix from scratch, we now know the secret. Secret herbs and spices be damned: that staggering, mouth-filling, umami facepunch of a flavour is down to the 15g of MSG.

(If you're worried about your MSG intake in this recipe, consider that it's mixed with the flour. The percentage of the main dose you consume will be similar to the percentage of the 200g of mixed flour coating that adheres to each piece.)

For the seasoning mix
5g English mustard powder ✻ 5g celery seed ✻ 5g dried onion flakes ✻ 5g dried oregano ✻ 5g chilli powder ✻ 5g dried sage ✻ 5g dried basil ✻ 5g garlic powder ✻ 5g ground black pepper ✻ 5g salt (optional) ✻ 5g sugar (optional) ✻ or: 15g MSG (optional)

For the chicken
8 pieces free-range skin-on chicken drumsticks and thighs ✻ 1 litre milk ✻ 250g plain flour ✻ 1.5 litres vegetable oil

1. Marinate the chicken pieces overnight in milk in a covered bowl.

2. Put the chicken pieces and their marinade into a pan and simmer for 20 minutes, turning the pieces occasionally to cook evenly. Allow to cool in the marinade for 1 hour.

3. Take 200g of the cooled marinade for dipping. (The rest makes a superb cream of chicken soup if slightly thickened with a roux.)

4. Blitz all the seasoning ingredients together and combine thoroughly with the flour. If you're not using MSG, use salt and sugar instead. Pour into a shallow tray for dipping.

5. Remove the chicken pieces from the milk and roll them straight in the flour all over. Leave them to stand for a minute, then dip them in the milk and roll them again in the flour.

6. Pour the oil into a large saucepan and heat to 180°C. Deep-fry the chicken in two or three batches, testing the temperature in between batches to make sure the oil is still at 180°C. Drain on kitchen paper and serve.

MSG

It was long believed that the human palate could only distinguish four separate tastes: sweet, sour, bitter and salt. (Tastes are sensations that take place solely in the mouth, while flavour is a combination of taste and olfactory sensation.) In 1908 Professor Kikunae Ikeda of Tokyo posited a fifth taste which he called 'umami' – Japanese for 'delicious' or 'savoury'. Most importantly, umami was found to improve or enhance the tastes and flavours of other ingredients.

This new taste was present in several common Eastern ingredients – soy sauce, nam pla fish sauce, dried shrimp, dried seaweed – and Ikeda was able to isolate the compound that created it: monosodium glutamate. Ikeda's company still extracts the naturally occurring compound from seaweed and it is sold as Aji-no-moto in Japan and Accent in the US. In the UK it's sold as 'flavour enhancer' or as the main ingredient in proprietary 'steak flavouring' or 'chicken seasoning'. We're a little more coy about MSG in the UK than in other countries, so the best thing is to take a good hard look at the ingredients list.

Many of us use MSG's qualities without realizing it. Western ingredients with an umami taste and a glutamate content are less common but include some varieties of mushroom, anchovies and, of course, Parmesan cheese. We also use ketchups and sauces which feature it in large dosages, stock cubes, in which it's a major constituent, and it's in most varieties of 'cook-in' sauce.

Is this a good or bad thing?

There's been very little science that indicates that MSG is harmful in any way – though a very few people have a genuine allergy to it. In commercial food production it's one of the things that enables manufacturers to reduce both salt and fat content in a recipe while still keeping it delicious.

There's a long-standing myth that food served in Chinese restaurants contains so much MSG that it creates symptoms ranging from headache to blackouts. This is palpable, borderline racist rubbish that was put conclusively to rest in one of my favourite pieces of food writing by the incomparable Jeffrey Steingarten. It's in his book *It Must Have Been Something I Ate*, an essay that almost doesn't need its 1,000-plus elegant words of brilliantly incisive argument, because the title does all the work: 'Why Doesn't Everyone in China Have a Headache?'

DUCK TALES

I spent a couple of very happy years living in San Francisco. It was back in the days before the dotcom boom, when the wealthy lived out in the fashionable suburbs and only skanky restaurant people lived downtown. My flat overlooked Chinatown from the top of a hill and every morning I'd watch men come out on to the roofs of their restaurant buildings, take the ducks from the little wooden sheds in which they hung, dip them in a big barrel of glaze, then replace them on their hooks where the heat of the day and the salt breeze off the Pacific would dry them.

I promised myself that one day I'd glaze and dry my own duck, though at the time I imagined I'd be doing it on my own balcony overlooking the ocean.

Things rarely turn out the way you imagine them at twenty-three.

DUCK HISTORY

The Chinese have naturally been roasting ducks for centuries, but, like many set-piece specialities, the recipe only really became set in stone with the arrival of restaurants for international travellers in the mid nineteenth century. Large-scale banquet dining is an important part of Chinese culture, and Peking duck, with its long preparation and rituals of service, is a popular course at a big celebratory meal. Most British fans of Chinese food are used to 'crispy fried duck', where the spiced and slow-roasted meat is shredded and served with pancakes, spring onions, cucumber and hoisin sauce. Though the meat of the Peking duck is eaten with the same trimmings, the skin is served separately as a first course with a dipping sauce and the carcass is used to make a broth to be served with rice towards the end of the meal.

After glazing, the ducks were originally roasted by dangling them in a pot oven, not unlike a tandoor or beanhole, after the main fuel of aromatic wood had burned out, leaving a slow residual heat and the merest hint of fragrant smoke.

If you want to replicate this effect, take a look at the chapters on cold-smoking and beanhole cooking (see pages 141 and 231).

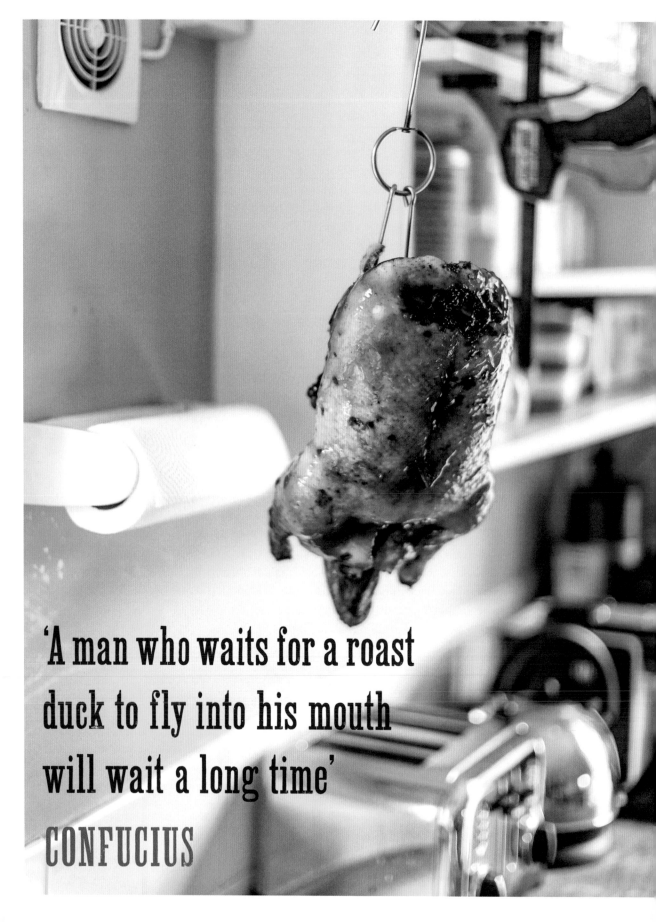

'A man who waits for a roast duck to fly into his mouth will wait a long time'

CONFUCIUS

PEKING DUCK

From a Chinese grocery, pick up a duck-hanging hook if you can find one. It's just a couple of light butcher's hooks attached to a metal ring and a handle – you can knock one up yourself out of a coathanger in two minutes, but the real thing is cheap, authentic and makes the job a whole lot easier. While you're there, pick up a jar of 'maltose'. This is a basic syrup of malt sugar, a common ingredient in Chinese cooking. It caramelizes beautifully but is less sweet than either regular sugar syrup or honey.

Thread the duck on to the hook, then lower it into a large pot of boiling water acidulated with 100g or so of vinegar and leave for 5 minutes.

Remove the duck from the boiling water, pat it dry, then season the inside of the cavity with a mixture of salt, dried mandarin peel, star anise, Szechuan peppercorns, fennel seed, cinnamon and cloves, finely ground in a pestle and mortar (commercial 'five-spice' mix will be fine if your spice cupboard is limited). Use a wooden skewer to stitch the lower vent closed, then insert a clean bicycle pump under the skin and pump it until it's loosened all over.

Hang the duck up to dry. If you don't have a flat roof with a reliable sea breeze and a small wooden hut, you're going to need something a little more practical for home use.

Find a large, strong corrugated cardboard box and stand it on end so the lids open like cupboard doors. Cut a 3cm hole in the top and lay a garden cane or a chopstick across it. This will let you hang the duck inside and form a drying cabinet. An oven dish or roasting tin forms a good drip tray.

Use a desk fan to create a breeze around your duck or, to speed things up, play over it with a hairdryer. A little heat may speed things up, but don't use so much that the fat begins to liquify and run. A greasy bird is much more difficult to handle and we need the skin papery dry if the glaze is to adhere properly.

Make up a mix of 100g of maltose, 50g of vinegar and 500g of boiling water. Paint it on to the dry skin of the duck and then dry again.

Repeat the painting and drying cycle as many times as you can over a 24-hour period, until the skin has built up a good glaze and has a parchment-like texture.

Finally, place the duck on a cooling rack over an oven dish of boiling water and roast slowly (around 160°C) until done (this depends on the size of your duck). In the last 15 minutes of cooking, whack the heat up to caramelize and crisp up the skin.

Break up the duck, tearing the flesh from the bones and piling it prettily on a serving platter. Serve with steamed Chinese pancakes, slivered spring onions and cucumber sliced into shards, with a small dish of hoisin dipping sauce.

DONER KEBAB

DIY DONER

It would be really easy to dismiss the doner kebab with a series of well-worn gags about food poisoning, 'elephant's leg' and a long string of drinking anecdotes. To be fair, the great cylinder of mystery meat, rotating in the late-night snack bar, may well conceal all the elements of a nutritional horror story, but then that's probably a logical market forces response to an audience who are too drunk to discern and too broke to pay more than £2.50 for emergency nourishment.

In fact, the doner is assembled from cheap but flavourful offcuts of lamb (usually halal), minced to the point of emulsification with a little seasoning and some cereal binder. Lamb is a naturally pretty healthy meat – grass-fed, impossible to battery-farm – and the same process of chilled fine-grinding is also used to make mortadella, saveloy, kosher salami, frankfurter and the less artisanal supermarket breakfast sausages.

Slices from a giant, hot, free-range lamb meatloaf with fresh salad, in a hot pitta. Hell, that's a sustainable health food. If we can find a way to rescue and repackage it, then the dodgy doner takes meat wasted in the trimming of a decent-quality meat and turns it into the kind of thing your personal trainer would implore you to snack on. It doesn't get much better than this – I can feel a halo forming above my head as I think of it. If you have any remaining doubts about the doner, our own St Elizabeth David took broadly the same ingredients – lamb breast, breadcrumbs and flavourings – and used them to make the legendary 'Lamb Ste Ménéhould'. Funnily enough, nobody ever associated her with strong continental lager, fighting on the night bus or weeing against lampposts.

Lamb breast is an often neglected cheap cut. It comes as a thin sheet formed of interleaved layers of muscle and fat and is usually served rolled and stuffed with a breadcrumb mixture. Cut 500g of it into 2cm squares and chill them in the fridge before passing once through a mincer, using a coarse plate.

The whole of this process should be carried out at as low a temperature as possible so the fat in the lamb doesn't get a chance to melt before it's emulsified. In commercial preparation, the butcher would probably add a little transglutaminase, known as 'meat glue', which is a blood extract that does exactly what it says on the tin. Meat glue means the ingredients will hold together without you having to be so careful about the emulsification. It's harmless, present in many prepared foods and ready meals, but it doesn't appear on the shelves of your local supermarket so let's press on with the Old School method.

Add around 100g of stale breadcrumbs, 7.5g of salt, a good grind of black pepper and a medium onion, coarsely grated. Mix thoroughly, using a rubber spatula, and place back in the fridge to chill down again.

Add 2.5g each of ground cumin and coriander seed and a couple of cloves of grated garlic, then mince the chilled ingredients again through the finest plate, which should render a smooth, meaty pâté. In making something like a hamburger you want to keep the mixture loose, to allow a good texture when cooked; with doner meat we're looking for as near a homogeneous slab of flavoured protein as possible, so you can't overwork it – as long as the whole thing remains as cold as possible so the fat can't soften and escape.

You could cook the meat in a regular terrine dish, but bear with me here. Honestly, it's worth it.

Clean a big, empty food tin – mine used to contain about half a kilo of puréed spinach – and line with two layers of clingfilm. Be careful of the edge, it's lethal. Work the chilled mixture quickly, podging it through your fingers until it looks homogeneous, then form it into fat burger shapes that will just fit into the tin. In the real thing, discs of the paste are piled on to a skewer, which gives the shape and a slight horizontal grain structure. We'll try to keep to that idea. Pack the pucks into the tin and then close the clingfilm tightly to seal the top.

Place the tin in the bottom of a big casserole and fill with boiling water to about half its depth. Put into a medium oven, around 150°C, and cook until the internal temperature reaches 75°C – mine took around an hour and a half. Then turn the oven off and leave for 15 minutes while you prepare a salad mix, like a dry coleslaw, heavy on the white cabbage, dressed with lemon.

Turn out and unwrap your mini-elephant leg and trim the bottom so it will stand on end on an oven tray or metal plate.

To serve, play a blowlamp over the surface of the meat and then slice vertically, stabilizing the cylinder with a carving fork if necessary.

If you've ever spent a night on the lash, the rest of the assembly process will come back to you through the haze the minute you see the chilli sauce, the tahini, the yoghurt and the freshly toasted pitta. If it doesn't . . . drink more.

If you have any doubts about the doner, our own St Elizabeth David took broadly the same ingredients and used them to make the legendary 'Lamb Ste Ménéhould'. And nobody ever associated her with strong continental lager or fighting on the night bus.

COFFEE SHOP

There's an enormous amount of arcane mystery in coffee-roasting. If you chat to the bloke with the piercings behind the counter at your local coffee shop you could be forgiven for thinking that it was somewhere between programming a supercomputer and launching a space shuttle.

Truth is, people all over the world have been roasting coffee adequately with little more than a heat source and a container since the bean was first discovered.

The big, shiny, computer-controlled roaster at your local CostaBucks has but three main elements. A source of dry heated air, a mechanical means of agitating the beans while roasting, and a cooling system. Everything else is an optional accessory.

A professional roaster follows the process by using all his senses to read exactly what happens to the heated bean so that he can intervene at just the right point.

The method outlined here isn't likely to become part of your breakfast routine but, with a minimal investment in equipment, you'll be able to watch the process close up and understand how it affects your final brew. You'll probably end up with something tastier than the warm coffee-flavoured milkshake you'd get in a big chain and, best of all, you'll be able to astonish the barista with your superior geekery.

You'll need a heat gun. These are available online or from hardware stores and are usually used for paint stripping. (I've just spotted a 2000w model online for £12 with a two-minute search.) The vessel for agitating the beans will be a wok – powered by you – and the cooling device a sieve or colander and a wooden spoon.

(You can do this directly over the heat of the stove but it's less controllable than the heat gun.)

You should be able to buy green beans from any independent who roast their own, or there are several suppliers of hobbyist quantities online (see pages 370–71).

Lay out all the equipment on a single worktop so you can get to everything quickly when things get real in the wok. Pour in enough green beans to form a layer about four beans deep, then start playing the heat gun over them with one hand while swirling the wok with the other.

Stage 1: Yellowing

After a few minutes you'll notice a smell a little like new-mown grass and the beans will begin to shift colour from green to yellow.

Stage 2: Steaming

Moisture inside the beans is being driven off wherever it is able to escape. This can be seen as steam.

Stage 3: First crack

Not all the steam can escape, though, and, as the oil in the beans begins to heat and the steam expands further, it bursts free with tiny explosions. Listen for the 'crack'.

Stage 4: First roast

At this point the bean has been roasted. There's a little caramelization of sugars, moisture has been given off and oils have been freed. The bean is ready to give up its flavours into hot water as soon as it's been ground. Most of the flavours liberated are directly attributable to the original bean and its treatment at harvest.

Stage 5: Caramelization

The remaining stages use the effects of heat to alter some flavours, to concentrate others and to introduce combustion products into the mix as things begin to 'burn'. Caramelization is effectively the burning of sugars. It can create richness and depth of flavour, though at the expense of sweetness. The caramelization phase can be stopped at any time, depending on the depth of roast you favour. For many, the trick is to go as far as they can in caramelization before...

Stage 6: Second crack

A secondary bout of explosive releases inside the bean creates more audible cracking. By now almost none of the original character of the bean will be evident – everything you can taste will be a result of the roast.

Beware that at this point the beans may be jumping about a bit, as the explosions can be vigorous.

Stage 7: Darkening roast

This is the dark, smoky, 'French' roast in which all sugars are burned, producing a strong, pungent flavour.

In a professional roasting machine the beans are pulled the instant they hit the point the roaster is looking for, and the process is halted as fast as possible. The beans pour into a flat tray through which cold air is forced, while a mechanical paddle ensures each bean is cooled equally quickly.

Time for the sieve or colander and spoon.

As soon as your experimental batch reaches the stage you want, pour it straight into the sieve or colander and begin stirring. Some heat guns allow you to switch off the elements and blow cold air, in which case you can continue blowing with one hand and tossing the colander with the other.

As soon as the beans are cool, run them between your hands to remove as much chaff as possible.

The flavours in the roasted bean continue to develop for a while before they then deteriorate, so most roasters recommend resting the beans for 24 hours before grinding and tasting.

A good roastery will work with blends of roasted beans to create the best cup of coffee they can. Now you understand the process, your next exercise is to imagine all the different ways a less scrupulous roaster works with both ingredients and process to make coffee more cheaply.

COFFEE ICE CREAM

75g roasted coffee beans ★ **500g whole milk** ★ **6 egg yolks** ★ **75g caster sugar** ★ **300g double cream**

1. Crush up some of your coffee beans in a pestle and mortar or with the end of a rolling pin. Put them in a pan with the milk, raise the temperature to just short of boiling, then cool, cover and refrigerate overnight. This will extract all the smooth, aromatic elements of the coffee without any of the bitterness.

2. Strain the milk through a sieve lined with a clean piece of J-cloth or muslin.

3. Make a double boiler with a mixing bowl over a pan of simmering water and in it, whisk together the egg yolks and sugar until pale and thickened. Now pour in the infused milk and keep whisking until you have a custard thick enough to coat the back of a spoon.

4. Pass the custard through a sieve, mix well with the cream, then chill well. Pour into an ice cream maker and churn until set.

This is quite a grown-up ice cream, low on sugar and high in coffee flavours. It works well in small servings, unadorned, or, for a really quite perky finish to a long meal, try it affogato style with a single shot of espresso poured over the top.

DAIRY & CHEESE

CHAPTER ELEVEN

Milk is the first food we eat. The ideal form of nourishment for us mammals, bound up in the ideal natural, on-demand delivery system – in fact milk was never designed to be kept at all. In spite of that, man has tirelessly invented ways of turning milk into butters, cheeses, yoghurts and thousands of strange regional dairy products. What's odd about these processes is that most of them seem to have begun as accidents, occasions when lovely fresh milk was mishandled, kept too long or somehow adulterated and, as a result, turned into something more interesting.

Over the centuries, methods of cheese-making have evolved in very particular ways. Simple cheeses can be infected with certain moulds to give them veining and complex flavours. They can be pressed, cooked, aged; their rinds can be encouraged, developed, washed, and in each case a new and more special flavour will develop.

A while ago I was invited to a farm that produced artisanal Beaufort, a washed-rind cheese made in the Haute-Savoie region of France. The cheese was made and aged in a vast barn built on to the side of a mountain. At the top of the barn was stored the winter fodder – a fragrant hay called 'sainfoin'. The next floor down contained the milking parlour – an admirably clean and modern set-up – at the end of which was an open door over a large mound of the dung, mucked out of the parlour. The smell was not unpleasant, just a rich, slightly poopy concentration of the sainfoin above. Finally I walked into the cheese-making and ageing rooms, where the racks of gorgeous, ripe, soft-rinded Beauforts smelled of . . . yes, sainfoin and cowpat.

The truth about cheese is that the cultures that develop their flavours are a product of the microbiological ecology in which they are aged. For the DIY-er, then, many of these cheeses will be out of reach. Without an ancient cave under a monastery we'll simply never make Camembert, without a gigantic pile of cowdung and a mountain full of sainfoin, we won't make Beaufort, but that shouldn't stop us experimenting, and by taking the first steps towards cheese-making we can create some delicious things.

Whole milk is treated in various ways to extend its shelf-life and make it a more desirable product commercially:

A. Pasteurization: Milk is raised in temperature and held there for a fixed time before re-chilling. This kills any bacteria in the milk.

B. UHT: Ultra Heat Treating is a little like a faster, harsher version of pasteurization which partially denatures some of the proteins in the milk and makes it stable and long-lasting at room temperature. It also changes some of the natural sugars in the milk, giving it its characteristic sweet taste.

C. Homogenization: The milk is forced through a grid of tiny holes, ensuring that the fat globules stay small and don't cling together to form any cream or lumps. Homogenized milk will not separate.

D. Skimming: Fat solids are lifted off the milk as cream, leaving a lower-fat final product.

Milk is a suspension of butterfat in a solution of carbohydrates and proteins. Like most suspensions in the food world, it's prone to splitting. Left to stand, the butterfat in fresh milk will float to the surface, from where it can be scraped or lifted off. This light cream can be slow-cooked in large flat pans to drive off more moisture, which produces clotted cream. Devon and Jersey cows produce a milk naturally high in creamy solids, which explains why we associate clotted cream with those regions.

Ferociously agitating milk causes the suspended particles of butterfat to knock together and form globules and clumps of butter. In commercial churning this is done in vast tanks with motorized beaters, though you can achieve the same effect with a small child and a jam jar.

Making butter manually is a great experiment to try with kids. Just put some room-temperature double cream into a jar and get them to shake it hard. Then shake it some more. Then, assuming that their attention span can take it . . . just a little longer. At some point, little golden grains of butter will begin to form, which you can strain out, wash, salt a little and spread on toast.

Child labour laws being what they are, this is not an experiment you're likely to repeat too many times, so you can also make quite useful quantities of butter using an electric mixer as a churn.

MAKING BUTTER

A big 2 litre jug of double cream will make nearly a kilo of butter, so, once it's reached room temperature, pour it into the mixer bowl and start beating. It will go through the usual stages of forming stiff peaks and then, quite suddenly, it'll be over-beaten and split. Big lumps of butter will begin to form, at which point you can strain everything through clean muslin in a sieve.

Save the liquid. This is buttermilk, a naturally acidic product which makes a terrific baking ingredient. Particularly when used with bicarb, it can give an excellent rise to things like scones, soda bread and pancakes.

The butter solids will need to be rinsed, repeatedly and carefully, in cold water, to remove the last of the buttermilk (that acidity would cause the butter to ferment – known as 'going rancid') and should be lightly salted to increase the butter's storage life.

Finally, shape it into pats with your fingers (keep your hands cold while you do it by regularly dunking them in cold water) and refrigerate.

CLARIFIED BUTTER (FOR COOKING OR POTTING)

When melted, butter separates, with the oily elements floating clear on the surface. Pure or 'clarified' butter fat has a much longer shelf-life than ordinary butter (it can remain good for months without refrigeration if kept airtight), so it's an excellent medium for potting or sealing food for preservation.

To clarify butter, put a whole pat into a small saucepan and place it somewhere on the top of your stove, where it will gently liquify without boiling up – too much heat will cause the creamy parts to fry and blacken, giving a bitter taste. Once the butter has separated into a clear yellow layer, floating on milk, put the whole saucepan into the fridge and leave it overnight to set.

In the morning, lever out the solid lump of butter – you can put it into a colander if it breaks up – drain off the milky liquid and wash off any remaining white, creamy deposits with cold water. Pat the lumps dry with kitchen paper and then put them back into the clean, dried pan and melt them gently again before using or storing in a sealed jar in the fridge.

You can buy clarified butter as 'ghee' in shops selling South Asian goods.

COMPOUND BUTTERS

Compound butters are an old-fashioned hangover of the professional kitchen. Unused fresh herbs or garlic that would otherwise dry up and be thrown out can be minced finely and mashed into unsalted butter.

Roll the flavoured butter into log shapes, a couple of centimetres thick, wrap them like a Christmas cracker in greaseproof paper and freeze them.

Café de Paris butter sounds like one of those lovely Edwardian, Escoffian standbys redolent of the gentleman's club, like devilling or rissoles. It probably has more recent and less glamorous roots but I prefer to stick with my romantic prejudices. It's also the only compound butter that really requires a recipe. It's usually prescribed for grilled steak but it works equally brilliantly on a surprising number of things . . . poached eggs on toast by no means least.

CAFÉ DE PARIS BUTTER

25g tomato ketchup ★ 25g fresh parsley ★ 25g fresh chives ★ 15g Dijon mustard ★ 15g capers ★ 5g Madeira ★ 10g salt ★ 5g fresh thyme ★ 5g fresh tarragon ★ 5g paprika ★ a pinch of dried marjoram ★ 6 anchovy fillets ★ 2 cloves of garlic ★ 1 sploosh of Worcestershire sauce ★ 1 sploosh of Tabasco sauce ★ 8 white peppercorns ★ zest of 1 lemon ★ 5g lemon juice ★ 500g unsalted butter, at room temperature

1. Purée all the ingredients except the butter, using a grinder or stick blender.

2. With the butter at room temperature, work the purée through it with a fork or wooden spoon until smoothly incorporated.

3. Allow to stand in the refrigerator for 3 days for the flavours to properly combine before forming into logs and freezing.

HERB BUTTER

Simple herb butters are easy to store in the freezer and are a good way of using up any fresh herbs you have left over. Pound the herbs in a pestle and mortar and combine thoroughly with softened butter before forming into pats and freezing. Remember to label them carefully, as thyme, tarragon, basil, sage, parsley, dill and sorrel butters can be all but indistinguishable. Use a big kitchen knife to chop chunks off the frozen pats of butter and whip straight into sauces or dab on to grilling meat.

Garlic butter, prepared similarly, is a good freezer standby, as are lemon or lime butters.

A few anchovies, mashed with a fork into softened butter, don't just enliven grilled lamb but can transform breakfast toast into a sophisticated retro savoury.

USING RENNET

As well as physical separation by churning, milk can be split into solids and liquids by several other means. Raising the acidity of milk causes it to 'curdle', so adding, for example, lemon juice will cause the butterfat to form into rubbery lumps almost immediately. This material can be used as the base of some cheeses. If left long enough, milk will also begin to ferment, raising its own acidity which also causes it to split – the kind of thing we see if we leave milk in the fridge too long past its sell-by date.

By far the most efficient way of separating milk, though, is the most natural: the use of rennet, an enzyme complex that occurs in the stomach linings of calves. Rennet is added to warm milk and rapidly sets the fatty material into 'curds', leaving behind a liquid 'whey'.

Rennet comes in liquid or tablet form, usually from health food shops or the bakery section of the supermarket.

The fresh set curds still contain a lot of moisture but taste of creamy fresh milk, so they make an excellent dessert, particularly with the addition of a simple sweetening or flavouring.

To further preserve the curds as cheese, they need to be drained of more liquid and salted.

Hanging the curds in a cheesecloth overnight creates the easiest and freshest farmhouse white cheese, which can be either used as a cooking ingredient or salted and flavoured for use at the table.

JUNKET WITH PORT JELLY

400g whole milk ✱ **15g caster sugar** ✱ **5g rennet** ✱ **2 sheets of gelatine** ✱ **200g port (Marsala also works well)**

1. Warm the milk to 32°C and stir in the sugar.

2. The quantity of rennet may vary depending on the brand and whether or not it's a vegetarian version; 5g of the liquid rennet I use is sufficient, but you'll find recommended amounts on the package. Pour it into the warm sweetened milk and stir it quickly but thoroughly. It will begin to set very quickly, so have your serving dishes standing by and ladle it in as fast as possible.

3. The junket should set fully after an hour in the fridge.

4. Soak the gelatine sheets in cold water. The standard domestic stuff I use (around 160 Bloom[37]) will take 2 sheets to set 150g of liquid to a good stiff jelly. Check your own packet, as brands differ.

5. Simmer the port gently in a pan so some of the alcohol boils off and it's reduced by about 25%, then take off the heat and allow to cool a little.

6. Squeeze out the gelatine sheets, which by now will be puffed up and soft, and stir them into the warm concentrated port.

7. The jelly will set as it cools, so you can pour it in a layer over the junket, or set it separately in a shallow tray or on a dinner plate in the fridge, then chop it into fine dice which you can sprinkle over the surface.

---

37 'Bloom' is the standard measurement of gelling strength in gelatine. It's usually given on the packet.

CURD TART

1.5 litre whole milk ★ 25g rennet ★ 125g plain flour, plus extra to dust ★ 160g cold unsalted butter ★ salt ★ 50g cold water ★ 50g caster sugar ★ 2 free-range eggs ★ 3g nutmeg, plus extra for dusting ★ 20g fresh white breadcrumbs

1. Use the milk and rennet to make curds as described page 359. Drain overnight in a muslin-lined sieve.

2. Put the flour, 60g of butter and a pinch of salt into a bowl and begin cutting it together using a spatula or butter knife. Once it's reduced to a lumpy mess, begin rubbing the butter in with your fingertips until it achieves the consistency of coarse sand. Try to keep everything cool, and work quickly.

3. Add enough water, a splash at a time, to bring everything together into a single mass using a knife or spatula. As soon as the dough coheres into a single ball, wrap it in clingfilm and get it back into the fridge to rest and cool for anything up to 20 minutes.

4. Preheat the oven to 170°C and place a baking tray on a central rack. Grease a 20cm tart tin. I like the fluted, loose-bottom jobs but 'other types are available'. Roll the dough on a floured work surface into a circle larger than the tin, lay it over the top and gently ease it down inside. Opinions vary on this, but I leave the spare hanging over the edges when I blind bake and trim it when it's hot out of the oven. Prick the base all over with a fork and put it back into the fridge for another quarter of an hour to firm up.

5. Line the dish with crumpled baking paper, pour in your favourite baking beans/beads and bake in the oven for 15–20 minutes, or until it's golden brown. You can, if you wish, lift the beans out and bake for another 5 minutes to ensure the base browns nicely. Remove, trim the edges of the pastry and allow to cool.

6. Cream the remaining 100g of softened butter with the sugar until pale and light, then gradually beat in the eggs, nutmeg and a pinch of salt. Finally, loosely mix in the breadcrumbs and the drained curds.

7. Pour the lumpy mixture into the cooled case and bake for 30–40 minutes, or until the internal temperature of the custard reaches 70°C and the custard is just set.

8. This is best served warm, with a further light dusting of freshly grated nutmeg.

'WHITE' OR 'FARMHOUSE' CHEESE

Gently warm a couple of litres of full-cream milk to 'blood heat' (around 38°C) and pour into a clean wide bowl. Quantities of rennet recommended can vary according to the brand you're using, so check the packaging, but it's usually around 10g per litre of milk. Stir the rennet in quickly, using a whisk to distribute it completely through the milk, then cover with a clean tea towel and leave to stand for a couple of hours at room temperature.

Test the set of the curds by dragging your finger across the surface. If it's properly set it will 'split' as you pull.

Use a knife to slice into the curds in parallel lines 1cm apart, then do it again at 90 degrees to the first cut. This increases the surface area of the curds to improve drainage.

Finally, pour the cut curds into a clean piece of muslin. Tie up the corners and hang it in the fridge to drain, at least overnight.

The set curds of white cheese are pretty bland by themselves. They work well to add creaminess to some sweet things (excellent with rum-soaked raisins beaten in and served rolled in a hot pancake), or they can be salted – just sprinkle some over the surface and work it in with a fork.

Some cheese-makers, including big commercial ones, make this quick, cheap cheese into a far more delicious product by moulding it into log shapes and rolling it in flavourings which combine brilliantly with the bland cheese when spread. Use a sushi mat lined with clingfilm to help with the rolling, and coat in chopped chives, nuts or fresh herbs and grated garlic, smoked paprika or crushed peppercorns.

PRESSING CHEESE AND BRINING

The more water that can be extracted, the better the cheese will last, so some mechanical methods can be introduced. In mozzarella-making, the curds are heated, kneaded and stretched, whereas in something as simple as a Cheddar, the curds are placed in a press and the moisture is driven out with pressure.

A dried block of drained curds is the basic material of all the great cheeses. It can be simply preserved in brine, like feta, or aged under a variety of conditions.

Line your cheese-press (see suppliers list on pages 370–71) with muslin and shovel in salted curds. Wrap the muslin tightly over the top and apply weight or pressure with the clamp.

If you don't have a cheese press, you can pack the curds in a similar way into a potato ricer and use elastic bands to apply a constant pressure to the handles.

Allow the press to do its work overnight, and save all the whey that's extracted; this will form the base of your pickling brine.

Add the extracted whey to the whey from the first draining of the curds and add water, if necessary, to bring it up to 500g. Dissolve 75g of salt into the liquid and allow it to stand at room temperature overnight – this allows the brine to develop the acidity that's vital for preservation.

Finally, cut the pressed cheese into cubes and store them in a jar, covered with the brine.

Made from goat's milk this would be a reasonably authentic feta. Made from cow's milk it's an excellent crumbly cheese that gets better with age in its brine. You can also experiment with adding live yoghurt to the original milk prior to warming it, which, as the curds set, will create a more sour taste.

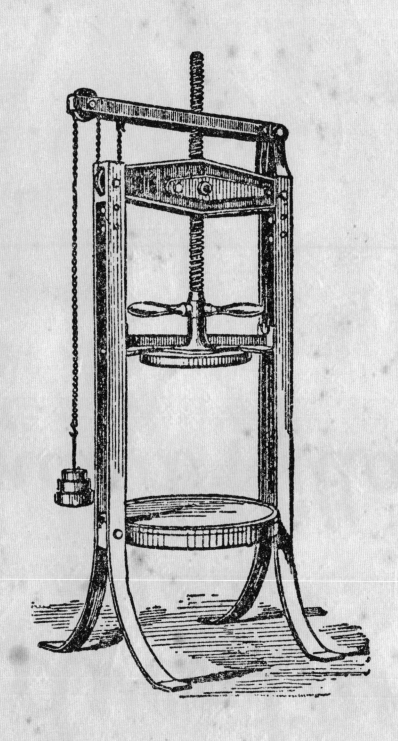

PUY LENTIL AND FETA SALAD

The sharp and salty taste of feta makes it a great accompaniment to the traditional ingredients of a horiatiki or Greek salad, but I prefer it with cold Puy lentils, dressed in a good vinaigrette and set on a bed of Little Gem hearts and torn herbs.

2 Little Gem hearts ★ 120g Puy lentils ★ a handful of fresh flat-leaf parsley ★ a large chunk of feta cheese ★ black pepper ★ olive oil

1. Rip the Little Gem hearts into separate leaves, then wash, pat dry, and divide between two plates.

2. Rinse the lentils under cold running water and drain. Put them into a saucepan and cover with double the amount of water (around 240g), then bring to the boil and simmer for 15–20 minutes. Drain and leave to cool.

3. Once cool, spoon the lentils over the leaves.

4. Tear over the parsley leaves, crumble the feta over the top and season with black pepper and olive oil, or a simple vinaigrette. Serve to 2 people.

CONTACTS, ADDRESSES, SUPPLIERS AND SITES

The Nisbets catalogue is a sort of bible in professional kitchens. Pots, pans and general professional catering equipment. Also a good source for cheap probe thermometers.

www.nisbets.co.uk

The Japanese Knife Company are the best UK importer I know of Japanese knives. They have an extensive selection, ranging from the reasonable to the staggeringly luxurious.

www.japaneseknifecompany.com

Franco's Famous Sausagemaking.org is the 'go-to' site for sausage skins, filling machines and brine pumps in the smaller quantities you will need. Best supplier for Prague Powders, or, if you're not confident in your measuring, of pre-made brine mixes.

www.sausagemaking.org

Lakeland Between the odd gadgets there's a matchless range of plastic storage containers, heavyweight freezer bags and vac-packing gear. In some branches, Lakeland now has a small department selling cheese-making gear.

www.lakeland.co.uk

Bradley If you're not up to building your own, Bradley are the Rolls-Royce of ready-made smokers.

www.bradleysmoker.co.uk

Weber Their barbecue gear isn't cheap but it lasts well and can survive abuse. Their barbecue lighting chimney is a lifesaver and a genuine blessing from the fire-gods.

www.weberbbq.co.uk

Mac's BBQ sell the ProQ cold smoke generator, various wood dusts and other smoking and grilling requisites. If you want to introduce a friend to smoking, their cardboard box smoker kit is the ideal way to do it.

www.macsbbq.co.uk

Thermapen Once you have the hang of internal temperatures, you'll never want to be without a probe thermometer again and you might want to fork out an extra few quid for a really swish one.

www.thermapen.co.uk

Cream Supplies is the secret hangout of the molecular cooks. They're the UK importer of the 'Smoking Gun', plus a great range of scientific cooking gear.

www.creamsupplies.co.uk

Weschenfelder are one of the world's foremost professional butchery suppliers. Knives, hooks, twine, saws and sausage stuffers.

www.weschenfelder.co.uk

Japanese Kitchen Regarded as a godsend by Japanese expats. Ingredients, tableware and utensils. UK-based and with a fast postal service.

www.japanesekitchen.co.uk

Heal Farm Your butcher might be able to supply you with a small quantity of caul fat, but it's usually sold by wholesalers in quantities too large to be useful. Heal Farm Fine Foods helpfully sell it in 250g packs.

www.healfarm.co.uk

The Coffee Bean Shop If you can't blag them from a friendly barista, try here for green unroasted coffee beans.

www.coffeebeanshop.co.uk

Welders Warehouse While tongs and forks are usually regarded as the acme of barbecuing technology, they can be a bit limiting. Welding gloves are an excellent idea for handling hot stuff; they cost around a fiver and if they work for white-hot metal they should be OK for a carbonized banger.

www.thewelderswarehouse.com

The Cheesemaking Shop Everything for the cheese-maker short of a cow.

www.cheesemakingshop.co.uk

Breadmatters Bread-making equipment and supplies, including hard-to-find proving baskets which give your loaves professionally rustic shapes.

www.breadmatters.com

Le Parfait There's nothing quite as frustrating as losing a batch of preserves when mismatched lids on jars don't seal. Bite the bullet and standardize on a single type.

www.leparfait.co.uk

Gas Products The gas boiling ring used for turkey frying can be turned to a variety of other uses when cooking outdoors. This site has a great selection in all sizes.

www.gasproducts.co.uk

Opies Pickled walnuts are probably the only ingredient I use regularly that's a bit tricky to find. As far as I know, Opies are the only UK manufacturer of this astonishingly lovely British ingredient, which is sometimes, though not reliably, stocked in supermarkets. Buy online or find a local supplier via . . .

www.b-opie.com

Wood If you're a real outdoorsman you'll relish collecting your own smoking woods with a chainsaw and an axe, but if not, smoking and barbecuing woods are available from . . .

Goulden's Barbecue Smoking Woods
www.bbqsmokingwood.co.uk

Hot Smoked
www.hotsmoked.co.uk

ACKNOWLEDGEMENTS

I'd like to thank my wife, Alison, for giving me freedom to write, tolerating my bonkers theorizing and helping me do what I love for a living. There's a cliché that usually fits here... something about 'without you, none of this would have been possible', and in Al's case, only she knows how totally true that is. I'd also like to thank Liberty, whose own tireless enthusiasm at ten continues to inspire mine at five times her age. She approaches the challenges of trying new stuff and learning new things with a joy that gives me constant delight and enormous hope for her future. This book is theirs.

THANKS TO...

Juliet Annan, my editor and publisher; John Hamilton, art director, who designed the book with help from Sarah Fraser, Alison O'Toole and Gail Jones; Sophie Missing; Ellie Smith, managing editor; Ilaria Rovera, production; Caroline Craig and Matt Clacher, who promoted and publicized the book; and all the team at Penguin.

Annie Lee, my copy editor.

Chris Terry, whose calm under fire makes him the most inspiring photographer to work with.

Nicholas John Frith, who drew the illustrations.

Susan Smillie at the *Guardian*, who let me get away with some truly odd work, and Sue Matthias and Natalie Whittle at the *FT*, who continue to do so.

Marina O'Loughlin, Jay Rayner, Matthew Fort, Rosie Stark, Kate Hawkings, Tom Williams and Sarah Lavelle for continued support and encouragement in the writing part of my job.

Leo Riethoff, a brilliantly talented cook with an excellent eye.

Catherine Phipps for continued help and sanity.

Rosie Sykes, the most inspiring cook I know.

Gill Abbs, Tom Whithead, 'Chinese' Dan Peirce, Kirsty Chapman, Mike Sim, Malgo Dzierugo, Rachel Blythe and the team at Fitzbillies for putting up with my nonsense.

Uyen Luu, Richard Bertinet, Ray Smith, 'Farmer' Sharp, Chris Bragg and Karl Smith, Bruno Zoccola, Fi Kirkpatrick and Fergus Henderson for sharing their expertise.

Big thanks to our suppliers – small businesses that make us look great.

Andrew Northrop and Martin Young, skilled butchers with enquiring minds and a seemingly unquenchable willingness to help.

Sticklebacks for strange fish requests.

The Small Works department at Mackays, the finest ironmongery in the known universe, for handling anything you throw at them with cheerful equanimity – and suggesting improvements.

And Tim Bates, Special Agent.

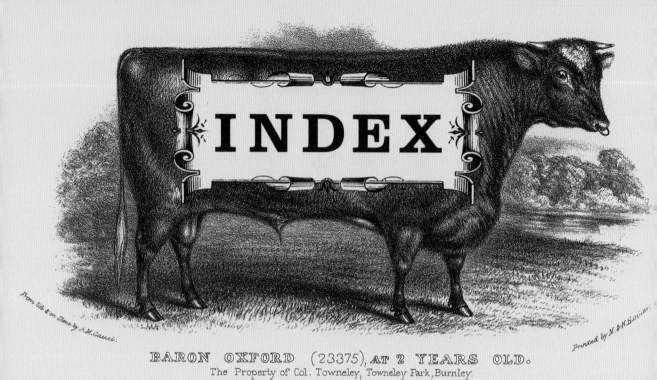

INDEX

BARON OXFORD (23375), AT 2 YEARS OLD.
The Property of Col. Towneley, Towneley Park, Burnley.

Page references for illustrations and photographs are in **bold**

Tim Hayward is a food writer and broadcaster. He is a contributing writer at the *Financial Times* and a regular contributor to the *Guardian* 'Word of Mouth' Food Blog and Radio 4 Food Programme, among others. Tim is the publisher and editor of *Fire & Knives*, a quarterly magazine of new food writing and winner of the 'Best Food Magazine' at the 2012 Guild of Food Writers Awards, and the publisher of *Gin & It*, a quarterly journal of new writing for drinkers and thinkers. He is the proprietor of the Fitzbillies bakery and restaurant in Cambridge. *Food DIY* is his first book.

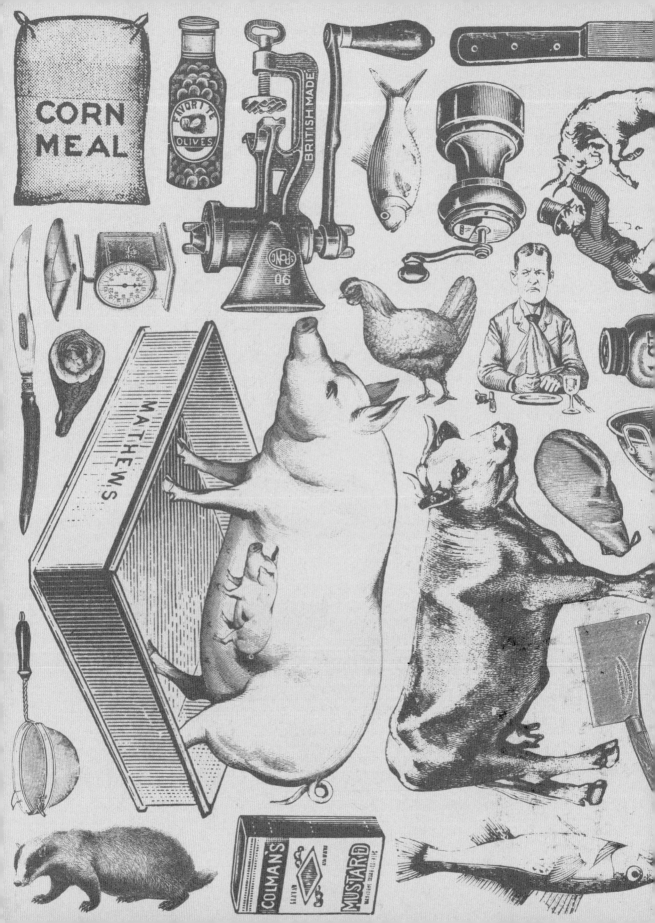